Virtual Reality: Concepts and Applications

Virtual Reality: Concepts and Applications

Edited by
Maxwell Oliver

Larsen & Keller
www.larsen-keller.com

Virtual Reality: Concepts and Applications
Edited by Maxwell Oliver
ISBN: 978-1-63549-284-2 (Hardback)

▤ Larsen & Keller

Published by Larsen and Keller Education,
5 Penn Plaza,
19th Floor,
New York, NY 10001, USA

Cataloging-in-Publication Data

Virtual reality : concepts and applications / edited by Maxwell Oliver.
    p. cm.
Includes bibliographical references and index.
ISBN 978-1-63549-284-2
1. Virtual reality. 2. Computer simulation. I. Oliver, Maxwell.
QA76.9.V5 V57 2017
006.8--dc23

The publisher's policy is to use permanent paper from mills that operate a sustainable forestry policy. Furthermore, the publisher ensures that the text paper and cover boards used have met acceptable environmental accreditation standards.

Printed and bound in the United States of America.

For more information regarding Larsen and Keller Education and its products, please visit the publisher's website www.larsen-keller.com

Table of Contents

Preface

Virtual reality refers to advanced and complex computer technologies and softwares which create sounds, images and environments around the user in order to provide with an interactive and realistic surrounding. It enables the user to walk around, interact with the objects of the artificially made world with the help of display screens, projectors or a virtual reality headset. This book is a compilation of chapters that discuss the most vital concepts in the field of virtual reality. The various subfields within this area of study along with the technological progress that have future implications are glanced at in this text. It is an essential guide for both graduates and postgraduates in the fields of software engineering, educational technology research and information system.

A short introduction to every chapter is written below to provide an overview of the content of the book:

Chapter 1 - The progress in technology has been immense and it is now possible to experience simulated reality with the help of software and devices. These devices provide the user with an artificial augmentation of the senses. This chapter introduces the reader to the world of virtual reality. It provides a brief overview to what virtual reality is and its methods.; **Chapter 2** - There are several facets to virtual reality; many of these can be represented by the reality–virtuality continuum. This chapter informs the reader about concepts of virtual reality like haptic technology, virtual body, virtual globe, cyberspace, motion simulator, Cave automatic virtual environment (CAVE), collaborative virtual environment and immersion. The chapter incorporates in-depth information with engaging examples that facilitate an extensive understanding of these concepts.; **Chapter 3** - Without technology one is unable to experience virtual reality, this chapter introduces the reader to technology like virtual reality headset, head-mounted display, EyeTap, head-up display, helmet-mounted display, virtual retinal display, MotionParallax3D, Leonar3Do etc. These state-of-the-art technologies give users a heightened and configurable digital reality.; **Chapter 4** - Due to its immense potential, virtual reality has become the choice of technology in a method of psychotherapy called virtual reality therapy (VRT) or virtual reality exposure therapy (VRET). This application of virtual reality in therapy enables the clinician to control and stimulate the exposure of the patient to triggers and triggering levels. This chapter examines this novel use of virtual reality in psychotherapy and in telerehabilitation and helps the reader consider the possibilities that exist for virtual reality in the sphere of medicine and therapeutics.; **Chapter 5** - Virtual reality simulation helps formulate and create real-life scenarios with no liability and hence has found application in diverse fields like disaster management, pilot training, recreation of locations, enhancing amusement park experience etc. This chapter illustrates these applications by the use of examples like advanced disaster management simulator, flight simulator, Unmanned Aircraft System Simulation, VR Coaster, Virtual tour and Google Street View.; **Chapter 6 -** The reality created by the ability to add, subtract and/or manipulate a person's perception through the use of technology like wearable computer or handheld devices like smartphones is known as computer-mediated reality. The chapter aids the reader in understanding the concepts of mixed reality, simulated reality, extended reality, augmented reality and computer-mediated reality with clarity.; **Chapter 7 -** Virtual reality uses a wide array of software to simulate the user's perception. This chapter details the various file formats used in VR like VRML, COLLADA, X3D, universal3D, 3DMLW etc. These specialized file formats help in dynamic and interactive digital content creation-graphics, textures etc.

Finally, I would like to thank my fellow scholars who gave constructive feedback and my family members who supported me at every step.

Editor

Introduction to Virtual Reality

The progress in technology has been immense and it is now possible to experience simulated reality with the help of software and devices. These devices provide the user with an artificial augmentation of the senses. This chapter introduces the reader to the world of virtual reality. It provides a brief overview to what virtual reality is and its methods.

Virtual Reality

Virtual reality or virtual realities (VR), also known as immersive multimedia or computer-simulated reality, is a computer technology that replicates an environment, real or imagined, and simulates a user's physical presence and environment to allow for user interaction. Virtual realities artificially create sensory experience, which can include sight, touch, hearing, and smell.

Assembled Google Cardboard VR

Most up-to-date virtual realities are displayed either on a computer monitor or with a virtual reality headset (also called head-mounted display), and some simulations include additional sensory information and focus on real sound through speakers or headphones targeted towards VR users. Some advanced haptic systems now include tactile information, generally known as force feedback in medical, gaming and military applications. Furthermore, virtual reality covers remote communication environments which provide virtual presence of users with the concepts of telepresence and telexistence or a virtual artifact (VA) either through the use of standard input devices such as a keyboard and mouse, or through multimodal devices such as a wired glove or omnidirectional treadmills. The immersive environment can be similar to the real world in order to create a lifelike experience—for example, in simulations for pilot or combat training—or it can differ significantly from reality, such as in VR games.

Concept Origins

In 1938, Antonin Artaud described the illusory nature of characters and objects in the theatre as "la réalité virtuelle" in a collection of essays, *Le Théâtre et son double*. The English translation of this book, published in 1958 as The Theater and its Double, is the earliest published use of the term "virtual reality".

The term "artificial reality", coined by Myron Krueger, has been in use since the 1970s. The term "Virtual Reality" was used in *The Judas Mandala*, a 1982 science-fiction novel by Damien Broderick. The Oxford English Dictionary cites a 1987 article titled *"Virtual reality"*, but the article is not about VR technology. Virtual Reality in its modern usage was popularized by Jaron Lanier through his company VPL Research. VPL Research held many of the mid eighties VR patents, and they developed the first widely used HMD: EyePhone and Haptic Input DataGlove The concept of virtual reality was popularized in mass media by movies such as *Brainstorm* and *The Lawnmower Man*. The VR research boom of the 1990s was accompanied by the non-fiction book *Virtual Reality* (1991) by Howard Rheingold. The book served to demystify the subject, making it more accessible to less technical researchers and enthusiasts.

History

Before the 1950s

The Sensorama was released in the 1950s.

View-Master, a stereoscopic visual simulator, was introduced in 1939.

The first traces of virtual reality came from the world of science fiction. Stanley G. Weinbaum's 1935 short story "Pygmalion's Spectacles" is recognized as one of the first works of science fiction that explores virtual reality. It describes a goggle-based virtual reality system with holographic recording of fictional experiences including smell and touch.

1950–1970

Morton Heilig wrote in the 1950s of an "Experience Theatre" that could encompass all the senses in an effective manner, thus drawing the viewer into the onscreen activity. He built a prototype of his vision dubbed the Sensorama in 1962, along with five short films to be displayed in it while engaging multiple senses (sight, sound, smell, and touch). Predating digital computing, the Sensorama was a mechanical device, which reportedly still functions today. Around the same time, Douglas Engelbart used computer screens as both input and output devices.

In 1968, Ivan Sutherland, with the help of his student Bob Sproull, created what is widely considered to be the first virtual reality and augmented reality (AR) head-mounted display (HMD) system. It was primitive both in terms of user interface and realism, and the HMD to be worn by the user was so heavy that it had to be suspended from the ceiling. The graphics comprising the virtual environment were simple wire-frame model rooms. The formidable appearance of the device inspired its name, The Sword of Damocles.

1970–1990

Also notable among the earlier hypermedia and virtual reality systems was the Aspen Movie Map, which was created at MIT in 1978. The program was a crude virtual simulation of Aspen, Colorado in which users could wander the streets in one of three modes: summer, winter, and polygons. The first two were based on photographs—the researchers actually photographed every possible movement through the city's street grid in both seasons—and the third was a basic 3-D model of the city.

Battlezone, an arcade video game from 1980, used 3D vector graphics to immerse the player in a VR world.(Atari).

Atari founded a research lab for virtual reality in 1982, but the lab was closed after two years due to Atari Shock (North American video game crash of 1983). However, its hired employees, such as Tom Zimmerman, Scott Fisher, Jaron Lanier and Brenda Laurel, kept their research and development on VR-related technologies.

By the 1980s the term "virtual reality" was popularized by Jaron Lanier, one of the modern pioneers of the field. Lanier had founded the company VPL Research in 1985. VPL Research has developed several VR devices like the Data Glove, the Eye Phone, and the Audio Sphere.VPL Research authorized the warrant of the Data Glove to New York video game company Mattel. Mattel used this technology and made an accessory known as the Power Glove. It was hard to use and not popular at all. However, the price for this accessory was $75. It might be the earliest affordable VR device.

During this time, virtual reality was not well known, though it did receive media coverage in the late 80s. Most of its popularity came from marginal cultures, like cyberpunks, who viewed the technology as a potential means for social change, and drug culture, who praised virtual reality not only as a new art form, but as an entirely new frontier. Once the industry began to attract media coverage, people started realizing that potential. Some even compared the innovations in virtual reality to the Wright Brothers' pioneering invention of the airplane.

In 1990, Jonathan Waldern, a VR Ph.D, demonstrates "Virtuality" at the Computer Graphics 90 exhibition staged at London's Alexandra Palace. This new system was an arcade machine that would use a virtual reality headset to immerse players.

CyberEdge and PCVR, VR industry focused magazines, started to publish in the early 90s. However, most ideas about VR remained theoretical due to the limited computing power available at the time. The extremely high cost of the technology made it impossible for most consumers to adopt. The public turned their focus to the Internet after it came out. The VR industry went silent in the U.S. and only provided VR devices for medical, flight simulation, automobile industry design, and military training purposes.

1990–2000

In 1991, Sega announced the Sega VR headset for arcade games and the Mega Drive console. It used LCD screens in the visor, stereo headphones, and inertial sensors that allowed the system to track and react to the movements of the user's head.

In the same year, Virtuality launched and went on to become the first mass-produced, networked, multiplayer VR entertainment system. It was released in many countries, including a dedicated VR arcade at Embarcadero Center in San Francisco. Costing up to $73,000 per multi-pod Virtuality system, they featured headsets and exoskeleton gloves that gave one of the first "immersive" VR experiences.

Antonio Medina, a MIT graduate and NASA scientist, designed a virtual reality system to "drive" Mars rovers from Earth in apparent real time despite the substantial delay of Mars-Earth-Mars signals. The system, termed "Computer-Simulated Teleoperation" as published by Rand, is an extension of virtual reality.

In 1991, Carolina Cruz-Neira, Daniel J. Sandin and Thomas A. DeFanti from the Electronic Visualization Laboratory created the first cubic immersive room, replacing goggles by a multi-projected environment where people can see their body and other people around.

In 1991, *Computer Gaming World* predicts "Affordable VR by 1994".

By 1994, Sega released the Sega VR-1 motion simulator arcade attraction, in SegaWorld amusement arcades. It was able to track head movement and featured 3D polygon graphics in stereoscopic 3D, powered by the Sega Model 1 arcade system board.

Also in 1994 Apple released QuickTime VR. A widely available product for interacting with VR models.

A year later, the artist Maurice Benayoun created the first VR artwork connecting in real time 2 continents: the "Tunnel under the Atlantic" between the Pompidou Centre in Paris and the Museum of Contemporary Art in Montreal. The installation included dynamic real time 3d modeling, video chat, spatialized sound and AI content management.

The Virtual Boy was created by Nintendo and was released in Japan on July 21, 1995 and in North America on August 15, 1995.

Also in 1995, a group in Seattle created public demonstrations of a "CAVE-like" 270 degree immersive projection room called the Virtual Environment Theater, produced by entrepreneurs Chet Dagit and Bob Jacobson. Then in 1996 the same system was shown in tradeshow exhibits sponsored by Netscape Communications, and championed by Jim Barksdale, for the first time showing VR connected to the Internet with World Wide Web content feeds embedded in VRML 3D virtual world models.

Forte released the VFX1, a PC-powered virtual reality headset in 1995, which was supported by games including *Descent, Star Wars: Dark Forces, System Shock* and *Quake*.

In 1999, entrepreneur Philip Rosedale formed Linden Lab with an initial focus on the development of hardware that would enable computer users to be fully immersed in a 360 degree virtual reality experience. In its earliest form, the company struggled to produce a commercial version of "The Rig," which was realized in prototype form as a clunky steel contraption with several computer monitors that users could wear on their shoulders. That vision soon morphed into the software-based, 3D virtual world Second Life.

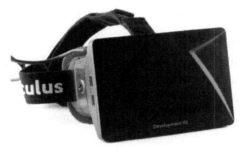

A 2013 developer version of Oculus Rift from Oculus VR, a company Facebook acquired in 2014 for $2 billion

Another VR headset called the "HTC Vive" Developed in co-production between HTC and Valve Corporation.

2000–Present

In 2001, SAS3 or SAS Cube became the first PC based cubic room, developed by Z-A Production (Maurice Benayoun, David Nahon), Barco, Clarté, installed in Laval France in April 2001. The SAS library gave birth to Virtools VRPack.

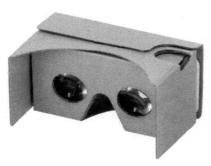

The affordable and accessible Google Cardboard standard.

By 2007, Google introduced Street View, a service that shows panoramic views of an increasing number of worldwide positions such as roads, indoor buildings and rural areas. It also features a stereoscopic 3D mode, introduced in 2010.

In 2010, Palmer Luckey, who later went on to found Oculus VR, designed the first prototype of the Oculus Rift. This prototype, built on a shell of another virtual reality headset, displayed only 2-D images and was noticeably cumbersome to wear. However, it boasted a 90-degree field of vision that was previously unseen anywhere in the market at the time. This initial design would later serve as a basis from which the later designs came.

In 2013, Nintendo filed a patent for the concept of using VR technology to produce a more realistic 3D effect on a 2D television. A camera on the TV tracks the viewer's location relative to the TV, and if the viewer moves, everything on the screen reorients itself appropriately. "For example, if you were looking at a forest, you could shift your head to the right to discover someone standing behind a tree."

In July 2013, Guild Software's Vendetta Online was widely reported as the first MMORPG to support the Oculus Rift, making it potentially the first persistent online world with native support for a consumer virtual reality headset.

On March 25, 2014, Facebook purchased a company that makes virtual reality headsets, Oculus VR, for $2 billion. Sony announces Project Morpheus (its code name for PlayStation VR), a virtual reality headset for the PlayStation 4. Google announces Cardboard, a do-it-yourself stereoscopic viewer for smartphones.

Since 2013, there have been several virtual reality devices that seek to enter the market to complement Oculus Rift to enhance the game experience. One, Virtuix Omni, is based on the ability to move in a three dimensional environment through an omnidirectional treadmill.

In 2015, the Kickstarter campaign for Gloveone, a pair of gloves providing motion tracking and haptic feedback, was successfully funded, with over $150,000 in contributions.

In February–March 2015, HTC partnered with Valve Corporation announced their virtual reality headset HTC Vive and controllers, along with their tracking technology called Lighthouse, which utilizes "base stations" mounted to the wall above the user's head in the corners of a room for positional tracking of the Vive headset and its motion controllers using infrared light. The company announced its plans to release the Vive to the public in April 2016 on December 8, 2015. Units began shipping on April 5, 2016.

In July 2015, OnePlus became the first company to launch a product using virtual reality. They used VR as the platform to launch their second flagship device the OnePlus 2, first viewable using an app on the Google Play Store, then on YouTube. The launch was viewable using OnePlus Cardboard, based on the Google's own Cardboard platform. The whole VR launch had a runtime of 33 minutes, and was viewable in all countries.

Also in 2015, Jaunt, a startup company developing cameras and a cloud distribution platform, whose content will be accessible using an app, reached $100 million in funding from such sources as Disney and Madison Square Garden.

On April 27, 2016, Mojang announced that Minecraft is now playable on the Gear VR. Minecraft is still being developed for the Oculus Rift headset but a separate version was released to the Oculus Store for use with the Gear VR. This version has everything that's in the Pocket Edition of Minecraft.

Use

Education and Training

Few are creating content that may be used for educational purposes, with most advances being made in the entertainment industry, yet research is being done on learning in virtual reality as many believe its immersive qualities have the potential to enhance learning.

Training

U.S. Navy personnel using a VR parachute training simulator.

The usage of VR in a training perspective is to allow professionals to conduct training in a virtual environment where they can improve upon their skills without the consequence of failing the operation. Thomas A. Furness III was one of the first to develop the use of VR for military training when, in 1982, he presented the Air Force with his first working model of a virtual flight simulator he called the Visually Coupled Airborne Systems Simulator (VCASS). By the time he started his work on VCASS, aircraft were becoming increasingly complicated to handle and virtual reality provided a better solution to previous training methods. Furness attempted to incorporate his knowledge of human visual and auditory processing to create a virtual interface that was more intuitive to use. The second phase of his project, which he called the "Super Cockpit," was even more advanced, with high resolution graphics (for the time) and a responsive display. Furness is often credited as a pioneer in virtual reality for this research.

VR plays an important role in combat training for the military. It allows the recruits to train under a controlled environment where they are to respond to different types of combat situations. A fully immersive virtual reality that uses head-mounted display (HMD), data suits, data glove, and VR weapon are used to train for combat. This setup allows the training's reset time to be cut down, and allows more repetition in a shorter amount of time. The fully immersive training environment allows the soldiers to train through a wide variety of terrains, situations and scenarios.

VR is also used in flight simulation for the Air Force where people are trained to be pilots. The simulator would sit on top of a hydraulic lift system that reacts to the user inputs and events. When the pilot steer the aircraft, the module would turn and tilt accordingly to provide haptic feedback. The flight simulator can range from a fully enclosed module to a series of computer monitors providing the pilot's point of view. The most important reasons on using simulators over learning with a real aircraft are the reduction of transference time between land training and real flight, the safety, economy and absence of pollution. By the same token, virtual driving simulations are used to train tank drivers on the basics before allowing them to operate the real vehicle. Finally, the same goes for truck driving simulators, in which Belgian firemen are for example trained to drive in a way that prevents as much damage as possible. As these drivers often have less experience than other truck drivers, virtual reality training allows them to compensate this. In the near future, similar projects are expected for all drivers of priority vehicles, including the police.

Medical personnel are able to train through VR to deal with a wider variety of injuries. An experiment was performed by sixteen surgical residents where eight of them went through laparoscopic cholecystectomy through VR training. They then came out 29% faster at gallbladder dissection than the controlled group. With the increased commercial availability of certified training programs for basic skills training in VR environments, students have the ability to familiarize themselves with necessary skills in a corrective and repetitive environment; VR is also proven to help students familiarize themselves with skills not specific to any particular procedure.

VR application was used to train road crossing skills in children. It proved to be rather successful. However some students with autistic spectrum disorders after such training might be unable to distinguish virtual from real. As a result, they may attempt quite dangerous road crossings.

Video Games

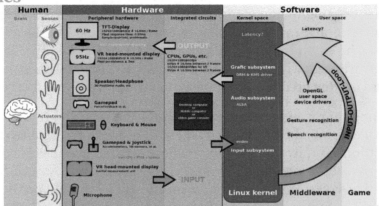

Paramount for the **immersion** into **virtual reality** are a high frame rate (at least 95 fps), as well as a low latency. Furthermore, a pixel persistence lower than 3 ms is required to not get sick when moving the head around.

The use of graphics, sound and input technology in video games can be incorporated into VR. Several Virtual Reality head mounted displays (HMD) were released for gaming during the early-mid 1990s. These included the Virtual Boy developed by Nintendo, the iGlasses developed by Virtual I-O, the Cybermaxx developed by Victormaxx and the VFX1 Headgear developed by Forte Technologies. Other modern examples of narrow VR for gaming include the Wii Remote, the Kinect, and the PlayStation Move/PlayStation Eye, all of which track and send motion input of the players to the game console somewhat accurately.

Several companies are working on a new generation of VR headsets: Oculus Rift is a head-mounted display for gaming purposes developed by Oculus VR, an American technology company that was acquired for US$2 billion by Facebook in 2014. One of its rivals was named by Sony as PlayStation VR (codenamed Morpheus), which requires a PS4 instead of a PC to run. In 2015, Valve Corporation announced their partnership with HTC to make a VR headset capable of tracking the exact position of its user in a 4.5 by 4.5 meters area, the HTC Vive. All these virtual reality headsets are tethered headsets that use special curved lenses to magnify and stretch a 5.7-inch screen (in the case of Morpheus) across your field of vision. There are many more gaming VR headsets in development, each with its own special abilities. StarVR, for instance, offers a 210° field of view, whereas FOVE tracks the position of your eyes as an input method.

Fine Arts

David Em was the first fine artist to create navigable virtual worlds in the 1970s. His early work was done on mainframes at Information International, Inc., Jet Propulsion

Laboratory, and California Institute of Technology. Jeffrey Shaw explored the potential of VR in fine arts with early works like *Legible City* (1989), *Virtual Museum* (1991), and *Golden Calf* (1994). Canadian artist Char Davies created immersive VR art pieces *Osmose* (1995) and *Ephémère* (1998). Maurice Benayoun's work introduced metaphorical, philosophical or political content, combining VR, network, generation and intelligent agents, in works like *Is God Flat?* (1994), "Is the Devil Curved?" (1995), *The Tunnel under the Atlantic* (1995), and *World Skin, a Photo Safari in the Land of War* (1997). Other pioneering artists working in VR have include Luc Courchesne, Rnmnmita Addison, Knowbotic Research, Rebecca Allen, Perry Hoberman, Jacki Morie, Margaret Dolinsky and Brenda Laurel. All mentioned artists are documented in the Database of Virtual Art.

Engineering

The use of 3D CAD data had been trapped in the confines of 2D monitors and paper printouts until the mid-to-late 1990's when projector , 3D tracking, and computer technology enabled a new renaissance in the consumption of 3D CAD data in virtual reality caves. With the use of active shutter glasses and multi-surface projection units immersive engineering was made possible by companies like VRcom and IC.IDO. Virtual reality has proven valuable to automotive, aerospace, and ground transportation OEMs in their product engineering and manufacturing engineering activities. Virtual reality adds more dimension to virtual prototyping, virtual product build, virtual assembly, virtual service, virtual performance use-cases enable engineers from different disciplines to review their individual designs integrated into the final product in an immersive environment. Immersive engineering reviews of this kind give the responsible management the ability to interact with the virtual prototypes weeks and months prior to the availability of any prototype components or tooling.

Heritage and Archaeology

The first use of a VR presentation in a heritage application was in 1994, when a museum visitor interpretation provided an interactive "walk-through" of a 3D reconstruction of Dudley Castle in England as it was in 1550. This consisted of a computer controlled laserdisc-based system designed by British-based engineer Colin Johnson. The system was featured in a conference held by the British Museum in November 1994, and in the subsequent technical paper, *Imaging the Past – Electronic Imaging and Computer Graphics in Museums and Archaeology*.

Virtual reality enables heritage sites to be recreated extremely accurately, so that the recreations can be published in various media. The original sites are often inaccessible to the public or, due to the poor state of their preservation, hard to picture. This technology can be used to develop virtual replicas of caves, natural environment, old towns, monuments, sculptures and archaeological elements.

Architectural Design

One of the first recorded uses of virtual reality in architecture was in the late 80s when the University of North Carolina modeled its Sitterman Hall, home of its computer science department, in a virtual environment.

A visitor at Mozilla Berlin Hackshibition trying Oculus Rift virtual reality experience on Firefox.

Several companies, including IrisVR and Floored, Inc., provide software or services that allow architectural design firms and various clients in the real estate industry to tour virtual models of proposed building designs. IrisVR currently provides software that allows users to convert design files created in CAD programs like SketchUp and Revit into files viewable with an Oculus Rift, HTC Vive, or a smartphone "in one click," without the need for complex tiered workflows or knowledge of game engines such as Unity3D. Floored, meanwhile, manually constructs and refines Rift-viewable 3D models in-house from either CAD files for un-built designs or physical scans of already built, brick-and-mortar buildings, and provides clients with access to its own viewing software, which can be used with either an Oculus Rift or a standard 2D web browser, afterward.

VR software products like these can provide a number of benefits to architects and their clients. During the design process, architects themselves can use VR in order to actually experience the designs they are working on before they are built. In particular, seeing a design in VR can help impress upon the architect a correct sense of scale and proportion. Having an interactive VR model on hand also eliminates the need to waste time and resources constructing physical miniatures in order to demonstrate or examine a design concept to clients or the public. Later on, after a building is constructed, developers and owners can create a VR model of a space that allows potential buyers or tenants to tour a space in VR, even if real-life circumstances make a physical tour unfeasible. For instance, if the owner of an apartment building in Manhattan has a VR model of a space while the building is under construction, they can begin showing and renting the units before they are even ready to be occupied. Furthermore, this sort of showing can be conducted over any distance, as long as the potential customer has access to a VR setup (or, even, with the help of Google Cardboard or a similar phone-based VR headset, nothing but an ordinary smartphone.)

Urban Design

In 2010, 3D virtual reality was beginning to be used for urban regeneration and planning and transport projects.

In 2007 development began on a virtual reality software which took design coordinate geometry used by land surveyors and civil engineers and incorporated precision spatial information created automatically by the lines and curves typically shown on subdivision plats and land surveying plans. These precise spatial areas cross referenced color and texture to an item list. The item list contained a set of controls for 3D rendering such as water reflective surface or building height. The land surface in software to create a contour map uses a digital terrain model (DTM). By 2010, prototype software was developed for the core technology to automate the process leading from design to virtualization. The first beta users in 2011 were able to press a single function and automatically drape the design or survey data over the digital terrain to create data structures that are passed into a video gaming engine to create a virtual interactive world showing massing of buildings in relation to man made improvements.

A Coved land development plan using 4th generation design and principals of Prefurbia

It was the first application where virtual reality was made effortless for Urban Planning principals using technology. The software was improved to implement massing or 3D models from other free or commercially sold software to create more realistic virtual reality with very little time and effort. The software is marketed as LandMentor and is the first precision design technology to make Urban Planning widely available with a short learning curve.

A Coved Streetscape with homes using architectural shaping and blending in Viera Florida

Therapy

The primary use of VR in a therapeutic role is its application to various forms of exposure therapy, including phobia treatments.

Theme Parks

Since 2015, virtual reality has been installed onto a number of roller coasters, including Galactica at Alton Towers, The New Revolution at Six Flags Magic Mountain and Alpenexpress at Europapark, amongst others.

Concerts

In Oslo Spektrum on May the 3rd 2016, Norwegian band a-ha cleared away their normal stage-production to give room for a very different concert performance in collaboration with Void, a Norwegian computational design studio working in the intersection between design, architecture, art and technology. The collaboration resulted in a unique one-of-a-kind concert with advanced scenography using 360 virtual reality technology.

The concept involved several movement sensors that reacted to the bands movements, voices and instruments. 3D cameras, 20000 lines of codes, 1000 square meters of projection film and massive projectors was set up into a visual show that made the Oslo Spektrum arena in Oslo, Norway into a light installation and visual experience that unfolded live for the audience instead of a pre programmed sequence. The stereoscopic VR-experience was made available for Android users directly through a YouTube app and also made available for iPhone users and other platforms.

Retail

Lowe's, IKEA, and Wayfair have developed systems that allow these company's products to be seen in virtual reality, to give consumers a better idea of how the product will fit into their home, or to allow the consumer to get a better look at the product from home.

Charity

Non-profit organisations such as Amnesty International, UNICEF, and World Wide Fund for Nature (WWF) have started using virtual reality to bring potential supporters closer to their work, effectively bringing distant social, political and environmental issues and projects to members of the public in immersive ways not possible with traditional media. Panoramic 360 views of conflict in Syria and face to face encounters with CGI tigers in Nepal have been used in experiential activations and shared online to both educate and gain financial support for such charitable work.

Film

Many companies, including GoPro, Nokia, Samsung, Ricoh and Nikon, develop omnidirectional cameras, also known as 360-degree cameras or VR cameras, that have the ability to record in all directions. These cameras are used to create images and videos that can be viewed in VR. Films produced for VR permit the audience to view the entire environment in every scene, creating an interactive viewing experience.

Production companies, such as Fox Searchlight Pictures and Skybound, utilize VR cameras to produce films that are interactive in VR. Fox Searchlight, Oculus and Samsung Gear VR collaborated on a project titled "Wild – The Experience", starring Reese Witherspoon. The VR film was presented at the Consumer Electronics Show as well as the Sundance Film Festival in January 2015.

On December 8, 2015, the production company Skybound announced their VR thriller titled "Gone". In collaboration with the VR production company WEVR, and Samsung Gear VR, the 360-degree video series was released on January 20, 2016.

Media

Companies such as Paramount Pictures, and Disney have applied VR into marketing campaigns creating interactive forms of media.

In October 2014 Paramount Pictures, in collaboration with the media production company Framestore, created a VR experience utilizing the Oculus DK2. The experience was dubbed a "time sensitive adventure in space" that took place in a portion of the Endurance space ship from the film "Interstellar." The experience was available to the public at limited AMC theater locations.

In May 2016, Disney released a VR experience titled Disney Movies VR on Valve Corporation's Steam software, free for download. The experience allows users to interact with the characters and worlds from the Disney, Marvel, and Lucasfilm universes.

Pornography

Pornographic studios such as Naughty America and Kink have applied VR into their products since late 2015 or early 2016. The clips and videos are shot from an angle that resembles a POV-style porn.

In Fiction

Many science fiction books and films have imagined characters being "trapped in virtual reality".

A comprehensive and specific fictional model for virtual reality was published in 1935 in the short story "Pygmalion's Spectacles" by Stanley G. Weinbaum. A more modern work to use this idea was Daniel F. Galouye's novel *Simulacron-3*, which was made into a German teleplay titled *Welt am Draht* ("World on a Wire") in 1973. Other science fiction books have promoted the idea of virtual reality as a partial, but not total, substitution for the misery of reality, or have touted it as a method for creating virtual worlds in which one may escape from Earth.

Stanisław Lem's 1961 story "I (Profesor Corcoran)", translated in English as "Further Reminiscences of Ijon Tichy I", dealt with a scientist who created a number of computer-simulated people living in a virtual world. Lem further explored the implications of what he termed "phantomatics" in his nonfictional 1964 treatise *Summa Technologiae*. The Piers Anthony novel *Killobyte* follows the story of a paralyzed cop trapped in a virtual reality game by a hacker, whom he must stop to save a fellow trapped player slowly succumbing to insulin shock.

A number of other popular fictional works use the concept of virtual reality. These include William Gibson's 1984 *Neuromancer*, which defined the concept of cyberspace, and his 1994 *Virtual Light*, where a presentation viewable in VR-like goggles was the MacGuffin. Other examples are Neal Stephenson's *Snow Crash*, in which he made extensive reference to the term avatar to describe one's representation in a virtual world, and Rudy Rucker's *The Hacker and the Ants*, in which programmer Jerzy Rugby uses VR for robot design and testing. The Otherland series of 4 novels by Tad Williams, published from 1996 to 2001 and set in the 2070s, shows a world where the Internet has become accessible via virtual reality.

The *Doctor Who* serial "The Deadly Assassin", first broadcast in 1976, introduced a dream-like computer-generated reality, known as the Matrix. British BBC2 sci-fi series *Red Dwarf* featured a virtual reality game titled "Better Than Life", in which the main characters had spent many years connected. Saban's syndicated superhero television series *VR Troopers* also made use of the concept.

The holodeck featured in *Star Trek: The Next Generation* is one of the best known examples of virtual reality in popular culture, including the ability for users to interactively modify scenarios in real time with a natural language interface. The depiction differs from others in the use of a physical room rather than a neural interface or headset.

The popular *.hack* multimedia franchise is based on a virtual reality MMORPG dubbed "The World". The French animated series *Code Lyoko* is based on the virtual world of *Lyoko* and the Internet.

In 2009, British digital radio station BBC Radio 7 broadcast *Planet B*, a science-fiction drama set in a virtual world. *Planet B* was the largest ever commission for an original drama programme.

The 2012 series *Sword Art Online* involves the concept of a virtual reality MMORPG of the same name, with the possibility of dying in real life when a player dies in the game. Also, in its 2014 sequel, *Sword Art Online II*, the idea of bringing a virtual character into the real world via mobile cameras is posed; this concept is used to allow a bedridden individual to attend public school for the first time.

Featured in 2012, *Accel World* expands the concept of virtual reality using the game *Brain Burst*, a game which allows players to gain and receive points to keep accelerating; accelerating is when an individual's brain perceives the images around them 1000 times faster, heightening their sense of awareness.

Motion Pictures

World Skin (1997), Maurice Benayoun's virtual reality interactive installation

- Rainer Werner Fassbinder's 1973 film *Welt am Draht*, based on Daniel F. Galouye's novel Simulacron-3, shows a virtual reality simulation inside a virtual reality simulation

- In 1983, the Natalie Wood / Christopher Walken film *Brainstorm* revolved around the production, use, and misuse of a VR device.

- *Total Recall*, directed by Paul Verhoeven and based on the Philip K. Dick story "We Can Remember It for You Wholesale"

- A VR-like system, used to record and play back dreams, figures centrally in Wim Wenders' 1991 film *Until the End of the World*.

- The 1992 film *The Lawnmower Man* tells the tale of a research scientist who uses a VR system to jumpstart the mental and physical development of his mentally handicapped gardener.

- The 1993 film *Arcade* is centered around a new virtual reality game (from which the film gets its name) that actively traps those who play it inside its world.

- The 1995 film *Johnny Mnemonic* has the main character Johnny (played by Keanu Reeves) use virtual reality goggles and brain–computer interfaces to access the Internet and extract encrypted information in his own brain.

- The 1995 film *Virtuosity* has Russell Crowe as a virtual reality serial killer name SID 6.7 (Sadistic, Intelligent and Dangerous) who is used in a simulation to train real-world police officer, but manages to escape into the real world.

- The 1999 film *The Thirteenth Floor* is an adaptation of Daniel F. Galouye's novel *Simulacron-3*, and tells about two virtual reality simulations, one in another.

- In 1999, *The Matrix* and later sequels explored the possibility that our world is actually a vast virtual reality (or more precisely, simulated reality) created by artificially intelligent machines.

- *eXistenZ* (1999), by David Cronenberg, in which level switches occur so seamlessly and numerously that at the end of the movie it is difficult to tell whether the main characters are back in "reality".

- In the film *Avatar*, the humans are hooked up to experience what their avatars perform remotely.

- *Surrogates* (2009) is based on a brain–computer interface that allows people to control realistic humanoid robots, giving them full sensory feedback.

Concerns and Challenges

There are certain health and safety considerations of virtual reality. For example, a number of unwanted symptoms have been caused by prolonged use of virtual reality, and these may have slowed proliferation of the technology. Most virtual reality systems come with consumer warnings.

In addition, there are social, conceptual, and philosophical considerations with virtual reality. What the phrase "virtual reality" means or refers to, is not always unambiguous. In the book *The Metaphysics of Virtual Reality* by Michael R. Heim, seven different concepts of virtual reality are identified: simulation, interaction, artificiality, immersion, telepresence, full-body immersion, and network communication.

There has been an increase in interest in the potential social impact of new technologies, such as virtual reality. In the book *Infinite Reality: Avatars, Eternal Life, New Worlds, and the Dawn of the Virtual Revolution*, Blascovich and Bailenson review the literature on the psychology and sociology behind life in virtual reality.

In addition, Mychilo S. Cline, in his book *Power, Madness, and Immortality: The Future of Virtual Reality*, argues that virtual reality will lead to a number of important changes in human life and activity. He argues that virtual reality will be integrated into daily life and activity, and will be used in various human ways. Another such speculation has been written up on how to reach ultimate happiness via virtual reality. He also argues that techniques will be developed to influence human behavior, interpersonal communication, and cognition. As we spend more and more time in virtual space, there would be a gradual "migration to virtual space", resulting in important changes in economics, worldview, and culture.

Philosophical implications of the concept of VR are discussed in books including Philip Zhai's *Get Real: A Philosophical Adventure in Virtual Reality* (1998) and *Digital Sensations: Space, Identity and Embodiment in Virtual Reality* (1999), written by Ken Hillis.

Virtual reality technology faces a number of challenges, most of which involve motion sickness and technical matters. Users might become disoriented in a purely virtual environment, causing balance issues; computer latency might affect the simulation, providing a less-than-satisfactory end-user experience; the complicated nature of head-mounted displays and input systems such as specialized gloves and boots may require specialized training to operate, and navigating the non-virtual environment (if the user is not confined to a limited area) might prove dangerous without external sensory information.

In January 2014, Michael Abrash gave a talk on VR at Steam Dev Days. He listed all the requirements necessary to establish presence and concluded that a great VR system will be available in 2015 or soon after. While the visual aspect of VR is close to being solved, he stated that there are other areas of VR that need solutions, such as 3D audio, haptics, body tracking, and input. However, 3D audio effects exist in games and simulate the head-related transfer function of the listener (especially using headphones). Examples include Environmental Audio Extensions (EAX), DirectSound and OpenAL.

VR audio developer Varun Nair points out that from a design perspective, sound for VR is still very much an open book. Many of the game audio design principles, especially those related to FPS games, crumble in virtual reality. He encourages more sound designers to get involved in virtual reality audio to experiment and push VR audio forward.

There have been rising concerns that with the advent of virtual reality, some users may experience virtual reality addiction.

Pioneers and Notables

- Thomas A. Furness III
- Maurice Benayoun
- Mark Bolas
- Fred Brooks
- Anshe Chung
- Edmond Couchot
- James H. Clark
- Doug Church

- Char Davies
- Tom DeFanti
- David Em
- Scott Fisher
- William Gibson
- Morton Heilig
- Eric Howlett
- Myron Krueger
- Knowbotic Research
- Jaron Lanier
- Brenda Laurel
- Palmer Luckey
- Michael Naimark
- Randy Pausch
- Mark Pesce
- Warren Robinett
- Philip Rosedale
- Louis Rosenberg
- Dan Sandin
- Susumu Tachi
- Ivan Sutherland

Commercial Industries

The companies working in the virtual reality sector fall broadly into three categories of involvement: hardware (making headsets and input devices specific to VR), software (producing software for interfacing with the hardware or for delivering content to users) and content creation (producing content, whether interactive or passive, for consumption with VR hardware).

HMD devices

- Altergaze
- Carl Zeiss (Carl Zeiss Cinemizer)

- Durovis Dive
- Facebook (Oculus Rift)
- Gameface
- Google (Google Cardboard)
- HTC (HTC Vive)
- Microsoft (Microsoft HoloLens)
- Razer (OSVR Hacker Dev Kit)
- Samsung (Samsung Gear VR)
- Sony Computer Entertainment (PS VR)
- Starbreeze Studios (StarVR)
- VRVana (Totem)

Input devices

- Cyberith Virtualizer
- Intugine
- Leap Motion
- Nokia (Nokia OZO camera)
- Sixense
- Virtuix Omni
- ZSpace (company)
- VicoVR

Software

- VREAM

Content

- Clone Mediaworks
- Framestore
- iClone
- Innervision

- Moving Picture Company
- Reel FX
- xRes

Emerging technologies

- 360 degree video
- Augmented reality
- HoloLens
- Intel RealSense
- Magic Leap
- Mixed reality
- Ultrahaptics
- VRVana

Companies

- Google
- Facebook
- Apple
- HTC
- Valve
- Samsung
- Microsoft
- Intel
- Campustours
- Sketchfab

Artists

- Rebecca Allen
- Maurice Benayoun
- Sheldon Brown
- Char Davies

- David Em

- Myron Krueger

- Jaron Lanier

- Brenda Laurel

- Michael Naimark

- Jeffrey Shaw

- Nicole Stenger

- Tamiko Thiel

Methods of Virtual Reality

There are a number of methods by which virtual reality (VR) can be realized.

Simulation-Based VR

The first method is simulation-based virtual reality. Driving simulators, for example, give the driver on board the impression that he/she is actually driving an actual vehicle by predicting vehicular motion caused by driver input and feeding back corresponding visual, motion, audio and proprioceptive cues to the driver. The simulator normally consists of several systems as follows: a real-time vehicle simulation system performing real-time simulation of vehicle dynamics; motion, visual and audio systems reproducing vehicle motion, driving environment scenes and noise sensed by a driver during driving; a control force roading system acting as an interface between the driver and the simulator; an operator console for monitoring system operation; and system integration managing information and data transfer among subsystems and synchronization. The driving simulators have been used effectively for vehicle system development, safety improvement and human factor study.

Avatar Image-Based VR

With avatar image-based virtual reality, people can join the virtual environment in the form of real video as well as an avatar. The proposed image VR system can handle two types of users. One can participate in the 3D distributed virtual environment as form of either a conventional avatar or a real video. Background of the video is effectively eliminated to enhance the sense of reality. A user can select his/her own type of participation based on the system capability. Users with capture board and camera may select a video avatar while others select a conventional computer graphics-based avatar. Avatar image-based VR now provides pretty good interaction environment between human and computer far beyond the conventional desktop computer systems. High-speed networks become available with the advance of network technologies.

Projector-based VR

In projector-based virtual reality, modeling of the real environment plays a vital role in various virtual reality applications, such as robot navigation, construction modeling and airplane simulation. Image based virtual reality system is gaining popularity in computer graphics as well as computer vision communities. The reason is that is it provides more realism by using photo realistic images and the modeling procedure is rather simple. In generating realistic models, it is essential to accurately register acquired 3D data. Usually, camera is used for modeling small objects at a short distance.

Desktop-based VR

Desktop-based virtual reality involves displaying a 3-dimensional virtual world on a regular desktop display without use of any specialized movement-tracking equipment. Many modern computer games can be used as an example, using various triggers, responsive characters, and other such interactive devices to make the user feel as though they are in a virtual world. A common criticism of this form of immersion is that there is no sense of peripheral vision, limiting the user's ability to know what is happening around them.

True Immersive Virtual Reality

Hypothetical virtual reality as immersive as consensus reality. Most likely to be produced using a brain–computer interface. An intermediate stage may be produced by "Virtual Space" using a head-mounted display with head tracking and computer control of the image presented to the helmet.

References

- Choi, SangSu, Kiwook Jung, and Sang Do Noh. "Virtual reality applications in manufacturing industries: Past research, present findings, and future directions." Concurrent Engineering (2015): 1063293X14568814.

- Kulkarni, S.D.; Minor, M.A.; Deaver, M.W.; Pardyjak, E.R.; Hollerbach, J.M.Design, Sensing, and Control of a Scaled Wind Tunnel for Atmospheric Display, Mechatronics, IEEE/ASME Transactions on, vol.17, no.4, pp. 635–645, Aug. 2012

- Blascovich, J Bailenson, J. Infinite Reality: Avatars, Eternal Life, New Worlds, and the Dawn of the Virtual Revolution, Harper Collins, 2011.

- Roudavski, S. (2010). Virtual Environments as Techno-Social Performances: Virtual West Cambridge Case-Study, in CAADRIA2010: New Frontiers, the 15th International Conference on Computer Aided Architectural Design Research in Asia, ed. by Bharat Dave, Andrew I-kang Li, Ning Gu and Hyoung-June Park, pp. 477–486

2

Aspects of Virtual Reality

There are several facets to virtual reality; many of these can be represented by the reality–virtuality continuum. This chapter informs the reader about concepts of virtual reality like haptic technology, virtual body, virtual globe, cyberspace, motion simulator, Cave automatic virtual environment (CAVE), collaborative virtual environment and immersion. The chapter incorporates in-depth information with engaging examples that facilitate an extensive understanding of these concepts.

Cave Automatic Virtual Environment

A cave automatic virtual environment (better known by the recursive acronym CAVE) is an immersive virtual reality environment where projectors are directed to between three and six of the walls of a room-sized cube. The name is also a reference to the allegory of the Cave in Plato's *Republic* in which a philosopher contemplates perception, reality and illusion.

General Characteristics of the CAVE

The CAVE

A CAVE is typically a video theater situated within a larger room. The walls of a CAVE are typically made up of rear-projection screens, however flat panel displays are becoming more common. The floor can be a downward-projection screen, a bottom projected screen or a flat panel display. The projection systems are very high-resolution due to the near distance viewing which requires very small pixel sizes to retain the illusion of reality. The user wears 3D glasses inside the CAVE to see 3D graphics generated by the CAVE. People using the CAVE can see objects apparently floating in the air, and can walk around them, getting a proper view of what they would look like in reality. This was initially made possible by electromagnetic sensors, but has converted to infrared cameras. The frame of early CAVEs had to be built from non-magnetic materials such as wood to minimize interference with the electromagnetic sensors; the change to infrared tracking has removed that limitation. A CAVE user's movements are tracked by the sensors typically attached to the 3D glasses and the video continually adjusts to retain the viewers perspective. Computers control both this aspect of the CAVE and the audio aspect. There are typically multiple speakers placed at multiple angles in the CAVE, providing 3D sound to complement the 3D video.

Technology

A lifelike visual display is created by projectors positioned outside the CAVE and controlled by physical movements from a user inside the CAVE. A motion capture system records the real time position of the user. Stereoscopic LCD shutter glasses convey a 3D image. The computers rapidly generate a pair of images, one for each of the user's eyes, based on the motion capture data. The glasses are synchronized with the projectors so that each eye only sees the correct image. Since the projectors are positioned outside the cube, mirrors are often used to reduce the distance required from the projectors to the screens. One or more computers drive the projectors. Clusters of desktop PCs are popular to run CAVEs, because they cost less and run faster.

Software and libraries designed specifically for CAVE applications are available. There are several techniques for rendering the scene. There are 3 popular scene graphs in use today: OpenSG, OpenSceneGraph, and OpenGL Performer. OpenSG and OpenSceneGraph are open source; while OpenGL Performer is free, its source code is not included.

CAVELib is the original application programmer's interface (API) developed for the CAVE(TM) system created at the Electronic Visualization Lab at University of Illinois Chicago. The software was commercialized in 1996 and further enhanced by Mechdyne Corporation. The CAVELib is a low level VR software package in that it abstracts for a developer window and viewport creation, viewer-centered perspective calculations, displaying to multiple graphics channels, multi-processing and multi-threading, cluster synchronization and data sharing, and stereoscopic viewing. Developers create all of the graphics for their environment and the CAVELib makes it display properly. The CAVELib API is platform-independent, enabling developers to create high-end virtual reality applications on Windows and Linux operating systems (IRIX, Solaris, and HP-UX are no longer supported). CAVELib-based applications are externally configurable at run-time, making an application executable independent of the display system.

Mechdyne's Conduit is a commercial software package that makes a small number of existing 3D OpenGL application (like CATIA V5, Pro/E, Unigraphics...) work directly in a CAVE, without any source code modification. Working like an OpenGL driver, it takes the model definitions of the existing application, streams them on a PC cluster, and changes the camera so that the viewpoint is dependent on the tracking system.

EON Icube is a hardware & software package developed by EON Reality that uses PC-based technology to create a multi-sided immersive environment in which participants may be completely surrounded by virtual imagery and 3D sound. The Icube software supports edge blending and the capability to create full quad buffer stereo images in 3D.

VR Juggler is a suite of APIs designed to simplify the VR application development process. VR Juggler allows the programmer to write an application that will work with any VR display device, with any VR input devices, without changing any code or having to recompile the application. Juggler is used in over 100 CAVEs worldwide.

CoVE is a suite of APIs designed to enable the creation of reusable VR applications. CoVE provides programmers with an API to develop multi-user, multi-tasking, collaborative, cluster-ready applications with rich 2D interfaces using an immersive window manager and windowing API to provide windows, menus, buttons, and other common widgets within the VR system. CoVE also supports running X11 applications within the VR environment.

Equalizer (software) is an open source rendering framework and resource management system for multipipe applications, ranging from single pipe workstations to VR installations. Equalizer provides an API to write parallel, scalable visualization applications which are configured at run-time by a resource server.

Syzygy (software) is a freely-distributed grid operating system for PC cluster virtual reality, tele-collaboration, and multimedia supercomputing, developed by the Integrated Systems Laboratory at the Beckman Institute of the University of Illinois at Urbana–Champaign. This middleware runs on Mac OS, Linux, Windows, and Irix. C++, OpenGL, and Python applications (as well as other regular computer apps) can run on this and be distributed for VR.

Avango is a framework for building distributed virtual reality applications. It provides a field/fieldcontainer based application layer similar to VRML. Within this layer a scene graph, based on OpenGL Performer, input sensors, and output actuators are implemented as runtime loadable modules (or plugins). A network layer provides automatic replication/distribution of the application graph using a reliable multi-cast system. Applications in Avango are written in Scheme and run in the scripting layer. The scripting layer provides complete access to fieldcontainers and their fields; this way distributed collaborative scenarios as well as render-distributed applications (or even both at the same time) are supported. Avango was originally developed at the VR group at GMD, now Virtual Environments Group at Fraunhofer IAIS and was open-sourced in 2004.

CaveUT is an open source mutator for Unreal Tournament 2004. Developed by PublicVR, CaveUT leverages existing gaming technologies to create a CAVE environment. By using Unreal Tournament's spectator function CaveUT can position virtual viewpoints around the player's "head". Each viewpoint is a separate client that, when projected on a wall, gives the illusion of a 3D environment.

Quest3D, a real-time 3D engine and development platform, suitable for CAVE implementations.

Vrui (Virtual Reality User Interface) is a development toolkit that handles real-time rendering, head tracking, etc. in multi-display environments such as the CAVE. 3DVisualizer, LidarViewer, and several other software packages were developed using Vrui to provide visualization tools for specific data types. These tools have been publicly released with continuing development by the Keck Center for Active Visualization in Earth Sciences. Oliver Kreylos maintains Vrui documentation and source code on his website.

inVRs The inVRs framework provides a clearly structured approach for the design of highly interactive and responsive VEs and NVEs. It is developed following open-source principles (LGPL) easy to use with CAVEs and a variety of input devices.

VR4MAX is a package for real-time 3D rendering and development of interactive 3D models and simulators based on Autodesk 3ds Max content. VR4MAX Extreme supports multi-projection for CAVE implementations and provides extensive tracking support.

Cave5D is an adaptation of Vis5D to the CAVE. It enables users to interactively explore animated 3D output from weather models and similar data sets.

libGlass is a general purpose distributed computing library, but has been used extensively in distributed computer graphic applications. There are many applications running at the five-sided CAVE. For example: astronomic application,arcade-like flight simulator and OpenGL demos.

P3D VirtualSight is a software solution designed to provide an immersive, photorealistic 3D experience of Digital Aspect Mockups on a 1:1 scale. P3D Virtual Sight supports multiple stereoscopic display modes. It can be interfaced with various tracking systems and can power configurations such as multi-screen devices, image walls based on juxtaposed projections, CAVE systems, or Head Mounted Displays.

Vizard (software) is a multi-purpose virtual reality development platform by WorldViz for building, rendering, and deploying 3D visualization & simulation applications in stereoscopic multi-display environments such as the CAVE. The software lets users control 3D content, CAD workflows, rendering clusters, visual displays, motion tracking, and user interaction from one single platform. A joint solution with SensoMotoric Instruments also allows to incorporate eye tracking.

Quazar3D Immersive (software) commercial software package for building and managing immersive digital environments including CAVE, PowerWalls, cylindrical projection systems, etc. The key feature is a powerful management console for easy configuration of the whole rendering cluster . Features such as VRPN, quadbuffer stereo, hardware and software synchronization, off-axis stereo for planar and cylindrical projections are supported.

Dice by Immersion is an acronym for Digital Immersive and Compact Environment. This is an affordable Premium turnkey CAVE-type solution developed by Immersion SAS (Fr), including hardware (screens, mechanics, projectors, tracking, workstation...), software suite (Middle VR and Unity) and Services (3-year warranty: parts & labour and consumables included).

3D Virtual Spaces by Satavision are CAVE-type solutions including both the hardware and the software developed by Satavision Ltd. The 3D Virtual Spaces are built to customer specific requirements and the content the customer wishes to use is converted into a CAVE compatible stereoscopic content. These spaces are used for multiple purposes: as a tool for planning, research or marketing, in educational settings or as an effective way to increase sales.

VisCube by Visbox affordable high performance CAVE systems that fit within existing spaces, eliminating time-consuming and costly room modifications. VisCube CAVE systems are available as either standalone displays or turn-key VR systems with tracking and software.

Calibration

To be able to create an image that will not be distorted or out of place, the displays and sensors must be calibrated. The calibration process depends on the motion capture technology being used. Optical or Inertial-acoustic systems only requires to configure the zero and the axes used by the tracking system. Calibration of electromagnetic sensors (like the ones used in the first cave) is more complex. In this case a person will put on the special glasses needed to see the images in 3D. The projectors then fill the CAVE with many one-inch boxes set one foot apart. The person then takes an instrument called an "ultrasonic measurement device" which has a cursor in the middle of it, and positions the device so that the cursor is visually in line with the projected box. This process can go on until almost 400 different blocks are measured. Each time the cursor is placed inside a block, a computer program records the location of that block and sends the location to another computer. If the points are calibrated accurately, there should be no distortion in the images that are projected in the CAVE. This also allows the CAVE to correctly identify where the user is located and can precisely track their movements, allowing the projectors to display images based on where the person is inside the CAVE.

Applications

The concept of the original CAVE has been reapplied and is currently being used in a variety of fields. Many universities own CAVE systems. CAVEs have many uses. Many engineering companies use CAVEs to enhance product development. Prototypes of parts can be created and tested, interfaces can be developed, and factory layouts can be simulated, all before spending any money on physical parts. This gives engineers a better idea of how a part will behave in the product in its entirety. CAVEs are also used more and more in the collaborative planning in construction sector.

The EVL team at UIC released the CAVE2 in October 2012. Similar to the original CAVE, it is a 3D immersive environment but is based on LCD panels rather than projection.

Haptic Technology

Haptic or kinesthetic communication recreates the sense of touch by applying forces, vibrations, or motions to the user. This mechanical stimulation can be used to assist in the creation of virtual objects in a computer simulation, to control such virtual objects, and to enhance the remote control of machines and devices (telerobotics). Haptic devices may incorporate tactile sensors that measure forces exerted by the user on the interface.

Rumble packs for controllers, such as this Dreamcast Jump Pack, provide haptic feedback through a user's hands

Most researchers distinguish three sensory systems related to sense of touch in humans: cutaneous, kinesthetic and haptic. All perceptions mediated by cutaneous and/ or kinesthetic sensibility are referred to as tactual perception. The sense of touch may be classified as passive and active, and the term "haptic" is often associated with active touch to communicate or recognize objects.

Haptic technology has made it possible to investigate how the human sense of touch works by allowing the creation of carefully controlled haptic virtual objects.

The word *haptic*, (*haptikos*), means "pertaining to the sense of touch" and comes from *haptesthai*, meaning "to contact" or "to touch".

History

One of the earliest applications of haptic technology was in large aircraft that use servomechanism systems to operate control surfaces. Such systems tend to be "one-way", meaning external forces applied aerodynamically to the control surfaces are not perceived at the controls. Here, the missing normal forces are simulated with springs and weights. In lighter aircraft without servo systems, as the aircraft approached a stall the aerodynamic buffeting (vibrations) was felt in the pilot's controls. This was a useful warning of a dangerous flight condition. This control shake is not felt when servo control systems are used. To replace this missing sensory cue, the angle of attack is measured and when it approaches the critical stall point, a stick shaker is engaged which simulates the response of a simpler control system. Alternatively, the servo force may be measured and the signal directed to a servo system on the control, known as *force feedback*. Force feedback has been implemented experimentally in some excavators and is useful when excavating mixed material such as large rocks embedded in silt or clay. It allows the operator to "feel" and work around unseen obstacles, enabling significant increases in productivity and less risk of damage to the machine.

The first US patent for a tactile telephone was granted to Thomas D. Shannon in 1973. An early tactile man-machine communication system was constructed by A. Michael Noll at Bell Telephone Laboratories, Inc. in the early 1970s and a patent issued for his invention in 1975.

Aura Interactor vest

In 1994, Aura Systems launched the Interactor Vest, a wearable force-feedback device that monitors an audio signal and uses Aura's patented electromagnetic actuator technology to convert bass sound waves into vibrations that can represent such actions as a punch or kick. The Interactor vest plugs into the audio output of a stereo, TV, or VCR and the user is provided with controls that allow for adjusting of the intensity of vibration and filtering out of high frequency sounds. The Interactor Vest is worn over the upper torso and the audio signal is reproduced through a speaker embedded in the vest. After selling 400,000 of its Interactor Vest, Aura began shipping the Interactor

Cushion, a device which operates like the Vest but instead of being worn, it's placed against a seat back and the user must lean against it. Both the Vest and the Cushion were launched with a price tag of $99.

In 1995 Norwegian Geir Jensen described a wrist watch haptic device with a skin tap mechanism, termed Tap-in. It would connect to a mobile phone via Blueteooth. Tapping-frequency patterns would identify callers to a mobile and enable the wearer to respond by selected short messages. It was submitted for a governmental innovation contest and received no award. It was not pursued or published until recovered in 2015. The Tap-in device by Jensen was devised facing the user to avoid twisting of the wrist. It would adapt across all mobile phone and watch brands. In 2015 Apple started to sell a wrist watch which included skin tap sensing of notifications and alerts to mobile phone of the watch wearer.

Commercial Applications

Tactile Electronic Displays

A tactile electronic display is a kind of display device that presents information in tactile form.

Teleoperators and Simulators

Teleoperators are remote controlled robotic tools—when contact forces are reproduced to the operator, it is called *haptic teleoperation*. The first electrically actuated teleoperators were built in the 1950s at the Argonne National Laboratory by Raymond Goertz to remotely handle radioactive substances. Since then, the use of force feedback has become more widespread in other kinds of teleoperators such as remote controlled underwater exploration devices.

When such devices are simulated using a computer (as they are in operator training devices) it is useful to provide the force feedback that would be felt in actual operations. Since the objects being manipulated do not exist in a physical sense, the forces are generated using haptic (force generating) operator controls. Data representing touch sensations may be saved or played back using such haptic technologies. Haptic simulators are used in medical simulators and flight simulators for pilot training. It is very critical to exert proper force magnitude to the user. It requires considering human force sensitivity.

Video Games

Haptic feedback is commonly used in arcade games, especially racing video games. In 1976, Sega's motorbike game *Moto-Cross*, also known as *Fonz*, was the first game to use haptic feedback which caused the handlebars to vibrate during a collision with another vehicle. Tatsumi's *TX-1* introduced force feedback to car driving games in 1983. The game *Earthshaker!* was the first pinball machine with haptic feedback in 1989.

Simple haptic devices are common in the form of game controllers, joysticks, and steering wheels. Early implementations were provided through optional components, such as the Nintendo 64 controller's *Rumble Pak* in 1997. In the same year, the Microsoft SideWinder Force Feedback Pro with built in feedback from Immersion Corporation was released. Many newer generation console controllers and joysticks feature built in feedback devices too, including Sony's DualShock technology. Some automobile steering wheel controllers, for example, are programmed to provide a "feel" of the road. As the user makes a turn or accelerates, the steering wheel responds by resisting turns or slipping out of control.

In 2007, Novint released the Falcon, the first consumer 3D touch device with high resolution three-dimensional force feedback; this allowed the haptic simulation of objects, textures, recoil, momentum, and the physical presence of objects in games.

In 2013, Valve announced a line of Steam Machines microconsoles, including a new Steam Controller unit that uses weighted electromagnets capable of delivering a wide range of haptic feedback via the unit's trackpads. These controllers' feedback systems are open to the user, which allows the user to configure the feedback to occur in nearly limitless ways and situations. Also, due to the community orientation of the controller, the possibilities to have games interact with the controller's feedback system are only limited to the game's design.

Personal Computers

In 2008, Apple's MacBook and MacBook Pro started incorporating a "Tactile Touchpad" design with button functionality and haptic feedback incorporated into the tracking surface. Products such as the Synaptics ClickPad followed thereafter.

Mobile Devices

Tactile haptic feedback is common in cellular devices. Handset manufacturers like Nokia, LG and Motorola are including different types of haptic technologies in their devices; in most cases, this takes the form of vibration response to touch. Alpine Electronics uses a haptic feedback technology named *PulseTouch* on many of their touch-screen car navigation and stereo units. The Nexus One features haptic feedback, according to their specifications. Samsung first launched a phone with haptics in 2007.

Surface haptics refers to the production of variable forces on a user's finger as it interacts with a surface, such as a touchscreen. Tanvas uses an electrostatic technology to control the in-plane forces experienced by a fingertip, as a programmable function of the finger's motion. The TPaD Tablet Project uses an ultrasonic technology to modulate the slipperiness of a glass touchscreen, as if a user's finger is floating on a cushion of air.

In February 2013, Apple Inc. was awarded the patent for a more accurate haptic feedback system that is suitable for multitouch surfaces. Apple's U.S. Patent for a "Method and apparatus for localization of haptic feedback" describes a system where at least two actuators are positioned beneath a multitouch input device to provide vibratory feedback when a user makes contact with the unit. More specifically, the patent provides for one actuator to induce a feedback vibration, while at least one other actuator creates a second vibration to suppress the first from propagating to unwanted regions of the device, thereby "localizing" the haptic experience. While the patent gives the example of a "virtual keyboard", the language specifically notes the invention can be applied to any multitouch interface.

Virtual Reality

Haptics are gaining widespread acceptance as a key part of virtual reality systems, adding the sense of touch to previously visual-only interfaces. Most of these use stylus-based haptic rendering, where the user interfaces to the virtual world via a tool or stylus, giving a form of interaction that is computationally realistic on today's hardware. Systems are being developed to use haptic interfaces for 3D modeling and design that are intended to give artists a virtual experience of real interactive modeling. Researchers from the University of Tokyo have developed 3D holograms that can be "touched" through haptic feedback using "acoustic radiation" to create a pressure sensation on a user's hands. The researchers, led by Hiroyuki Shinoda, had the technology on display at SIGGRAPH 2009 in New Orleans. Several companies are making full-body or torso haptic vests or haptic suits for use in immersive virtual reality so that explosions and bullet impacts can be felt.

Research

Research has been done to simulate different kinds of taction by means of high-speed vibrations or other stimuli. One device of this type uses a pad array of pins, where the pins vibrate to simulate a surface being touched. While this does not have a realistic feel, it does provide useful feedback, allowing discrimination between various shapes, textures, and resiliencies. Several haptics APIs have been developed for research applications, such as Chai3D, OpenHaptics, and the Open Source H3DAPI.

Medicine

Haptic interfaces for medical simulation may prove especially useful for training in minimally invasive procedures such as laparoscopy and interventional radiology, as well as for performing remote surgery. A particular advantage of this type of work is that surgeons can perform more operations of a similar type with less fatigue.

Tactile Imaging, as a medical imaging modality, translates the sense of touch into a digital image. The tactile image is a function of $P(x,y,z)$, where P is the pressure on soft tissue surface under applied deformation and x,y,z are coordinates where pressure P was measured. Tactile imaging closely mimics manual palpation, since the probe of the device with a pressure sensor array mounted on its face acts similar to human fingers during clinical examination, deforming soft tissue by the probe and detecting resulting changes in the pressure pattern. Clinical applications include imaging of the prostate, breast, elasticity assessment of vagina and pelvic floor support structures, muscle functional imaging of the female pelvic floor and myofascial trigger points in muscle.

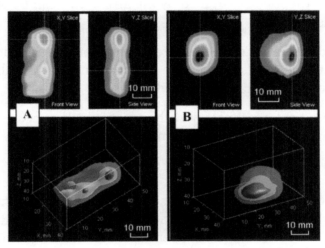

Tactile images for breast lesions. A – two cysts; B – invasive ductal carcinoma.

Mechanical imaging, as a modality of medical diagnostics using mechanical sensors, was introduced in mid 1990s.

A Virtual Haptic Back (VHB) was successfully integrated in the curriculum at the Ohio University College of Osteopathic Medicine.

Robotics

The Shadow Hand uses the sense of touch, pressure, and position to reproduce the strength, delicacy, and complexity of the human grip. The SDRH was developed by Richard Greenhill and his team of engineers in London as part of The Shadow Project, now known as the Shadow Robot Company, an ongoing research and development program whose goal is to complete the first convincing artificial humanoid. An early prototype can be seen in NASA's collection of humanoid robots, or robonauts. The Shadow Hand has haptic sensors embedded in every joint and finger pad, which relay information to a central computer for processing and analysis. Carnegie Mellon University in Pennsylvania and Bielefeld University in Germany found The Shadow Hand to be an invaluable tool in advancing the understanding of haptic awareness, and in 2006 they were involved in related research. The first PHANTOM, which allows one to interact with objects in virtual reality through touch, was developed by Thomas Massie while a student of Ken Salisbury at MIT.

Arts and Design

Touching is not limited to feeling, but allows interactivity in real-time with virtual objects. Thus, haptics are used in virtual arts, such as sound synthesis or graphic design and animation. The haptic device allows the artist to have direct contact with a virtual instrument that produces real-time sound or images. For instance, the simulation of a violin string produces real-time vibrations of this string under the pressure and expressiveness of the bow (haptic device) held by the artist. This can be done with physical modeling synthesis.

Designers and modellers may use high-degree-of-freedom input devices that give touch feedback relating to the "surface" they are sculpting or creating, allowing faster and more natural workflow than traditional methods.

Artists working with haptic technology such as vibrotactile effectors are Christa Sommerer, Laurent Mignonneau, and Stahl Stenslie.

Non-contact Haptic Technology

Non-contact haptic technology utilizes the sense of touch without physical contact of a device. This type of feedback involves interactions with a system that are in a 3D space around the user. Thus, the user is able to perform actions on a system in the absence of holding a physical input device.

Air Vortex Rings

Air vortex rings are donut-shaped air pockets that are concentrated gusts of air. Focused air vortices can have the force to blow out a candle or disturb papers from a few yards away. Two specific companies have done research using air vortices as a source for non-contact haptic feedback.

Disney Research

In 2013, Disney worked on a technology they called AIREAL. This system delivered non-contact haptic feedback through the use of air vortex rings. According to Disney, AIREAL helps users experience textures and "touch" virtual 3D objects in free space. This is all without the need for a glove or any other type of physical haptic feedback.

Disney took on this research because they believed that technology is advancing towards more virtual or augmented reality applications. According to Disney, the missing piece in this emerging computer-augmented world is the absence of physical feeling of virtual objects. Disney's main intention for this research was to encourage other research regarding new applications of non-contact haptic feedback.

Microsoft

In 2013, Microsoft explored the same area as Disney. They used air vortex rings in order to try and provide haptic feedback for an at-a-distance interaction. Microsoft mostly focused on the study of vortex formation theory and parameters that will provide the most effective air vortex ring that will impart haptic feedback onto the user. Microsoft concluded that in order to get the best experience from the air vortex rings, the aperture size that produces the rings does not constrain the design. However, the L/D Ratio is the most useful measurement. The optimal L/D ratio for an air vortex ring generator is between 5 and 6.

Ultrasound

Ultrasound is a form of sound wave that has a high frequency. The most popular use of ultrasound is the visualization of a baby in the mother's womb. These sound waves are not harmful to the human body and can be focused easily. One company called Ultrahaptics has been working with this technology to provide non-contact haptic feedback.

Ultrahaptics

Founded in 2013, Ultrahaptics has focused on providing users haptic feedback in free space using ultrasound technology. They use multiple ultrasound speakers to make changes in the air pressure around the user. This provides the ability to feel the pockets of air pressure focused in the environment. This gives the user tactile cues for gestures, invisible interfaces, textures, and virtual objects.

The company is continuing to grow and launched their evaluation programme in 2014. This programme includes a device that rests on the table. The various ultrasound speakers are laid out in a grid, which can focus the ultrasound waves directly above it. This type of technology is currently intended for use with a laptop or computer.

Future Applications

Future applications of haptic technology cover a wide spectrum of human interaction with technology. Current research focuses on the mastery of tactile interaction with holograms and distant objects, which if successful may result in applications and advancements in gaming, movies, manufacturing, medical, and other industries. The medical industry stands to gain from virtual and telepresence surgeries, which provide new options for medical care. The clothing retail industry could gain from haptic technology by allowing users to "feel" the texture of clothes for sale on the internet. Future advancements in haptic technology may create new industries that were previously not feasible nor realistic.

Holographic Interaction

Researchers at the University of Tokyo are working on adding haptic feedback to holographic projections. The feedback allows the user to interact with a hologram and receive tactile responses as if the holographic object were real. The research uses ultrasound waves to create acoustic radiation pressure, which provides tactile feedback as users interact with the holographic object. The haptic technology does not affect the hologram, or the interaction with it, only the tactile response that the user perceives. The researchers posted a video displaying what they call the Airborne Ultrasound Tactile Display. As of 2008, the technology was not ready for mass production or mainstream application in industry, but was quickly progressing, and industrial companies showed a positive response to the technology. This example of possible future application is the first in which the user does not have to be outfitted with a special glove or use a special control—they can "just walk up and use [it]".

Future Medical Applications

One currently developing medical innovation is a central workstation used by surgeons to perform operations remotely. Local nursing staff set up the machine and prepare the patient, and rather than travel to an operating room, the surgeon becomes a telepresence. This allows expert surgeons to operate from across the country, increasing availability of expert medical care. Haptic technology provides tactile and resistance feedback to surgeons as they operate the robotic device. As the surgeon makes an incision, they feel ligaments as if working directly on the patient.

As of 2003, researchers at Stanford University were developing technology to simulate surgery for training purposes. Simulated operations allow surgeons and surgical students to practice and train more. Haptic technology aids in the simulation by creating a realistic environment of touch. Much like telepresence surgery, surgeons feel simulated ligaments, or the pressure of a virtual incision as if it were real. The researchers, led by J. Kenneth Salisbury Jr., professor of computer science and surgery, hope to be able to create realistic internal organs for the simulated surgeries, but Salisbury stated that the task will be difficult. The idea behind the research is that "just as commercial pilots train in flight simulators before they're unleashed on real passengers, surgeons will be able to practice their first incisions without actually cutting anyone".

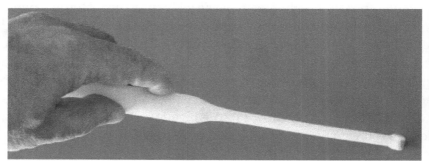

Laparoscopic Tactile Imaging probe (design concept).

According to a Boston University paper published in *The Lancet*, "Noise-based devices, such as randomly vibrating insoles, could also ameliorate age-related impairments in balance control." If effective, affordable haptic insoles were available, perhaps many injuries from falls in old age or due to illness-related balance-impairment could be avoided.

In February 2013, an inventor in the United States built a "spider-sense" bodysuit, equipped with ultrasonic sensors and haptic feedback systems, which alerts the wearer of incoming threats; allowing them to respond to attackers even when blindfolded.

During a laparoscopic surgery the video camera becomes a surgeon's eyes, since the surgeon uses the image from the video camera positioned inside the patient's body to perform the procedure. Visual feedback is either similar or often superior to open procedures. The greatest limitation to these minimally invasive approaches is the impairment (in the case of traditional laparoscopy) or complete lack of tactile sensation (in the case of robotic laparoscopy) normally used to assist in surgical dissection and decision making. Despite multiple attempts, no tactile imaging device or probe is currently commercially available for laparoscopic surgery. Figure on the right presents one of the proposed devices, which is in the development phase.

Reality–Virtuality Continuum

The virtuality continuum is a continuous scale ranging between the completely virtual, a virtuality, and the completely real, reality. The reality-virtuality continuum therefore encompasses all possible variations and compositions of real and virtual objects. It has been described as a concept in new media and computer science, but in fact it could be considered a matter of anthropology. The concept was first introduced by Paul Milgram.

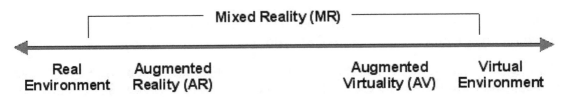

Reality-Virtuality Continuum.

The area between the two extremes, where both the real and the virtual are mixed, is called mixed reality. This in turn is said to consist of both augmented reality, where the virtual augments the real, and augmented virtuality, where the real augments the virtual.

Overview

This continuum has been extended into a two-dimensional plane of *virtuality* and *mediality*. Taxonomy of reality, virtuality, mediality. The origin R denotes unmodified reality. A continuum across the virtuality axis, V, includes reality augmented with graphics (augmented reality), as well as graphics augmented by reality (augmented virtuality). However, the taxonomy also includes modification of reality or virtuality or any combination of these. The modification is denoted by moving up the mediality axis. Further up this axis, for example, we can find mediated reality, mediated virtuality, or any combination of these. Further up and to the right we have virtual worlds that are responsive to a severely modified version of reality.

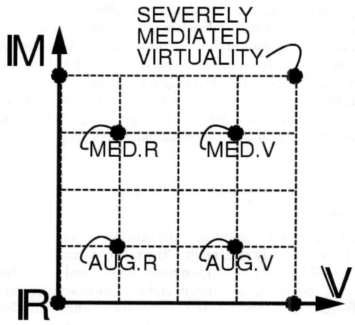

Mediated reality continuum showing four points: augmented reality, augmented virtuality, mediated reality, and mediated virtuality on the virtuality and mediality axes

While the term augmented virtuality is rarely used nowadays, augmented reality and mixed reality are now sometimes used as synonyms.

The virtuality continuum has grown and progressed past labels such as computer science and new media. As the concept has much to do with the way in which humans continue to change how they communicate; the way in which form identities and the way in which they interact to and within the world; it is more accurately described as a subject within anthropology.

Changes in attitudes towards and the increase in availability of technology and media have changed and progressed the way it is used. One to one (SMS), one to many (email), and many to many (chat rooms), have become ingrained in society. The use of such items have made once clear distinctions like *online* and *offline* obsolete, and the distinctions between reality and virtuality have become blurred as people are incorporating and relying heavily upon virtuality within their everyday personal realities.

Daniel Miller and Don Slater are prominent researchers pursuing the concept of the virtuality continuum and the media and its effect on communities, especially in the Caribbean, most notably Trinidad and Jamaica.

Steve Woolgar is another researcher who has established four rules of virtuality. These are:

- The way in which media and technology affect people relies on their non-information communication technology (ICT) related background which may include gender, age, social status, income amongst others.

- Risks and fears in regards to new media and technology are unevenly socially distributed.

- Advancements in media and technology supplement rather than replace existing activities in reality.

- New media and technology tends to create new kinds of localism rather than furthering globalization.

Virtual Body

A virtual body is the state of being when inhabiting virtual reality or a virtual environment.

A person connected to the internet is considered not only physically in the space in front of the computer but also virtually represented, with the opportunity to interact, in cyberspace. This indicates the potential for the body to simultaneously exist in two realities, internally and externally experiencing and being experienced. The virtual body is also recognized as an escape from the limits set by reality and different forms of conventionality.

Frequently Discussed Modes

There are two particular ways that the virtual body is frequently discussed; the disembodied essence of a person's mind in cyberspace and the consequent representation of a person's identity as a virtual body in cyberspace.

The 'disembodiment' discourse focuses around allowing the mind to wander without the physical inhibitions of the body. This discourse is regarded as an expansion of classic theories such as astral projection or 'out-of-body experiences'. Subsequently, the virtual body is regarded as psychologically created essence that is virtually floating between information. This information in turn, according to theories, affects the mind and the virtual body but has no interaction with the physical body, which has deployed a *technological gaze.*

An early issue frequently discussed about virtual bodies is that although the opportunity was presented to create and be any sort of virtual body imaginable, there was a tendency to reproduce old identities referring to gender and racial stereotypes. Therefore, the disembodiment of before transforms into 'a new body' with a new identity that is either entirely new or a representation of the real. When new identities are explored, it has been noticed that the virtual body effortlessly (and sometimes subconsciously) crosses traditional borders, not only concerning identities but also of human and machine, particularly in the sense of having a clear notion of what is real and what is only available through collaboration with the computer. This 'border crossing' implies that the virtual body in itself is a fluid state of being that conceals itself within social conventions.

Other Notions

The virtual body can also be regarded as needing the body for extra immersion into a virtual environment. This notion was initially discussed in reference to the original developments of Virtual Reality, where goggles and gloves were required to fully immerse the mind into virtual worlds. This type of virtual reality offers a different kind of virtual body because it generates the idea within the mind that the virtual body and the real physical body are one and the same.

A more common notion of the identities constructed by people (and therefore depicted through virtual bodies) is the representation people give on websites such as Facebook and MySpace. These websites offer a more direct way for people to exhibit how they want to be seen and understood, which in turn develops their virtual body representation. Along the same lines, is the identity significant idea behind chat rooms (particularly dating ones) where there would be issues regarding how different the represented virtual body and identity is to the real physical one. This is unlike virtual bodies created for the sake of playing games online where exaggeration and the use of the imagination is encouraged.

Virtual Globe

A virtual globe is a three-dimensional (3D) software model or representation of the Earth or another world. A virtual globe provides the user with the ability to freely move around in the virtual environment by changing the viewing angle and position. Compared to a conventional globe, virtual globes have the additional capability of representing many different views on the surface of the Earth. These views may be of geographical features, man-made features such as roads and buildings, or abstract representations of demographic quantities such as population.

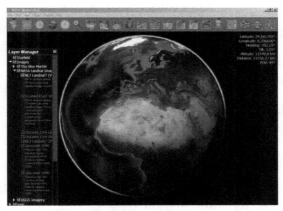

NASA World Wind, an open-source virtual globe with stars and advanced atmosphere & sunlight effects

On November 20, 1997, Microsoft released an *offline* virtual globe in the form of *Encarta Virtual Globe 98*, followed by Cosmi's 3D World Atlas in 1999. The first widely publicized *online* virtual globes were NASA World Wind (released in mid-2004) and Google Earth (mid-2005). NOAA released its virtual globe, Science On A Sphere (SOS) Explorer, in September 2015.

Types

Virtual globes may be used for study or navigation (by connecting to a GPS device) and their design varies considerably according to their purpose. Those wishing to portray a visually accurate representation of the Earth often use satellite image servers and are capable not only of rotation but also zooming and sometimes horizon tilting. Very often such virtual globes aim to provide as true a representation of the World as is possible with worldwide coverage up to a very detailed level. When this is the case the interface often has the option of providing simplified graphical overlays to highlight man-made features since these are not necessarily obvious from a photographic aerial view. The other issue raised by such detail available is that of security with some governments having raised concerns about the ease of access to detailed views of sensitive locations such as airports and military bases.

Another type of virtual globe exists whose aim is not the accurate representation of the planet but instead a simplified graphical depiction. Most early computerized atlases were of this type and, while displaying less detail, these simplified interfaces are still widespread since they are faster to use because of the reduced graphics content and the speed with which the user can understand the display.

List of Virtual Globe Software

As more and more high-resolution satellite imagery and aerial photography become accessible for free, many of the latest online virtual globes are built to fetch and display these images. They include:

- ArcGIS Explorer a lightweight client for ArcGIS Server, supports WMS and many other GIS file formats.

- Bing Maps 3D interface runs inside Internet Explorer and Firefox, and uses NASA Blue Marble: Next Generation.

- Bhuvan is an India-specific virtual globe.

- Cesium, a WebGL virtual globe and map engine. Cesium is free and open-source software (Apache 2.0).

- CitySurf Globe, fast adaptation and transfer secured data due to special data storage structure, dynamic spatial data editing on 3D client monitor, data stored in Oracle SDO or PostGIS, flexible authorization models for different user groups (LDAP and Active Directory support) also excellent quality and fast 2D map rendering.

- driveme.in is a street view application for India.

- Earth3D, a program that visualizes the Earth in a real-time 3D view. It uses data from NASA, USGS, the CIA and the city of Osnabrück. Earth3D is free software (GPL).

- EarthBrowser, an Adobe Flash/AIR-based virtual globe with real-time weather forecasts, earthquakes, volcanoes, and webcams.

- G3M is an open source multiplatform advanced 3D visualization framework, allowing very high performance in mobile native development (iOS and Android).

- Google Earth, satellite & aerial photos dataset (including commercial Digital-Globe images) with international road dataset, the first popular virtual globe along with NASA World Wind.

- MapJack is a map feature covering areas in Canada, France, Latvia, Macau, Malaysia, Puerto Rico, Singapore, Sweden, Thailand, and the United States.

- Marble, part of the KDE, with data provided by OpenStreetMap, as well as NASA Blue Marble: Next Generation and others. Marble is Free and open-source software (LGPL).

- NASA World Wind, USGS topographic maps and several satellite and aerial image datasets, the first popular virtual globe along with Google Earth. World Wind is open-source software (NOSA).

- NORC is a street view web service for Central and Eastern Europe.

- OpenWebGlobe, a virtual globe SDK written in JavaScript using WebGL. OpenWebGlobe is free and open-source software (MIT).

- osgEarth is an open-source (LGPL) C++ SDK for global terrain rendering. It can pull data from web services(WMS, WCS, TMS) as well as many GDAL supported formats.

- PYXIS WorldView, integrates multisource local and remote GIS content on a discrete global Grid (spatial index) system for analysis and sharing.

- Science On A Sphere (SOS) Explorer, free virtual globe from National Oceanic and Atmospheric Administration (NOAA) enables users to explore the world and environmental data.

- Worldwide Telescope features an Earth mode with emphasis on data import/export, time-series support and a powerful Tour authoring environment.

As well as the availability of satellite imagery, online public domain factual databases such as the CIA World Factbook have been incorporated into virtual globes.

Technical Info, Data, and Image Sources

Although by default the World Wind download only comes with public domain imagery from the USGS and Landsat 7, Community members have made available high resolution imagery for New Zealand and New York, here and additional countries, as well as Microsoft's Virtual Earth data (for non-commercial purposes)

Google Earth, NASA World Wind and Norkart Virtual Globe save a cache of downloaded imagery to the user's hard disk, enabling them to be used offline to view previously viewed areas. However, Google Earth cannot be activated without logging into its server the first time it is used.

The Google Earth's cache size is limited to 2000 MB whereas World Wind has no limit on cache size. In Norkart Virtual Globe the disk cache can be set by the user.

In addition to downloaded images, NASA World Wind also comes with the complete 500 m Blue Marble imagery and global placenames including countries, capitals, counties, cities, towns and historical references that are available from install.

World Wind is also capable of displaying MODIS imagery from the JPL Aqua and Terra satellites. An add-on allows for near-real-time MODIS imagery.

Google Earth and Virtual Earth 3D are both capable of displaying many more urban areas in high-resolution thanks to their private image sources. Both companies also hire chartered flights over major cities of the U.S. to take aerial images.

Science On A Sphere (SOS) Explorer is the desktop version of NOAA's Science On A Sphere which is installed in 130+ museums around the world. It includes environmental datasets, NASA blue marble imagery, and was developed using the Unity 3D game engine. Focusing on Earth science education, it supports videos, tours, web content, satellite imagery, and KML.

Marble (KDE) is designed for use in lightweight environments without 3D hardware acceleration and is capable of not only being used as a standalone application, but also as a component in other applications, such as in a "World Clock" Plasma (KDE) and for geolocation in the photo management software digiKam.

3D Weather Globe & Atlas comes with complete 1 km Blue Marble imagery, 40,000 locations database, countries and time zones overlays. Application requires Internet connection only for online features: satellite cloud cover and real-time weather and forecast data.

Worldwide Telescope data support includes raster and vector types, the latter including up to 700,000 points in a single layer..

osgEarth uses a .earth XML map description to configure both web map services and local data sources. osgEarth developers are able to use ReadyMap.org free data services that hosts a 15m global basemap derived from the GLCF Landsat imagery, 90M SRTM elevation dataset derived from CGIAR SRTM, and world-wide street vector overlay from OpenStreetMap.

History

The use of virtual globe software was widely popularized by (and may have been first described in) Neal Stephenson's famous science fiction novel *Snow Crash*. In the metaverse in Snow Crash there is a piece of software called Earth made by the Central Intelligence Corporation. The CIC uses their virtual globe as a user interface for keeping track of all their geospatial data, including maps, architectural plans, weather data, and data from real-time satellite surveillance.

Virtual globes (along with all hypermedia and virtual reality software) are distant descendants of the Aspen Movie Map project, which pioneered the concept of using computers to simulate distant physical environments (though the Movie Map's scope was limited to the city of Aspen, Colorado).

Many of the functions of virtual globes were envisioned by Buckminster Fuller who in 1962 envisioned the creation of a Geoscope that would be a giant globe connected by computers to various databases. This would be used as an educational tool to display large scale global patterns related to topics such as economics, geology, natural resource use, etc.

Comparison

Today's virtual globes can support various features:

Virtual Globe	Introduction year	OS - Windows, Mac, Linux, Unix	Program/data license	Multiple datasets	Guides			Overlays					Tools			
					School, Restaurant, Hotel	Transport	Park	Street map	Satellite and aerial image	Weather map	Topographic map	Real-time traffic report	GPS-integration	Distance measure	Drawing tools	Movie maker
SOS Explorer	2015	Windows and Mac	freeware	Yes	No	No	No	No	Yes	Yes	Yes	Yes	No	Yes	Yes	No
Google Earth	2005	all	freeware (Basic) proprietary(Pro)	No	Yes	Yes	Yes	Yes	Yes	Yes	Some	Yes	Yes	Yes	Yes	Yes
NASA World Wind	2004	Windows/all	open source, free domain	Yes	No	Yes	No	No	Yes	Yes	Yes	No	Yes	Yes	No	Yes
Bing Maps	2006	Windows only	freeware	No	No	Yes	No	Yes	Yes	No	No	No	No	Yes	Yes	Yes
Marble (KDE)	2006	all	LGPL	Yes	No	No	No	Yes: OpenStreetMap	Yes	Some: Shows real-time cloud images	Yes	No	Yes	Yes	No	No
osgEarth	2009	all	LGPL	Yes	No	No	No	Yes: OpenStreetMap	Yes	Some: Can display from OWM	Yes	No	No	Yes	Yes	No
Virtual Globe	Introduction year	OS - Windows, Mac, Linux, Unix	Program/data license	Multiple datasets	School, Restaurant, Hotel	Transport	Park	Street map	Satellite and aerial image	Weather map	Topographic map	Real-time traffic report	GPS-integration	Distance measure	Drawing tools	Movie maker

Virtual Globe	3D Modelling				Planetarium	Day/night views	Imagery of other planets	Telescope/Sky mode	Simulators		Online community user input	Extensibility	Wikipedia integration
	3D Graphics	Buildings	Terrain	Seafloor					Flight Simulator	Sunlight Simulator			
SOS Explorer	Yes	Yes	Yes	Yes	No	Yes	Yes	No	No	Yes	Yes	No	No
Google Earth	Yes	Yes	Yes	Yes	Yes	Yes	Yes	Yes	Yes	Yes	Yes	Some	Yes
NASA World Wind	Yes	No	Yes	Yes	Yes	Yes	Yes	Some	No	Yes	Yes	Yes	Yes
Bing Maps	Yes	Yes	Yes	No	Yes	No	No	No	No	No	No	No	Yes
Marble (KDE)	No	No	No	No	No	Yes	Yes	No	No	Yes	Yes	Yes	Yes
os-gEarth	Yes	Yes	Yes	Yes	No	Yes	Yes	No	Yes	Yes	Yes	Yes	No
Virtual Globe	3D Modelling				Planetarium	Day/night views	Imagery of other planets	Telescope/Sky mode	Simulators		Online community user input	Extensibility	Wikipedia integration
	3D Graphics	Buildings	Terrain	Seafloor					Flight Simulator	Sunlight Simulator			

Virtual Globe	languag-es sup-ported	Hi-resolution data set areas	street-level address search areas	driving direc-tion areas	business listing areas	hotel listing areas
Google Earth	45 different languag es	Some: Austra-lia, Belgium, Canada, China, Denmark, France, Germa-ny, Italy, Japan, Netherlands, Spain, United Kingdom, Unit-ed States	Some: Australia, Belgium, Brazil, Canada, China, Czech Republic, Sweden, Denmark, Estonia, France, Germany, Hungary, Italy, Japan, Lithu-ania, Netherlands, Poland, Spain, United Kingdom, United States	Some: Austra-lia, Belgium, Canada, China, Denmark, France, Ger-many, Italy, Netherlands, Spain, United Kingdom, Unit-ed States	Some: Austra-lia, Belgium, Canada, China, Den-mark, France, Germany, Italy, Japan, Netherlands, Spain, United Kingdom, Unit-ed States	Some: Austra-lia, Belgium, Canada, China, Den-mark, France, Germany, Italy, Japan, Netherlands, Spain, United Kingdom, United States
NASA World Wind	English	Some: United States, New Zealand (par-tially)	Some: Australia, Germany, France, Japan, United States, United Kingdom	No	No	No
Bing Maps	English	Some: United States, Can-ada, United Kingdom, Italy, France, Austra-lia, Germany	Some: United States, United King-dom, Australia	Some: United States, United Kingdom, Australia	No	No
Marble (KDE)	Translat-ed as part of KDE, which has 88 lan-guages	No	Yes: via Open-streetmap	Yes: Worldwide via Openstreet-map	No	No
os-gEarth	English	Some: hires data located on ReadyMap	No	No	No	No
Virtual Globe	language support	Hi-resolution data set areas	street-level address search areas	driving direc-tion areas	business listing areas	hotel listing areas

Avatar (Computing)

In computing, an **avatar** is the graphical representation of the user or the user's alter ego or character. It may take either a three-dimensional form, as in games or virtu-al worlds, or a two-dimensional form as an icon in Internet forums and other online communities. Avatar images have also been referred to as "picons" (personal icons) in the past, though the usage of this term is uncommon now. It can also refer to a text construct found on early systems such as MUDs. The term "avatar" can also refer to the personality connected with the screen name, or handle, of an Internet user. Common avatars may be Internet memes.

Origins

The word *avatar* originates in Hinduism, where it stands for the "descent" of a deity in a terrestrial form (deities in India are popularly thought to be formless and capable of manifesting themselves in any form).

The earliest use of the word *avatar* in a computer game was the 1979 PLATO role-playing game *Avatar*.

The use of the term *avatar* for the on-screen representation of the user was coined in 1985 by Richard Garriott for the computer game *Ultima IV: Quest of the Avatar*. In this game, Garriott desired the player's character to be his earth self manifested into the virtual world. Garriott did this because he wanted the real player to be responsible for the character's in game actions due to the ethical parables he designed into the story. Only if you were playing "yourself" Garriott felt, could you be judged based on your character's actions. Because of its ethically-nuanced, story-driven approach, he took the Hindu word associated with a deity's manifestation on earth in physical form, and applied it to a player manifesting in the game world.

The term *avatar* was also used in 1986 by Chip Morningstar in Lucasfilm's online role-playing game *Habitat*.

Another early use of the term was in the pen and paper role-playing game *Shadowrun* (1989).

Popular Fiction

Norman Spinrad

In Norman Spinrad's novel *Songs from the Stars* (1980), the term *avatar* is used in a description of a computer generated virtual experience. In the story, humans receive messages from an alien galactic network that wishes to share knowledge and experience with other advanced civilizations through "songs". The humans build a "galactic receiver" that describes itself:

The galactic receiver is programmed to derive species specific full sensory input data from standard galactic meaning code equations. By controlling your sensorium input along species specific parameters galactic songs astral back-project you into approximation of total involvement in artistically recreated broadcast realities...

From the last page of the chapter titled "The Galactic Way" in a description of an experience that is being relayed via the galactic receiver to the main characters:

You stand in a throng of multifleshed being, mind avatared in all its matter, on a broad avenue winding through a city of blue trees with bright red foliage and living buildings growing from the soil in a multitude of forms.

Neal Stephenson

The use of *avatar* to mean online virtual bodies was popularised by Neal Stephenson in his cyberpunk novel *Snow Crash* (1992). In *Snow Crash,* the term *avatar* was used to describe the virtual simulation of the human form in the *Metaverse,* a fictional virtual-reality application on the Internet. Social status within the Metaverse was often based on the quality of a user's avatar, as a highly detailed avatar showed that the user was a skilled hacker and programmer while the less talented would buy off-the-shelf models in the same manner a beginner would today. Stephenson wrote in the "Acknowledgments" to *Snow Crash*:

The idea of a "virtual reality" such as the Metaverse is by now widespread in the computer-graphics community and is being used in a number of different ways. The particular vision of the Metaverse as expressed in this novel originated from idle discussion between me and Jaime (Captain Bandwidth) Taaffe...The words *avatar* (in the sense used here) and *Metaverse* are my inventions, which I came up with when I decided that existing words (such as *virtual reality*) were simply too awkward to use...after the first publication of *Snow Crash,* I learned that the term *avatar* has actually been in use for a number of years as part of a virtual reality system called *Habitat*...in addition to avatars, *Habitat* includes many of the basic features of the Metaverse as described in this book.

Use

Internet forums

Despite the widespread use of avatars, it is unknown which Internet forums were the first to use them; the earliest forums did not include avatars as a default feature, and they were included in unofficial "hacks" before eventually being made standard. Avatars on Internet forums serve the purpose of representing users and their actions, personalizing their contributions to the forum, and may represent different parts of their persona, beliefs, interests or social status in the forum.

The traditional avatar system used on most Internet forums is a small (80x80 to 100x100 pixels, for example) square-shaped area close to the user's forum post, where the avatar is placed in order for other users to easily identify who has written the post without having to read their username. Some forums allow the user to upload an avatar image that may have been designed by the user or acquired from elsewhere. Other forums allow the user to select an avatar from a preset list or use an auto-discovery algorithm to extract one from the user's homepage.

Some avatars are animated, consisting of a sequence of multiple images played repeatedly. In such animated avatars, the number of images as well as the time in which they are replayed vary considerably.

Other avatar systems exist, such as on Gaia Online, WeeWorld, Frenzoo or Meez, where a pixelized representation of a person or creature is used, which can then be customized to the user's wishes. There are also avatar systems (e.g. Trutoon) where a representation is created using a person's face with customized characters and backgrounds.

Another avatar-based system is one wherein an image is automatically generated based on the identity of the poster. Identicons are formed as visually distinct geometric images derived from a digest hash of the poster's IP address. In this way, a particular anonymous user can be uniquely identified from session to session without the need for registration or authentication. In the cases where registration has occurred, the identicon serves as a means to associate a particular user with a particular geometric representation. If an account is compromised, a dissimilar identicon will be formed as the attacker is posting from an unfamiliar IP address.

Internet Chat

GIF avatars were introduced as early as 1990 in the ImagiNation Network (also known as Sierra On-Line) game and chat hybrid.

In 1994, Virtual Places offered VOIP capabilities which were later abandoned for lack of bandwidth.

In 1995, KeepTalking, a product of UNET2 Corporation, was one of the first companies to implement an avatar system into their web chat software.

In 1995, Cybertown first introduced three dimensional avatars to internet chat.

In 1996 Microsoft Comic Chat, an IRC client that used cartoon avatars for chatting, was released.

Instant Messaging Programs

America Online introduced instant messaging for its membership in 1996 and included a limited number of "buddy icons," picking up on the avatar idea from PC games. When AOL later introduced the free version of its messenger, AIM, for use by anyone on the Internet, the number of icons offered grew to be more than 1,000 and the use of them grew exponentially, becoming a hallmark feature of instant messaging. In 2002, AOL introduced "Super Buddies," 3D animated icons that talked to users as they typed messages and read messages. The term Avatar began to replace the moniker of "buddy icon" as 3D customizable icons became known to its users from the mainstream popularity of PC Games. Yahoo's instant messenger was the first to adopt the term "avatar" for its icons. Today, many other instant-messaging services support the use of avatars.

Instant messaging avatars are usually very small. AIM icons, have been as small as 16x16 pixels but are used more commonly at the 48x48 pixels size, although many icons can be found online that typically measure anywhere from 50x50 pixels to 100x100 pixels in size.

The latest use of avatars in instant messaging is dominated by dynamic avatars. The user chooses an avatar that represents him while chatting and, through the use of text to speech technology, enables the avatar to talk the text being used at the chat window. Another form of use for this kind of avatar is for video chats/calls. Some services, such as Skype (through some external plugins) allow users to use talking avatars during video calls, replacing the image from the user's camera with an animated, talking avatar.

American Online began to use AIM buddy icons as a marketing tool, known as "Expressions," for music, movies, and computer games in 2001. Since then many advertising firms have as well.

Artificial Intelligence

An avatar used by an automated online assistant providing customer service on a web page

Avatars can be used as virtual embodiments of embodied agents, which are driven more or less by artificial intelligence rather than real people. Automated online assistants are examples of avatars used in this way.

Such avatars are used by organizations as a part of automated customer services in order to interact with consumers and users of services. This can avail for enterprises to reduce their operating and training cost. A major underlying technology to such systems is natural language processing. Some of these avatars are commonly known as "bots". Famous examples include Ikea's Anna, an avatar designed to guide users around the Ikea website.

Such avatars can also be powered by a digital conversation which provides a little more structure than those using NLP, offering the user options and clearly defined paths to an outcome. This kind of avatar is known as a Structured Language Processing or SLP Avatar.

Both types of avatar provide a cost effective and efficient way of engaging with consumers.

Video Games

Avatars in video games are the player's representation in the game world. The first video game to include a representation of the player was Maze War in 1973, which was the first first person shooter. This game represented the players as an eyeball.

In some games, the player's representation is fixed, however many games offer a basic character model, or template, and then allow customization of the physical features as the player sees fit. For example, Carl Johnson, the avatar from *Grand Theft Auto: San Andreas*, can be dressed in a wide range of clothing, can be given tattoos and haircuts, and can even body build or become obese depending upon player actions. One video game in which the avatar and player are two separate entities is the game Perspective, where the player controls both themself in a 3-dimensional world and the avatar in a 2-dimensional world.

Aside from an avatar's physical appearance, its dialogue, particularly in cut scenes, may also reveal something of its character. A good example is the crude, action hero stereotype, Duke Nukem. Other avatars, such as Gordon Freeman from *Half-Life*, who never speaks at all, reveal very little of themselves (the original game never showed the player what he looked like without the use of a console command for third-person view).

Game consoles such as the Wii, PlayStation 3, and Xbox 360 (shown here) feature universal animated avatars.

Massively multiplayer online games (MMOGs) are the source of the most varied and sophisticated avatars. Customization levels differ between games; For example, in *EVE Online*, players construct a wholly customized portrait, using a software that allows for several changes to facial structure as well as preset hairstyles, skin tones, etc. However, these portraits appear only in in-game chats and static information view of other players. Usually, all players appear in gigantic spacecraft that give no view of their pilot, unlike in most other RPGs. Alternatively, *City of Heroes* offers one of the most detailed and comprehensive in-game avatar creation processes, allowing players to construct anything from traditional superheroes to aliens, medieval knights, monsters, robots, and many more. Robbie Cooper's 2007 book "Alter Ego, Avatars and their creators" pairs photographs of players of a variety of MMO's with images of their in-game avatars and profiles; recording the player's motivations and intentions in designing and using their avatars. The survey reveals wide variation in the ways in which players of MMO's use avatars. Felicia Day, creator and star of *The Guild* web series, created a song called "(Do You Wanna Date My) Avatar" which satirizes avatars and virtual dating.

Nintendo's Wii console allows for the creation of avatars called "Miis" that take the form of stylized, cartoonish people and can be used in some games as avatars for players, as in Wii Sports. In some games, the ability to use a Mii as an avatar must be unlocked, such as in *Mario Kart Wii*.

On November 19, 2008, Microsoft released an Xbox 360 Dashboard update which featured the introduction of Avatars as part of the console's New Xbox Experience. With the update installed users can personalize the look of their Avatars by choosing from a range of clothing and facial features. On August 11, 2009, the NXE Avatar program was updated with the inclusion of an Avatar Marketplace feature that allows users to purchase additional product and game branded clothing, jewelry, full body suits, and animated props. On initial release of the update, game branded content included items from *Gears of War 2*, *BioShock 2*, *Star Wars*, *Fable II*, *Halo 3*, and *The Secret of Monkey Island* special edition. The Xbox LIVE Avatar Marketplace is updated weekly with new items.

PlayStation Home for Sony's PlayStation 3 console also features the use of avatars, but with a more realistic style than Nintendo's Miis or Microsoft's Avatars.

Non-Gaming Online Worlds

Avatars in non-gaming online worlds are used as two- or three-dimensional human or fantastic representations of a person's inworld self. Such representations are a tool which facilitates the exploration of the virtual universe, or acts as a focal point in conversations with other users, and can be customized by the user. Usually, the purpose and appeal of such universes is to provide a large enhancement to common online conversation capabilities, and to allow the user to peacefully develop a portion of a non-gaming universe without being forced to strive towards a pre-defined goal.

In non-gaming universes, the criteria avatars have to fulfill in order to become useful can depend to a great extent on the age of potential users. Research suggests that younger users of virtual communities put great emphasis on fun and entertainment aspects of avatars. They are also interested in the simple ease of use of avatars, and their ability to retain the user's anonymity. Meanwhile, older users pay great importance to an avatar's ability to reflect their own appearance, identity, and personality. Most older users also want to be able to use an avatar's expressive functionalities (such as showing emotions), and are prepared to learn new ways of navigation to do it. Surprisingly, some evidence suggests that avatars that are more anthropomorphic are perceived to be less credible and likeable than images that are less anthropomorphic. Social scientists at Stanford's Virtual Human Interaction Lab examine the implications, possibilities, and transformed social interaction that occur when people interact via avatars.

Avatar-based non-gaming universes are usually populated by age groups whose requirements concerning avatars are fulfilled. For example, most users of Habbo Hotel, Ty Girlz and Webkinz are aged 10 to 15 years, while users of Gaia Online and WeeWorld are 13 to 18. The reason may well be the properties and functionalities of the avatars of these virtual communities, as well as what the games are able to give to their players. In contrast, There and Kaneva Game Platform target users aged 22 to 49 and their avatars allow for a wide range of social interactions, including the expression of emotions: laughing, waving, blowing kisses, and rude gestures. The Palace, most of whose users seem to be older, allows users to use their own images as avatars. This turns the avatar into a direct reflection of users' real-life appearance, as desired by older users.

Lisa Nakamura has suggested that customizable avatars in non-gaming worlds tend to be biased towards lighter skin colors and against darker skin colors, especially in those of the male gender. In Second Life avatars are created by residents and take any form, and range from lifelike humans to robots, animals, plants and mythical creatures. Avatar customization is one of the most important entertainment aspects in non gaming virtual worlds, such as Second Life, IMVU, and Active Worlds. Many virtual worlds are providing users with tools to customize their representations, allowing them to change shapes, hair, skins and also genre. Moreover, there is a growing secondary industry devoted to the creations of products and items for the avatars. Some companies have also launched social networks and other websites for avatars such as Koinup, Myrl, and Avatars United.

Customization

Early examples of customizable avatars include multi-user systems, including MUDs. Most forums use a small JPEG, Portable Network Graphics (PNG) or Graphics Interchange Format (GIF) file to display a small image next to posts from a user. Gaia Online has a customizable avatar where users can dress it up as desired. Users may earn credits for completing sponsored surveys or certain tasks to purchase items and upgrades to customize their avatar. Linden Lab's *Second Life* creates a virtual world in which avatars, homes, decorations, buildings and land are for sale. Less-common items may be designed to appear better than common items, and an experienced player may be identified from a group of new characters before in-game statistics are seen. Sherry Turkle described a middle-aged man who played an aggressive, confrontational female character in his online communities, displaying personality traits he was embarrassed to display in the offline world. Research by Nick Yee of the Daedelus Project demonstrates that an avatar may differ considerably from a player's offline identity, based on gender. However, most players will make an avatar that is (proportionately) equal to their height (or slightly taller). Sherry Turkle has observed that some players seek an emotional connection they cannot establish in the real world. She described a case in which a man with a serious heart condition preventing him from ordinary socializing found acceptance and friendship through his online identity. Others have pointed out similar findings in those with mental disorders making social interaction difficult, such as those with autism or similar disabilities.

Academics

Avatars have become an area of study in the world of academics. The emergence of online avatars have profound implications for domains of scholarly research such as technoself studies, which is concerned with all aspects of human identity in a technological society and also the social avatar and its effects upon the psyche. Paul Hemp has written an article for the Harvard Business Review, where he analyses the effects of avatars on real-world business. He focuses on the game "Second Life", and shows that the creators of virtual avatars are willing to spend real money to purchase goods marketed solely to their virtual selves.

The Journal of Computer-Mediated Communication published a study of the reactions to certain types of avatars by a sample group of human users. The results showed that users commonly chose avatars which were humanoid and matched their gender. The conclusion was that in order to make users feel more "at home" in their avatars, designers should maximise the custimizability of visual criteria common to humans, such as skin and hair color, gender, hair styles and height.

Researchers at York University studied whether avatars reflected a user's real-life personality. Student test groups were able to infer upon extraversion, agreeableness, and neuroticism, but could not infer upon openness and conscientiousness.

Social Media

Another use of the avatar has emerged with the widespread use of Social Media platforms. There is a practice in Social Media sites, uploading Avatars in place of real profile image. Profile picture is a distinct graphics that represent the identity of profile holder. It is usually the portrait of an individual, logo of an organization, organizational building or distinctive character of book, cover page etc. Using avatars as profile pictures can increase users' perceived level of social presence which in turn fosters reciprocity and sharing behavior in online environments.

Avatar created with online Avatar making forms.

According to MIT professor Sherry Turkle: "... we think we will be presenting ourselves, but our profile ends up as somebody else - often the fantasy of who we want to be.".

In Popular Culture

Cartoons and stories sometimes have a character based on their creator, either a fictionalised version (e.g. the Matt Groening character in some episodes of The Simpsons) or an entirely fictional character (e.g. Hermione Granger in the Harry Potter series has been said by J. K. Rowling to be based upon herself). Such characters are sometimes known as "author avatars".

Generators

To meet the demand for millions of unique, customised avatars, generator tools and services have been created.

Portals

As avatars grow in use, services to centralize design, management, and transportation of digital avatars start to appear. They can offer to deployed in virtual worlds, online games, social networks, video clips, greeting cards, and mobile apps, as well as professional animation and pre-visualization projects. For example, Evolver (3D Avatar Web Portal) seems to be the first solution to bring together complex 3D modeling, consumer ease of use, and fully interoperable avatars.

Cyberspace

Cyberspace is "the notional environment in which communication over computer networks occurs." The word became popular in the 1990s when the uses of the Internet, networking, and digital communication were all growing dramatically and the term "cyberspace" was able to represent the many new ideas and phenomena that were emerging.

The parent term of cyberspace is "cybernetics", (steersman, governor, pilot, or rudder), a word introduced by Norbert Wiener for his pioneering work in electronic communication and control sci-ence. This word first appeared in the novel Neuromancer by William Gibson (Page 4, Phantasia Press Edition, Bloomfield, MI, 1986), one of the first cyberpunk hardbacks published.

As a social experience, individuals can interact, exchange ideas, share information, provide social support, conduct business, direct actions, create artistic media, play games, engage in political discussion, and so on, using this global network. They are sometimes referred to as *cybernauts*. The term *cyberspace* has become a conventional means to describe anything associated with the Internet and the diverse Internet culture. The United States government recognizes the interconnected information technology and the interdependent network of information technology infrastructures operating across this medium as part of the US national critical infrastructure. Amongst individuals on cyberspace, there is believed to be a code of shared rules and ethics mutually beneficial for all to follow, referred to as cyberethics. Many view the right to privacy as most important to a functional code of cyberethics. Such moral responsibilities go hand in hand when working online with global networks, specifically, when opinions are involved with online social experiences.

According to Chip Morningstar and F. Randall Farmer, cyberspace is defined more by the social interactions involved rather than its technical implementation. In their view, the computational medium in cyberspace is an augmentation of the communication channel between real people; the core characteristic of cyberspace is that it offers an environment that consists of many participants with the ability to affect and influence each other. They derive this concept from the observation that people seek richness, complexity, and depth within a virtual world.

Origins of the Term

The term "cyberspace" first appeared in the visual arts in the late 1960s, when Danish artist Susanne Ussing (1940-1998) and her partner architect Carsten Hoff (b. 1934) constituted themselves as Atelier Cyberspace. Under this name the two made a series of installations and images entitled "sensory spaces" that were based on the principle of open systems adaptable to various influences, such as human movement and the behaviour of new materials.

Atelier Cyberspace worked at a time when the Internet did not exist and computers were more or less off-limit to artists and creative engagement. In a 2015-interview with Scandinavian art magazine Kunstkritikk, Carsten Hoff recollects, that although Atelier Cyberspace did try to implement computers, they had no interest in the virtual space as such:

To us, 'cyberspace' was simply about managing spaces. There was nothing esoteric about it. Nothing digital, either. It was just a tool. The space was concrete, physical.

And in the same interview Hoff continues:

Our shared point of departure was that we were working with physical settings, and we were both frustrated and displeased with the architecture from the period, particularly when it came to spaces for living. We felt that there was a need to loosen up the rigid confines of urban planning, giving back the gift of creativity to individual human beings and allowing them to shape and design their houses or dwellings themselves – instead of having some clever architect pop up, telling you how you should live. We were thinking in terms of open-ended systems where things could grow and evolve as required.

For instance, we imagined a kind of mobile production unit, but unfortunately the drawings have been lost. It was a kind of truck with a nozzle at the back. Like a bee building its hive. The nozzle would emit and apply material that grew to form amorphous mushrooms or whatever you might imagine. It was supposed to be computer-controlled, allowing you to create interesting shapes and sequences of spaces. It was a merging of organic and technological systems, a new way of structuring the world. And a response that counteracted industrial uniformity. We had this idea that sophisticated software might enable us to mimic the way in which nature creates products – where things that belong to the same family can take different forms. All oak trees are oak trees, but no two oak trees are exactly alike. And then a whole new material – polystyrene foam – arrived on the scene. It behaved like nature in the sense that it grew when its two component parts were mixed. Almost like a fungal growth. This made it an obvious choice for our work in Atelier Cyberspace.

The works of Atelier Cyberspace were originally shown at a number of Copenhagen venues and have later been exhibited at The National Gallery of Denmark in Copenhagen as part of the exhibition "What's Happening?"

The term "cyberspace" first appeared in fiction in the 1980s in the work of cyberpunk science fiction author William Gibson, first in his 1982 short story "Burning Chrome" and later in his 1984 novel *Neuromancer*. In the next few years, the word became prominently identified with online computer networks. The portion of *Neuromancer* cited in this respect is usually the following:

Cyberspace. A consensual hallucination experienced daily by billions of legitimate operators, in every nation, by children being taught mathematical concepts... A graphic representation of data abstracted from the banks of every computer in the human system. Unthinkable complexity. Lines of light ranged in the nonspace of the mind, clusters and constellations of data. Like city lights, receding.

Now widely used, the term has since been criticized by Gibson, who commented on the origin of the term in the 2000 documentary *No Maps for These Territories*:

All I knew about the word "cyberspace" when I coined it, was that it seemed like an effective buzzword. It seemed evocative and essentially meaningless. It was suggestive of something, but had no real semantic meaning, even for me, as I saw it emerge on the page.

Metaphorical

Don Slater uses a metaphor to define cyberspace, describing the "sense of a social setting that exists purely within a space of representation and communication . . . it exists entirely within a computer space, distributed across increasingly complex and fluid networks." The term "Cyberspace" started to become a de facto synonym for the Internet, and later the World Wide Web, during the 1990s, especially in academic circles and activist communities. Author Bruce Sterling, who popularized this meaning, credits John Perry Barlow as the first to use it to refer to "the present-day nexus of computer and telecommunications networks." Barlow describes it thus in his essay to announce the formation of the Electronic Frontier Foundation (note the spatial metaphor) in June, 1990:

In this silent world, all conversation is typed. To enter it, one forsakes both body and place and becomes a thing of words alone. You can see what your neighbors are saying (or recently said), but not what either they or their physical surroundings look like. Town meetings are continuous and discussions rage on everything from sexual kinks to depreciation schedules. Whether by one telephonic tendril or millions, they are all connected to one another. Collectively, they form what their inhabitants call the Net. It extends across that immense region of electron states, microwaves, magnetic fields, light pulses and thought which sci-fi writer William Gibson named Cyberspace.

—John Perry Barlow, "Crime and Puzzlement," 1990-06-08

As Barlow, and the EFF, continued public education efforts to promote the idea of "digital rights", the term was increasingly used during the Internet boom of the late 1990s.

Virtual Environments

Although the present-day, loose use of the term "cyberspace" no longer implies or suggests immersion in a virtual reality, current technology allows the integration of a number of capabilities (sensors, signals, connections, transmissions, processors, and controllers) sufficient to generate a virtual interactive experience that is accessible regardless of a geographic location.

In 1989, Autodesk, an American multinational corporation that focuses on 2D and 3D design software, developed a virtual design system called Cyberspace.

Recent Definitions of Cyberspace

Although you can find several definitions of cyberspace both in scientific literature and in official governmental sources, there is no fully agreed official definition yet. According to F. D. Kramer there are 28 different definitions of the term cyberspace. The following links: "Cyberpower and National Security: Policy Recommendations for a Strategic Framework," in Cyberpower and National Security, FD Kramer, S. Starr, L.K. Wentz (ed.), National Defense University Press, Washington (DC) 2009.

The most recent draft definition is the following: Cyberspace is a global and dynamic domain (subject to constant change) characterized by the combined use of electrons and electromagnetic spectrum, whose purpose is to create, store, modify, exchange, share and extract, use, eliminate information and disrupt physical resources. Cyberspace includes: a) physical infrastructures and telecommunications devices that allow for the connection of technological and communication system networks, understood in the broadest sense (SCADA devices, smartphones/tablets, computers, servers, etc.); b) computer systems and the related (sometimes embedded) software that guarantee the domain's basic operational functioning and connectivity; c) networks between computer systems; d) networks of networks that connect computer systems (the distinction between networks and networks of networks is mainly organizational); e) the access nodes of users and intermediaries routing nodes; f) constituent data (or resident data). Often, in common parlance (and sometimes in commercial language), networks of networks are called Internet (with a lowercase i), while networks between computers are called intranet. Internet (with a capital I, in journalistic language sometimes called the Net) can be considered a part of the system a). A distinctive and constitutive feature of cyberspace is that no central entity exercises control over all the networks that make up this new domain.

Just as in the real world there is no world government, cyberspace lacks an institutionally predefined hierarchical center. To cyberspace, a domain without a hierarchical ordering principle, we can therefore extend the definition of international politics coined by Kenneth Waltz: as being "with no system of law enforceable." This does not mean that the dimension of power in cyberspace is absent, nor that power is dispersed and scattered into a thousand invisible streams, nor that it is evenly spread across myriad people and organizations, as some scholars had predicted. On the contrary, cyberspace is characterized by a precise structuring of hierarchies of power.

Cyberspace as an Internet Metaphor

While cyberspace should not be confused with the Internet, the term is often used to refer to objects and identities that exist largely within the communication network itself, so that a website, for example, might be metaphorically said to "exist in cyberspace". According to this interpretation, events taking place on the Internet are not happening in the locations where participants or servers are physically located, but "in cyberspace".

Firstly, cyberspace describes the flow of digital data through the network of interconnected computers: it is at once not "real", since one could not spatially locate it as a tangible object, and clearly "real" in its effects. Secondly, cyberspace is the site of computer-mediated communication (CMC), in which online relationships and alternative forms of online identity were enacted, raising important questions about the social psychology of Internet use, the relationship between "online" and "offline" forms of life and interaction, and the relationship between the "real" and the virtual. Cyberspace draws attention to remediation of culture through new media technologies: it is not just a communication tool but a social destination, and is culturally significant in its own right. Finally, cyberspace can be seen as providing new opportunities to reshape society and culture through "hidden" identities, or it can be seen as borderless communication and culture.

Cyberspace is the "place" where a telephone conversation appears to occur. Not inside your actual phone, the plastic device on your desk. Not inside the other person's phone, in some other city. The place between the phones. [...] in the past twenty years, this electrical "space," which was once thin and dark and one-dimensional—little more than a narrow speaking-tube, stretching from phone to phone—has flung itself open like a gigantic jack-in-the-box. Light has flooded upon it, the eerie light of the glowing computer screen. This dark electric netherworld has become a vast flowering electronic landscape. Since the 1960s, the world of the telephone has cross-bred itself with computers and television, and though there is still no substance to cyberspace, nothing you can handle, it has a strange kind of physicality now. It makes good sense today to talk of cyberspace as a place all its own.

> — *Bruce Sterling, Introduction to The Hacker Crackdown*

The "space" in cyberspace has more in common with the abstract, mathematical meanings of the term than physical space. It does not have the duality of positive and negative volume (while in physical space for example a room has the negative volume of usable space delineated by positive volume of walls, Internet users cannot enter the screen and explore the unknown part of the Internet as an extension of the space they are in), but spatial meaning can be attributed to the relationship between different pages (of books as well as webservers), considering the unturned pages to be somewhere "out there." The concept of cyberspace therefore refers not to the content being presented to the surfer, but rather to the possibility of surfing among different sites, with feedback loops between the user and the rest of the system creating the potential to always encounter something unknown or unexpected.

Videogames differ from text-based communication in that on-screen images are meant to be figures that actually occupy a space and the animation shows the movement of those figures. Images are supposed to form the positive volume that delineates the empty space. A game adopts the cyberspace metaphor by engaging more players in the game, and then figuratively representing them on the screen as avatars. Games do not have to stop at the avatar-player level, but current implementations aiming for more immersive playing space (i.e. Laser tag) take the form of augmented reality rather than cyberspace, fully immersive virtual realities remaining impractical.

Although the more radical consequences of the global communication network predicted by some cyberspace proponents (i.e. the diminishing of state influence envisioned by John Perry Barlow) failed to materialize and the word lost some of its novelty appeal, it remains current as of 2006.

Some virtual communities explicitly refer to the concept of cyberspace, for example Linden Lab calling their customers "Residents" of Second Life, while all such communities can be positioned "in cyberspace" for explanatory and comparative purposes (as did Sterling in *The Hacker Crackdown*, followed by many journalists), integrating the metaphor into a wider cyber-culture.

The metaphor has been useful in helping a new generation of thought leaders to reason through new military strategies around the world, led largely by the US Department of Defense (DoD). The use of cyberspace as a metaphor has had its limits, however, especially in areas where the metaphor becomes confused with physical infrastructure. It has also been critiqued as being unhelpful for falsely employing a spatial metaphor to describe what is inherently a network.

Alternate Realities in Philosophy and Art

Predating Computers

A forerunner of the modern ideas of cyberspace is the Cartesian notion that people might be deceived by an evil demon that feeds them a false reality. This argument is the direct predecessor of modern ideas of a brain in a vat and many popular conceptions of cyberspace take Descartes's ideas as their starting point.

Visual arts have a tradition, stretching back to antiquity, of artifacts meant to fool the eye and be mistaken for reality. This questioning of reality occasionally led some philosophers and especially theologians to distrust art as deceiving people into entering a world which was not real. The artistic challenge was resurrected with increasing ambition as art became more and more realistic with the invention of photography, film, and immersive computer simulations.

Influenced by Computers

Philosophy

American counterculture exponents like William S. Burroughs (whose literary influence on Gibson and cyberpunk in general is widely acknowledged) and Timothy Leary were among the first to extoll the potential of computers and computer networks for individual empowerment.

Some contemporary philosophers and scientists (e.g. David Deutsch in *The Fabric of Reality*) employ virtual reality in various thought experiments. For example, Philip Zhai in *Get Real: A Philosophical Adventure in Virtual Reality* connects cyberspace to the platonic tradition:

Let us imagine a nation in which everyone is hooked up to a network of VR infrastructure. They have been so hooked up since they left their mother's wombs. Immersed in cyberspace and maintaining their life by teleoperation, they have never imagined that life could be any different from that. The first person that thinks of the possibility of an alternative world like ours would be ridiculed by the majority of these citizens, just like the few enlightened ones in Plato's allegory of the cave.

Note that this brain-in-a-vat argument conflates cyberspace with reality, while the more common descriptions of cyberspace contrast it with the "real world".

A New Communication Model

The technological convergence of the mass media is the result of a long adaptation process of their communicative resources to the evolutionary changes of each historical moment. Thus, the new media became (plurally) an extension of the traditional media on the cyberspace, allowing to the public access information in a wide range of digital devices. In other words, it is a cultural virtualization of human reality as a result of the migration from physical to virtual space (mediated by the ICTs), ruled by codes, signs and particular social relationships. Forwards, arise instant ways of communication, interaction and possible quick access to information, in which we are no longer mere senders, but also producers, reproducers, co-workers and providers. New technologies also help to "connect" people from different cultures outside the virtual space, what was unthinkable fifty years ago. In this giant relationships web, we mutually absorb each other's beliefs, customs, values, laws and habits, cultural legacies perpetuated by a physical-virtual dynamics in constant metamorphosis (ibidem). In this sense, Professor Doctor Marcelo Mendonça Teixeira created, in 2013, a new model of communication to the virtual universe, based in Claude Elwood Shannon (1948) article "A Mathematical Theory of Communication".

Art

Having originated among writers, the concept of cyberspace remains most popular in literature and film. Although artists working with other media have expressed interest in the concept, such as Roy Ascott, "cyberspace" in digital art is mostly used as a synonym for immersive virtual reality and remains more discussed than enacted.

Computer Crime

Cyberspace also brings together every service and facility imaginable to expedite money laundering. One can purchase anonymous credit cards, bank accounts, encrypted global mobile telephones, and false passports. From there one can pay professional advisors to set up IBCs (International Business Corporations, or corporations with anonymous ownership) or similar structures in OFCs (Offshore Financial Centers). Such advisors are loath to ask any penetrating questions about the wealth and activities of their clients, since the average fees criminals pay them to launder their money can be as much as 20 percent.

5-level Model

In 2010, a 5-level model was designed in France. According to this model, cyberspace is composed of 5 layers based on information discoveries: language, writing, printing, Internet, etc. This original model links the world of information to telecommunication technologies.

Popular Culture Examples

- In October 1966, Doctor Who aired *The Tenth Planet,* in which a wandering planet enters the solar system. This planet, Mondas, is the home of the Cybermen.

- The anime *Digimon* is set in a variant of the cyberspace concept called the "Digital World". The Digital World is a parallel universe made up of data from the Internet. Similar to cyberspace, except that people could physically enter this world instead of merely using a computer.

- The anime *Ghost in the Shell* is set in the future where cyberization of humanity is commonplace and the world is connected by a vast electronic network. Explained in the *Philosophy of Ghost in the Shell.*

- The CGI series, *ReBoot,* takes place entirely inside cyberspace, which is composed of two worlds: the Net and the Web.

- In the film *Tron,* a programmer was physically transferred to the program world, where programs were personalities, resembling the forms of their creators.

- In the film *Virtuosity* a program encapsulating a super-criminal within a virtual world simulation escapes into the "real world".

- In the novel *Simulacron-3* the author Daniel F. Galouye explores multiple levels of "reality" represented by the multiple levels of computer simulation involved.

- The idea of "the matrix" in the film *The Matrix* resembles a complex form of cyberspace where people are "jacked in" from birth and do not know that the reality they experience is virtual.

- In the televised remote controlled robot competition series *Robot Wars*, the *Megahurtz* and subsequently *Terrorhurtz* team and their robot were introduced as being 'from Cyberspace', a nod to their online collaborative formation.

- In the 1984 novel *Neuromancer* the author William Gibson introduces the idea of a virtual reality data space called "the Matrix".

Motion Simulator

Simulator seating at the St. Louis Zoo

A motion simulator or motion platform is a mechanism that encapsulates occupants and creates the effect/feelings of being in a moving vehicle. A motion simulator can also be called a motion base, motion chassis or a motion seat. The movement is synchronous with visual display and is designed to add a tactile element to video gaming, simulation, and virtual reality. When motion is applied and synchronized to audio and video signals, the result is a combination of sight, sound, and touch. All *full motion* simulators move the entire occupant compartment and can convey changes in orientation and the effect of false gravitational forces. These motion cues trick the mind into thinking it is immersed in the simulated environment and experiencing kinematic changes in position, velocity, and acceleration. The mind's failure to accept the experience can result in motion sickness. Motion platforms can provide movement on up to six degrees of freedom: three rotational degrees of freedom (roll, pitch, yaw) and three translational or linear degrees of freedom (surge, heave, sway).

Types

Motion simulators can be classified according to whether the occupant is controlling the vehicle, or whether the occupant is a passive rider, also referred to as a simulator ride or motion theater.

- Common examples of occupant-controlled motion simulators are flight simulators, driving simulators, and auto racing games. Other occupant-controlled vehicle simulation games simulate the control of boats, motorcycles, rollercoasters, military vehicles, ATVs, or spacecraft, among other craft types.

- Examples of passive ride simulators are theme park rides where an entire theater system, with a projection screen in front of the seats, is in motion on giant actuators. An enhanced motion vehicle moves the motion base along a track in a show building.

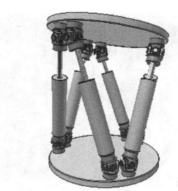

An example of a Stewart platform

Professional Stewart Hybrid Type Motion System with six degrees of freedom

Historically, motion platforms have varied widely in scale and cost. Those in the category of amusement park rides and commercial and military aircraft simulators are at the high end of this spectrum; arcade style amusement devices fall into the middle of the spectrum, while smaller and lower-costing home-based motion platforms comprise the other end.

Modern motion platforms have become complicated machines, but they have simpler roots. Many of the early motion platforms were flight simulators used to train pilots. One of the first motion platforms, the Sanders Teacher, was created in 1910. The Sanders Teacher was an aircraft with control surfaces fitted to the ground by a simple universal joint. When wind was present, the pilot in training was able to use the control surfaces to move the simulator in the three rotational degrees of freedom. Around 1930, a large advance in motion platform technology was made with the creation of the Link

Trainer. The Link Trainer used the control stick and external motors to control organ bellows located under the simulator. The bellows could inflate or deflate, causing the simulator to rotate with three degrees of freedom. In 1958 the Comet IV was designed using a three-degrees-of-freedom hydraulic system. After the Comet IV both the range of motion and the degrees of freedom exhibited by motion platforms was increased. The most expensive motion platforms utilize high-fidelity six-degrees-of-freedom motion, often coupled with advanced audio and visual systems. Today you will find motion platforms in many applications including: flight simulation, driving simulation, amusement rides, and even small home-based motion platforms.

Fly motion simulator with 6 rotational degrees of freedom

The high-end motion platform has been used in conjunction with military and commercial flight instruction and training applications. Today one can find high-end, multiple-occupant motion platforms in use with entertainment applications in theme parks throughout the world. The systems used in these applications are very large, weighing several tons, and are typically housed in facilities designed expressly for them. As a result of the force required to move the weight of these larger simulator systems and one or more occupants, the motion platform must be controlled by powerful and expensive hydraulic or electromagnetic cylinders. The cost of this type of motion platform exceeds US$100,000, and often goes well into the millions of dollars for the multi-occupant systems found at major theme park attractions. The complexity of these systems require extensive programming and maintenance, further extending the cost.

A typical high-end motion system is the Stewart platform, which provides full 6 degrees of freedom (3 translation and 3 rotation) and employs sophisticated algorithms to provide high-fidelity motions and accelerations. These are used in a number of applications, including flight simulators for training pilots. However, the complexity and expensive mechanisms required to incorporate all degrees of freedom has led to alternative motion simulation technology using mainly the three rotational degrees of freedom. An analysis of capabilities of these systems reveals that a simulator with three rotational degrees of freedom is capable of producing motion simulation quality and vestibular motion sensations comparable to that produced by a Stewart platform. Historically these systems used hydraulics or pneumatics; however, many modern systems use electric actuators.

Low-cost home motion system with 3 rotational degrees of freedom

The middle of the spectrum includes a number of disclosures involving powered motion platforms aimed at arcade-style amusement games, rides, and other arrangements. These systems fall into a price range from $10,000 to $99,000 USD. Typically the space requirements for such a platform are modest requiring only a portion of an arcade room and a smaller range of motion is provided via similar, less expensive, control systems than the high-end platforms.

The lower-cost systems include home-based motion platforms, which have recently become a more common device used to enhance video games, simulation, and virtual reality. These systems fall into a price range from $1,000 to $9,000 USD. Within the 2000s (decade), several individuals and business entities have developed these smaller, more affordable motion systems. Most of these systems were developed mainly by flight simulation enthusiasts, were sold as do it yourself projects, and could be assembled in the home from common components for around one thousand US dollars ($1,000). Recently, there has been increased market interest in motion platforms for more personal, in-home, use. The application of these motion systems extends beyond just flight training simulation into a larger market of more generalized "craft-oriented" simulation, entertainment, and virtual reality systems.

Common Uses

Engineering Analysis

Motion platforms are commonly used in the field of engineering for analysis and verification of vehicle performance and design. The ability to link a computer-based dynamic model of a particular system to physical motion gives the user the ability to feel how the vehicle would respond to control inputs without the need to construct expensive prototypes. For example, an engineer designing an external fuel tank for an aircraft could have a pilot determine the effect on flying qualities or a mechanical engineer could feel the effects of a new brake system without building any hardware, saving time and money.

Flight simulators are also used by aircraft manufacturers to test new hardware. By connecting a simulated cockpit with visual screen to a real flight control system in a laboratory, integrating the pilot with the electrical, mechanical, and hydraulic components that exist on the real aircraft, a complete system evaluation can be conducted prior to initial flight testing. This type of testing allows the simulation of "seeded faults" (i.e. an intentional hydraulic leak, software error, or computer shutdown) which serve to validate that an aircraft's redundant design features work as intended. A test pilot can also help identify system deficiencies such as inadequate or missing warning indicators, or even unintended control stick motion. This testing is necessary to simulate extremely high risk events that cannot be conducted in flight but nonetheless must be demonstrated. While 6 degree-of-freedom motion is not necessary for this type of testing, the visual screen allows the pilot to "fly" the aircraft while the faults are simultaneously triggered.

Ride Simulators

Motion simulators are sometimes used in theme parks to give the park guests a themed simulation of flight or other motion.

Some examples:

- *Star Tours* and its sequel, located at Disneyland and other Disney theme parks, use purpose-modified military flight simulators known as Advanced Technology Leisure Application Simulators (ATLAS) to simulate a flight through outer space.

- *Wild Arctic* at SeaWorld Orlando and SeaWorld San Diego.

- Soarin' Over California, located in Disney California Adventure, uses an IMAX dome screen and a hang glider simulation to provide a beautiful simulated flight over many of California's scenic places.

- StormRider is a simulator ride at Tokyo DisneySea.

- Star Trek: The Experience was located at the Las Vegas Hilton between 1998 and 2008. Its "Klingon Encounter" culminated with a state of the art, 6 degrees-of-freedom flight simulator ride including associated space battle movie footage.

- *Back to the Future: The Ride*, a simulator ride based on the *Back to the Future* film series, is located at Universal Studios Japan, and formerly at Universal Studios Florida and Universal Studios Hollywood. The ride used DeLorean-based simulator cars that faced a 70-foot-tall IMAX dome screen. In 2008, it was replaced at the Florida and Hollywood parks by another simulator ride, *The Simpsons Ride*.

- The Funtastic World of Hanna-Barbera (now closed) was one of the original attractions at Universal Studios Florida. The ride used rocket-based simulator cars and a theater-sized screen.

- Jimmy Neutron's Nicktoon Blast (now closed) was located at the Universal Studios Florida theme park where The Funtastic World of Hanna-Barbera had been located. The ride used rocket-based simulator cars and a theater-sized screen.

- The National Air and Space Museum in Washington, D.C., houses a gallery full of two-seat interactive flight simulators doing 360-degree barrel rolls in air combat.

- Europe in the Air, a simulator ride located in Busch Gardens Williamsburg, uses a motion platform, high-definition footage, and wind effects to simulate flight over Europe's notable icons.

Video Games

Some driving and flying simulation games allow the use of specialized controllers such as steering wheels, foot pedals or joysticks. Certain game controllers designed in recent years have employed haptic technology to provide realtime, tactile feedback to the user in the form of vibration from the controller. A motion simulator takes the next step by providing the player full-body tactile feedback. Motion gaming chairs can roll to the left and right and pitch forward and backward to simulate turning corners, accelerations and decelerations. Motion platforms permit a more stimulative and potentially realistic gaming experience, and allow for even greater physical correlation to sight and sound in game play.

How Human Physiology Processes and Responds to Motion

The way we perceive our body and our surroundings is a function of the way our brain interprets signals from our various sensory systems, such as sight, sound, balance and touch. Special sensory pick-up units (or sensory "pads") called receptors translate stimuli into sensory signals. External receptors (exteroceptors) respond to stimuli that arise outside the body, such as the light that stimulates the eyes, sound pressure that stimulates the ear, pressure and temperature that stimulates the skin and chemical substances that stimulate the nose and mouth. Internal receptors (enteroceptors) respond to stimuli that arise from within blood vessels.

Postural stability is maintained through the vestibular reflexes acting on the neck and limbs. These reflexes, which are key to successful motion synchronization, are under the control of three classes of sensory input:

- Proprioceptors are receptors located in your muscles, tendons, joints and the inner ear, which send signals to the brain regarding the body's position. Aircraft pilots sometimes refer to this type of sensory input as the "seat of your pants".

- The vestibular system contributes to balance and sense of spatial orientation and includes the vestibular organs, ocular system, and muscular system. The vestibular system is contained in the inner ear and interprets rotational motion and linear acceleration. The vestibular system does not interpret vertical motion.

- Visual input from the eye relays information to the brain about the craft's position, velocity, and attitude relative to the ground.

Proprioceptors

Proprioceptors are receptors located in your muscles, tendons, joints and the inner ear, which send signals to the brain regarding the body's position. An example of a "popular" proprioceptor often mentioned by aircraft pilots, is the "seat of the pants". In other words, these sensors present a picture to your brain as to where you are in space as external forces act on your body. Proprioceptors respond to stimuli generated by muscle movement and muscle tension. Signals generated by exteroceptors and proprioceptors are carried by sensory neurons or nerves and are called electrochemical signals. When a neuron receives such a signal, it sends it on to an adjacent neuron through a bridge called a synapse. A synapse "sparks" the impulse between neurons through electrical and chemical means. These sensory signals are processed by the brain and spinal cord, which then respond with motor signals that travel along motor nerves. Motor neurons, with their special fibres, carry these signals to muscles, which are instructed to either contract or relax.

The downfall with our internal motion sensors is that once a constant speed or velocity is reached, these sensors stop reacting. Your brain now has to rely on visual cues until another movement takes place and the resultant force is felt. In motion simulation, when our internal motion sensors can no longer detect motion, a "washout" of the motion system may occur. A washout allows the motion platform occupant to think they are making a continuous movement when actually the motion has stopped. In other words, washout is where the simulator actually returns to a central, home, or reference position in anticipation of the next movement. This movement back to neutral must occur without the occupant actually realizing what is happening. This is an important aspect in motion simulators as the human feel sensations must be as close to real as possible.

Vestibular System

The vestibular system is the balancing and equilibrium system of the body that includes the vestibular organs, ocular system, and muscular system. The vestibular system is contained in the inner ear. It consists of three semicircular canals, or tubes, arranged at right angles to one another. Each canal is lined with hairs connected to nerve endings and is partially filled with fluid. When the head experiences acceleration the fluid moves within the canals, causing the hair follicles to move from their initial vertical orientation. In turn the nerve endings fire resulting in the brain interpreting the acceleration as pitch, roll, or yaw.

There are, however, three shortcomings to this system. First, although the vestibular system is a very fast sense used to generate reflexes to maintain perceptual and postural stability, compared to the other senses of vision, touch and audition, vestibular input is perceived with delay. Indeed, although engineers typically try and reduce delays between physical and visual motion, it has been shown that a motion simulator should move about 130ms before visual motion in order to maximize motion simulator fidelity. Second, if the head experiences sustained accelerations on the order of 10 – 20 seconds, the hair follicles return to the "zero" or vertical position and the brain interprets this as the acceleration ceasing. Additionally, there is a lower acceleration threshold of about 2 degrees per second that the brain cannot perceive. In other words, slow and gradual enough motion below the threshold will not affect the vestibular system. As discussed in the preceding "Proprioceptors" section, this shortfall actually allows the simulator to return to a reference position in anticipation of the next movement.

Visual Inputs

The human eye is the most important source of information in motion simulation. The eye relays information to the brain about the craft's position, velocity, and attitude relative to the ground. As a result, it is essential for realistic simulation that the motion works in direct synchronization to what is happening on the video output screen. Time delays cause disagreement within the brain, due to error between the expected input and the actual input given by the simulator. This disagreement can lead to dizziness, fatigue and nausea in some people.

For example, if the occupant commands the vehicle to roll to the left, the visual displays must also roll by the same magnitude and at the same rate. Simultaneously, the cab tilts the occupant to imitate the motion. The occupant's proprioceptors and vestibular system sense this motion. The motion and change in the visual inputs must align well enough such that any discrepancy is below the occupant's threshold to detect the differences in motion.

In order to be an effective training or entertainment device, the cues the brain receives by each of the body's sensory inputs must agree.

Putting it Together - How Simulators Trick the Body

It is physically impossible to correctly simulate large scale ego-motion in the limited space of a laboratory. The standard approach to simulate motions (so called motion

cueing) is to simulate the "relevant" cues as closely as possible, especially the acceleration of an observer. Visual and auditory cues enable humans to perceive their location
in space on an absolute scale. On the other hand, the somatosensory cues, mainly proprioception and the signals from the vestibular system, code only relative information.
But fortunately (for our purpose), humans cannot perceive accelerations and velocities
perfectly and without systematic errors. And this is where the tricky business of motion
simulation starts. We can use those imperfections of the human sensory and perceptual
systems to cheat intelligently.

Linear Movements

In principle, velocity cannot be directly perceived by relative cues alone, like those from
the vestibular system. For such a system, flying in space with some constant velocity
is not different from sitting in a chair. However, changing the velocity is perceived as
acceleration, or force acting on the human body. For the case of constant linear acceleration, a substitute for the real situation is simple. Since the amplitude of the acceleration is not very well perceived by humans, one can tilt the subject backwards and use
the gravity vector as a replacement for correct resulting force from gravity and forward
acceleration. In this case, leaning backwards is therefore not perceived differently from
being constantly accelerated forwards.

Linear Accelerations

Linear accelerations are detected by otoliths. The otolith structure is simpler than the
three-axis semicircular canals that detect angular accelerations. The otoliths contain
calcium carbonate particles that lag behind head movement, deflecting hair cells.
These cells transmit motion information to the brain and oculomotor muscles.
Studies indicate that the otoliths detect the tangential component of the applied
forces. A transfer function model between the perceived force y(s) and the
applied forces f (s) is given by:

$$\frac{y(s)}{f(s)} = \frac{2.02(s+0.1)}{s+0.2}$$

Based on centrifuge experiments, threshold values of 0.0011 ft/s^2 have been reported;
values up to 0.4 ft/s^2 have been reported based on airborne studies in the USSR. The
same studies suggest that the threshold is not a linear acceleration but rather a jerk
motion (third time derivative of position), and the reported threshold value is on the
order of 0.1 ft/s^3. These findings are supported by early studies showing that human
movement kinematics is represented by characteristics of jerk profiles.

Rotational Movements

Unfortunately, there is no easy way of cheating for rotations. Hence, many motion simulations try to avoid the problem by avoiding quick and large rotations altogether. The only convincing way of simulating larger turns is an initial yaw rotation above threshold and a back-motion below threshold. For roll and pitch, the static (otolithic) cues cannot be modified easily due to the ambiguity of linear accelerations and changes in gravitational direction. In real life, the ambiguity is resolved by using the dynamical properties of the vestibular and other sensory signals (most importantly, vision).

Angular Accelerations

Angular accelerations are detected by semicircular canals while linear accelerations are detected by another structure in the inner ear called the otolith.

The three semicircular canals are mutually orthogonal (similar to three-axis accelerometer) and are filled with a fluid called the endolymph. In each canal, there is a section where the diameter is larger than the rest of the canal. This section is called the ampulla and is sealed by a flap called the cupula. Angular accelerations are detected as follows: an angular acceleration causes the fluid in the canals to move, deflecting the cupula. The nerves in the cupula report the motion to both the brain and oculomotor muscles, stabilizing eye movements. A transfer function model between the perceived angular displacement $y(s) \{\displaystyle y(s)\}$ $y(s)$ and the actual angular displacement $phi(s)$ is:

$$\frac{y(s)}{phi(s)} = \frac{0.07s^3(s+50)}{(s+0.05)(s+0.03)}$$

A second-order model of the angle of the cupula θ is given by

$$\ddot{\theta} + 2\zeta\omega_n\dot{\theta} + \omega_n\theta = u(t)$$

where ζ is the damping ratio, ω_n is the natural frequency of the cupula, and $u(t)$ is the input angular acceleration. ζ have been reported to be between 3.6 and 6.7 while values of ω_n have been reported to be between 0.75 and 1.9. Thus, the system is overdamped with distinct, real roots. The shorter time constant is 0.1 seconds, while the longer time constant depends on the axis about which the test subject is accelerating (roll, pitch, or yaw). These time constants are one to two orders of magnitude greater than the shorter time constant.

Experiments have shown that angular accelerations below a certain level cannot be detected by a human test subject. Values of $0.5° / \sec^2$ have been reported for pitch and roll accelerations in a flight simulator.

Implications

The above studies indicate that the pilot's vestibular system detects accelerations before the aircraft instruments displays them. This can be considered an inner control loop in which the pilots responds to accelerations that occur in full-motion simulators and aircraft, but not in fixed simulators. This effect shows that there is a potential negative training transfer when transitioning from a fixed-based simulator to an aircraft and indicates the need for motion systems for pilot training.

It is physically impossible to precisely simulate large scale egomotion in the limited space of a laboratory. There is simply no way around the physics. However, by exploiting some of the imperfections of the body's sensory and perceptual systems, it is possible to create an environment in which the body perceives motion without actually moving the subject more than a few feet in any one direction. This is where the tricky business of motion simulation begins.

The standard approach to simulating motion (so called motion cueing) is to simulate the "relevant" cues as closely as possible which trigger motion perception. These cues can be visual, auditory, or somatosensory in nature. Visual and auditory cues enable humans to perceive their location in space on an absolute scale, whereas somatosensory cues (mainly proprioception and other signals from the vestibular system) provide only relative feedback. Fortunately for us, humans cannot perceive velocity and acceleration directly without some form of error or uncertainty.

For example, consider riding in a car traveling at some arbitrary constant speed. In this situation, our sense of sight and sound provide the only cues (excluding engine vibration) that the car is moving; no other forces act on the passengers of the car except for gravity. Next, consider the same example of a car moving at constant speed except this time, all passengers of the car are blindfolded. If the driver were to step on the gas, the car would accelerate forward thus pressing each passenger back into their seat. In this situation, each passenger would perceive the increase in speed by sensing the additional pressure from the seat cushion. However, if the car were traveling in reverse and the driver stepped on the brake pedal instead of the gas, the deceleration of the vehicle would create the same feeling of increased pressure from the seat cushion as in the case of acceleration that the passengers would be unable to distinguish which direction the vehicle is actually moving.

Summary of Most Commonly used "Tricks"

- Moving the observer below detection threshold to gain additional simulation space

- Trading the gravity vector for acceleration (tilting the seat)

- Masking not-to-be-detected motions by noise (i.e., vibrations and jitter)

- Guiding the attention of the observer away from the imperfections of the motion simulation

Implementation Using Washout Filters

Washout filters are an important aspect of the implementation of motion platforms as they allow motion systems, with their limited range of motion, to simulate the range of vehicle dynamics being simulated. Since the human vestibular system automatically re-centers itself during steady motions, washout filters are used to suppress unnecessary low-frequency signals while returning the simulator back to a neutral position at accelerations below the threshold of human perception. For example, a pilot in a motion simulator may execute a steady, level turn for an extended period of time which would require the system stay at the associated bank angle, but a washout filter allows the system to slowly move back to an equilibrium position at a rate below the threshold which the pilot can detect. This allows the higher level dynamics of the computed vehicle to provide realistic cues for human perception, while remaining within the limitations of the simulator.

Three common types of washout filters include classical, adaptive and optimal washout filters. The classical washout filter comprises linear low-pass and high-pass filters. The signal into the filter is split into translation and rotational signals. High-pass filters are used for simulating transient translational and rotational accelerations, while the low-pass filters are used to simulate sustaining accelerations. The adaptive washout filter uses the classical washout filter scheme, but utilizes a self-tuning mechanism that is not featured with the classical washout filter. Finally, the optimal washout filter takes into account models for vestibular system.

Classical Control Representation

The classical washout filter is simply a combination of high-pass and low-pass filters; thus, the implementation of the filter is compatibly easy. However, the parameters of these filters have to be empirically determined. The inputs to the classical washout filter are vehicle-specific forces and angular rate. Both of the inputs are expressed in the vehicle-body-fixed frame. Since low-frequency force is dominant in driving the motion base, force is high-pass filtered, and yields the simulator translations. Much the same operation is done for angular rate.

To identify the tilt of the motion platform, the tilt mechanism first supplies the low-frequency component of force for rotation calculation. Then, the high-frequency component 'f' is used to orient the gravity vector 'g' of the simulator platform:

$$\beta = \sin^{-1}(\frac{f}{g})$$

Typically, to find position, the low-pass filter (in a continuous-time setting) is represented in the s-domain with the following transfer function:

$$LP(s) = \frac{1}{1 + sT}$$

The inputs to the high-pass filter are then calculated according to the following equation:

$$U(s) = (\beta + LP(s))X(s)$$

$X(s)$ are the force inputs. The high-pass filter may then be represented according to (for example) the following series:

$$HP(s) = \frac{Y(s)}{U(s)} = \frac{s^2 T_2^2}{1 + s2dT_2 + s^2 T_2^2}\left(\frac{1}{s}\right)\frac{sT_1}{1 + sT_1}\left(\frac{1}{s}\right)$$

The two integrators in this series represent the integration of acceleration into velocity, and velocity into position, respectively. T, T_1 T_2 represent the filter parameters. It is evident that the output of the filter will vanish in steady state, preserving the location of the open-loop equilibrium points. This means that while transient inputs will be "passed", steady-state inputs will not, thus fulfilling the requirements of the filter.

The present practice for empirically determining the parameters within the washout filter is a trial and error subjective tuning process whereby a skilled evaluation pilot flies predetermined maneuvers. After each flight the pilot's impression of the motion is communicated to a washout filter expert who then adjusts the washout filter coefficients in an attempt to satisfy the pilot. Researchers have also proposed using a tuning paradigm and the capturing of such using an expert system.

Nonlinear Washout Filter

This washout filter can be regarded as the result of a combination of an Adaptive and an Optimal washout filter. A nonlinear approach is desired to further maximize the available motion cues within the hardware limitations of the motion system, therefore resulting in a more realistic experience. For example, the algorithm described by Daniel and Augusto computes a gain, α, as a function of the system states; thus, the washout is time varying. The 'a' gain will increase as the platform states increase their magnitude, making room for a faster control action to quickly washout the platform to its original position. The opposite outcome occurs when the magnitude of the platform states is small or decreasing, prolonging the motion cues which will be sustained for longer durations.

Likewise, the work of Telban and Cardullo added an integrated perception model that includes both visual and vestibular sensation to optimize the human's perception of motion. This model as shown to improve pilot's responses to motion cues.

Adaptive Washout Filter

This adaptive approach was developed at NASA Langley. It is made up of a combination of empirically determined filters in which several of the coefficients are varied in a prescribed manner in order to minimize a set objective (cost) function. In a study conducted at the University of Toronto the coordinated adaptive filter provided the "most favorable pilot ratings" as compared with the other two types of washout filters. The benefits of this style of washout filter can be summarized with two major points. First, the adaptive characteristics give more realistic motion cues when the simulator is near its neutral position, and the motion is only reduced at the limits of the motions systems capabilities, allowing for better use of the motion system's capabilities. Second, the cost function or the objective function (by which the washout filter is optimized) is very flexible and various terms may be added in order to incorporate higher fidelity models. This allows for an expandable system that is capable of changing over time, resulting in a system that responds in the most accurate way throughout the simulated flight. The disadvantages are that the behavior is difficult to adjust, primarily due to the cross fed channels. Finally execution time is relatively high due to the large number of derivative function calls required. In addition as more complex cost functions are introduced the corresponding computing time required will increase.

Limitations

Although washout filters do provide great utility for allowing the simulation of a wider range of conditions than the physical capabilities of a motion platform, there are limitations to their performance and practicality in simulation applications. Washout filters take advantage of the limitations of human sensing to the appearance of a larger simulation environment than actually exists. For example, a pilot in a motion simulator may execute a steady, level turn for an extended period of time which would require the system stay at the associated bank angle. In this situation, a washout filter allows the system to slowly move back to an equilibrium position at a rate below the threshold which the pilot can detect. The benefit of this is that the motion system now has a greater range of motion available for when the pilot executes his next maneuver.

Such behavior is easily applied in the context of aircraft simulation with very predictable and gradual maneuvers (such as commercial aircraft or larger transports). However, these slow, smooth dynamics do not exist in all practical simulation environments and diminish the returns of washout filters and a motion system. Take training of fighter pilots, for example: while the steady, cruise regime of a fighter aircraft may be able to be well simulated within these limitations, in aerial combat situations flight maneuvers are executed in a very rapid manner to physical extremes. In these scenarios, there is not time for a washout filter to react to bring the motion system back to its range equilibrium resulting in the motion system quickly hitting its range of movement limitations and effectively ceasing to accurately simulate the dynamics. It is for this reason that motion and washout filter based systems are often reserved for those that experience a limited range of flight conditions.

The filters themselves may also introduce false cues, defined as: 1) a motion cue in the simulator that is in the opposite direction to that in the aircraft, 2) a motion cue in the simulator when none was expected in the aircraft, and 3) a relatively high-frequency distortion of a sustained cue in the simulator for an expected sustained cue in the air-craft. The previous definition groups together all of the cueing errors that lead to very large decreases in perceived motion fidelity. Six potential sources of false cues are:

- Software or Hardware Limiting:When the simulator approaches a displacement limit, two methods of protection are provided: 1) software limiting and 2) hard-ware limiting. In either case the simulator is decelerated to prevent damage to the motion system. Large false cues are often associated with this deceleration.

- Return to Neutral: This false cue is attributed to the overshoot of the high-pass filters to step-type inputs. This type of response only occurs if second- or third-order high-pass filters are used.

- G-Tilt

- Tilt-Coordination Angular Rate

- Tilt-Coordination Remnant: For sustained specific force input in sway or surge, the simulator will achieve a steady-state pitch or roll angle because of tilt-coor-dination. If the input ends abruptly, then the highpass specific force response will initially cancel out the specific force associated with the tilt, but only for a brief time before the restricted simulator displacement prohibits translational acceleration of the simulator. If the tilt is removed quickly, then a tilt-coordi-nation angular rate false cue will occur; if not, the remaining tilt will create a sensation of acceleration, called a tilt-coordination remnant false cue.

- Tilt Coordination Angular Acceleration: This false cue is caused by the angular acceleration generated by the tilt-coordination occurring about a point other than the pilot's head. The angular acceleration combined with the moment arm from the center of rotation to the pilot's head results in the specific force false cue at the pilot's head. The point about which angular rotations are simulated (the so-called reference point) is typically at the centroid of the upper bearing block frame for hexapod motion systems.

Impact

Impact of Motion in Simulation and Gaming

The use of physical motion applied in flight simulators has been a debated and researched topic. The Engineering department at the University of Victoria conducted a series of tests in the 1980s, to quantify the perceptions of airline pilots in flight simulation and the impact of motion on the simulation environment. In the end, it was found that there was a definite positive effect on how the pilots perceived the simulation environment when motion was present and there was almost unanimous dislike for the simulation environment that lacked motion. A conclusion that could be drawn on the findings of the Response of Airline Pilots study is that the realism of the simulation is in direct relationship to the accuracy of the simulation on the pilot. When applied to video gaming and evaluated within our own gaming experiences, realism can be directly related to the enjoyment of a game by the game player. In other words, – motion enabled gaming is more realistic, thus more iterative and more stimulating. However, there are adverse effects to the use of motion in simulation that can take away from the primary purpose of using the simulator in the first place such as Motion Sickness. For instance, there have been reports of military pilots throwing off their vestibular system because of moving their heads around in the simulator similar to how they would in an actual aircraft to maintain their sensitivity to accelerations. However, due to the limits on simulator acceleration, this effect becomes detrimental when transitioning back to a real aircraft.

Adverse Effects (Simulator Sickness)

Motion or simulator sickness: Simulators work by "tricking" the mind into believing that the inputs it is receiving from visual, vestibular and proprioceptive inputs are a specific type of desired motion. When any of the cues received by the brain do not correlate with the others, motion sickness can occur. In principle, simulator sickness is simply a form of motion sickness that can result from discrepancies between the cues from the three physical source inputs. For example, riding on a ship with no windows sends a cue that the body is accelerating and rotating in various directions from the vestibular system, but the visual system sees no motion since the room is moving in the same manner as the occupant. In this situation, many would feel motion sickness.

Along with simulator sickness, additional symptoms have been observed after exposure to motion simulation. These symptoms include feelings of warmth, pallor and sweating, depression and apathy, headache and fullness of head, drowsiness and fatigue, difficulty focusing eyes, eye strain, blurred vision, burping, difficulty concentrating, and visual flashbacks. Lingering effects of these symptoms were observed to sometimes last up to a day or two after exposure to the motion simulator.

Contributing Factors to Simulator Sickness

Several factors contribute to simulation sickness, which can be categorized into human variables, simulator usage, and equipment. Common human variable factors include susceptibility, flight hours, fitness, and medication/drugs. An individual's variance in susceptibility to motion sickness is a dominant contributing factor to simulator sickness. Increasing flight hours is also an issue for pilots as they become more accustomed to the actual motion in a vehicle. Contributing factors due to simulator usage are adaptation, distorted or complicated scene content, longer simulation length, and freeze/reset. Freeze/reset refers to the starting or ending points of a simulation, which should be as close to steady and level conditions as possible. Clearly, if a simulation is ended in the middle of an extreme maneuver then the test subjects IMU system is likely to be distorted. Simulator equipment factors that contribute to motion sickness are quality of motion system, quality of visual system, off-axis viewing, poorly aligned optics, flicker, and delay/mismatch between visual and motion systems. The delay/mismatch issue has historically been a concern in simulator technology, where time lag between pilot input and the visual and motion systems can cause confusion and generally decrease simulator performance.

Debate over Performance Enhancement from Motion Simulators

In theory, the concept of motion simulators seem self-explanatory: if the perception of events can be mimicked exactly, they will provide the user an identical experience. However, this ideal performance is next to impossible to achieve. Although the motion of vehicles can be simulated in 6 degrees of freedom (all that should be required to mimic motion), the impacts of simulated motion on pilots, and operators in many other fields, often leave trainees with a multitude of adverse side effects not seen in un-simulated motion. Further, there are many scenarios which may be difficult to simulate in training simulators exposing a concern that replacing real world exposure with motion simulations may be inadequate.

Due to the exorbitant cost of adding motion to simulators, military programs have established research units to investigate the impact of "skill acquisition" with the use of motion simulators. These units have provided results as recent as 2006 despite the use motion simulators over the last century. From an Army study, it was determined that "motion-based simulators are recommended for training when individuals must continue to perform skill-based tasks...while the ground vehicle negotiates rough terrain." However, if individuals are not required to negotiate rough terrain, or motion sickness does not detract from performance in the field, then "motion is not recommended."

The existence of adverse side effects of virtual environments has spawned a plethora of studies from predicting and measuring the impact of the side effects to identifying their specific causes.

Advantages and Disadvantages of Simulation in Training

Advantages

- Simulators provide a safe means of training in the operation of potentially dangerous craft (e.g., aircraft).

- The expense of training on real equipment can sometimes exceed the expense of a simulator.

- Time between training sessions may be reduced since it may be as simple as resetting the motion system to initial conditions.

Disadvantages

- The true environment may not be mimicked identically; therefore the pilot/rider may be confused by the lack of expected sensations or not properly prepared for the real environment.

- Lining up all sensor inputs to eliminate or at least mitigate the risk of "simulator sickness" can be challenging.

- Age of participant as well as amount of experience in true environment modifies reactions to simulated environment.

Collaborative Virtual Environment

Collaborative virtual environments, or CVEs, are used for collaboration and interaction of possibly many participants that may be spread over large distances. Typical examples are distributed simulations, 3D multiplayer games, collaborative engineering software, and others. The applications are usually based on the shared virtual environment. Because of the spreading of participants and the communication latency, some data consistency model have to be used to keep the data consistent.

The consistency model influences deeply the programming model of the application. One classification is introduced in based on several criteria, like centralized/distributed architecture, type of replication, and performance and consistency properties. Four types of consistency models were described, covering the most frequently used CVE architectures:

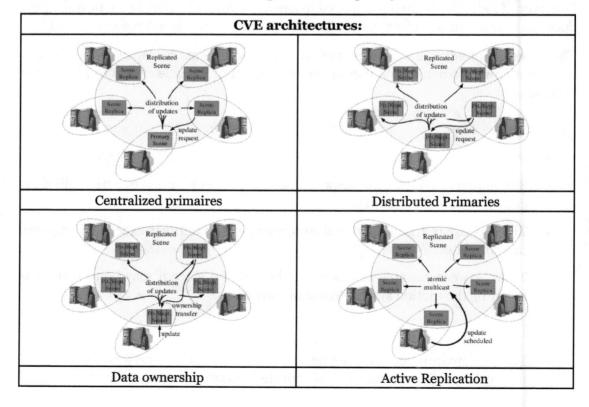

CVE architectures:	
Centralized primaires	Distributed Primaries
Data ownership	Active Replication

- Centralized primaries

  All primary replicas of each data item resides on the same computer called server.

  Advantages: complete server control over the scene

  Disadvantages: performance is limited by the server computer

- Distributed primaries

  Primary replicas are distributed among the computers.

  Advantages: high performance and scalability

  Disadvantages: difficult programming model, weaker consistency

  Used in: Distributed Interactive Simulation (DIS), Repo-3D, DIV, DOOM

- Data ownership

  Primaries are allowed to migrate among the computers. This approach is often called system with transferable data ownership.

  Advantages: more flexibility compared to Distributed Primaries

  Disadvantages: high amount of ownership requests may limit the system performance

  Used in: MASSIVE-3/HIVEK, Blue-c, CIAO, SPLINE

- Active replication

  Active replication uses peer-to-peer approach while all replicas are equal. Usually, atomic broadcast is used to deliver updates to all of them, thus they are kept synchronized.

  Advantages: complete scene synchronization (equal scene content on all computers)

  Disadvantages: the performance is limited by the slowest computer in the system

  Used in: active transactions, Age of Empires, Avango, DIVE

Immersion (Virtual Reality)

Immersion into virtual reality is a perception of being physically present in a non-physical world. The perception is created by surrounding the user of the VR system in images, sound or other stimuli that provide an engrossing total environment.

The name is a metaphoric use of the experience of submersion applied to representation, fiction or simulation. Immersion can also be defined as the state of consciousness where a "visitor" (Maurice Benayoun) or "immersant" (Char Davies)'s awareness of physical self is transformed by being surrounded in an artificial environment; used for describing partial or complete suspension of disbelief, enabling action or reaction to stimulations encountered in a virtual or artistic environment. The degree to which the virtual or artistic environment faithfully reproduces reality determines the degree of suspension of disbelief. The greater the suspension of disbelief, the greater the degree of presence achieved.

Types of Immersion

Classic Virtual reality HMD

According to Ernest W. Adams, author and consultant on game design, immersion can be separated into three main categories:

Tactical immersion

> Tactical immersion is experienced when performing tactile operations that involve skill. Players feel "in the zone" while perfecting actions that result in success.

Strategic immersion

> Strategic immersion is more cerebral, and is associated with mental challenge. Chess players experience strategic immersion when choosing a correct solution among a broad array of possibilities.

Narrative immersion

> Narrative immersion occurs when players become invested in a story, and is similar to what is experienced while reading a book or watching a movie.

Staffan Björk and Jussi Holopainen, in *Patterns In Game Design*, divide immersion into similar categories, but call them sensory-motoric immersion, cognitive immersion and emotional immersion, respectively. In addition to these, they add a new category:

Spatial immersion

Spatial immersion occurs when a player feels the simulated world is perceptually convincing. The player feels that he or she is really "there" and that a simulated world looks and feels "real".

Presence

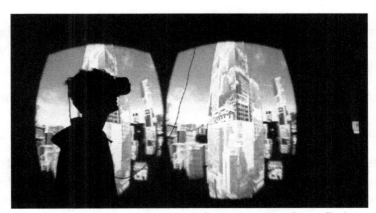

10.000 moving cities, Marc Lee, Telepresence-Based Installation

Presence, a term derived from the shortening of the original "telepresence," is a phenomenon enabling people to interact with and feel connected to the world outside their physical bodies via technology. It is defined as a person's subjective sensation of being there in a scene depicted by a medium, usually virtual in nature (Barfield et al., 1995). Most designers focus on the technology used to create a high-fidelity virtual environment; however, the human factors involved in achieving a state of presence must be taken into account as well. It is the subjective perception, although generated by and/or filtered through human-made technology, that ultimately determines the successful attainment of presence (Thornson, Goldiez, & Le, 2009).

Virtual reality glasses can produce a visceral feeling of being in a simulated world, a form of spatial immersion called Presence. According to Oculus VR, the technology requirements to achieve this visceral reaction are low-latency and precise tracking of movements.

Michael Abrash gave a talk on VR at Steam Dev Days in 2014. According to the VR research team at Valve, all of the following are needed to establish presence.

- A wide field of view (80 degrees or better)

- Adequate resolution (1080p or better)

- Low pixel persistence (3 ms or less)

- A high enough refresh rate (>60 Hz, 95 Hz is enough but less may be adequate)

- Global display where all pixels are illuminated simultaneously (rolling display may work with eye tracking.)

- Optics (at most two lenses per eye with trade-offs, ideal optics not practical using current technology)

- Optical calibration

- Rock-solid tracking – translation with millimeter accuracy or better, orientation with quarter degree accuracy or better, and volume of 1.5 meter or more on a side

- Low latency (20 ms motion to last photon, 25 ms may be good enough)

Immersive Virtual Reality

Immersive virtual reality is a hypothetical future technology that exists today as virtual reality art projects, for the most part. It consists of immersion in an artificial environment where the user feels just as immersed as they usually feel in consensus reality.

Direct Interaction of the Nervous System

The most considered method would be to induce the sensations that made up the virtual reality in the nervous system directly. In functionalism/conventional biology we interact with consensus reality through the nervous system. Thus we receive all input from all the senses as nerve impulses. It gives your neurons a feeling of heightened sensation. It would involve the user receiving inputs as artificially stimulated nerve impulses, the system would receive the CNS outputs (natural nerve impulses) and process them allowing the user to interact with the virtual reality. Natural impulses between the body and central nervous system would need to be prevented. This could be done by blocking out natural impulses using nanorobots which attach themselves to the brain wiring, whilst receiving the digital impulses of which describe the virtual world, which could then be sent into the wiring of the brain. A feedback system between the user and the computer which stores the information would also be needed. Considering how much information would be required for such a system, it is likely that it would be based on hypothetical forms of computer technology.

Requirements

Understanding of the nervous system

A comprehensive understanding of which nerve impulses correspond to which sensations, and which motor impulses correspond to which muscle contractions will be required. This will allow the correct sensations in the user, and actions in the virtual reality to occur. The Blue Brain Project is the current, most promising research with the idea of understanding how the brain works by building very large scale computer models.

Ability to manipulate CNS

The nervous system would obviously need to be manipulated. Whilst non-invasive devices using radiation have been postulated, invasive cybernetic implants are likely to become available sooner and be more accurate. Manipulation could occur at any stage of the nervous system – the spinal cord is likely to be simplest; as all nerves pass through here, this could be the only site of manipulation. Molecular Nanotechnology is likely to provide the degree of precision required and could allow the implant to be built inside the body rather than be inserted by an operation.

Computer hardware/software to process inputs/outputs

A very powerful computer would be necessary for processing virtual reality complex enough to be nearly indistinguishable from consensus reality and interacting with central nervous system fast enough.

Immersive Digital Environments

Cosmopolis (2005), Maurice Benayoun's Giant Virtual Reality Interactive Installation

An immersive digital environment is an artificial, interactive, computer-created scene or "world" within which a user can immerse themselves.

Immersive digital environments could be thought of as synonymous with virtual reality, but without the implication that actual "reality" is being simulated. An immersive digital environment could be a model of reality, but it could also be a complete fantasy user interface or abstraction, as long as the user of the environment is immersed within it. The definition of immersion is wide and variable, but here it is assumed to mean simply that the user feels like they are part of the simulated "universe". The success with which an immersive digital environment can actually immerse the user is dependent on many factors such as believable 3D computer graphics, surround sound, interactive user-input and other factors such as simplicity, functionality and potential for enjoyment. New technologies are currently under development which claim to bring realistic environmental effects to the players' environment – effects like wind, seat vibration and ambient lighting.

Perception

To create a sense of full immersion, the 5 senses (sight, sound, touch, smell, taste) must perceive the digital environment to be physically real. Immersive technology can perceptually fool the senses through:

- Panoramic 3D displays (visual)

- Surround sound acoustics (auditory)

- Haptics and force feedback (tactile)

- Smell replication (olfactory)

- Taste replication (gustation)

Interaction

Once the senses reach a sufficient belief that the digital environment is real (it is interaction and involvement which can never be real), the user must then be able to interact with the environment in a natural, intuitive manner. Various immersive technologies such as gestural controls, motion tracking, and computer vision respond to the user's actions and movements. Brain control interfaces (BCI) respond to the user's brainwave activity.

Examples and Applications

Training and rehearsal simulations run the gamut from part task procedural training (often buttonology, for example: which button do you push to deploy a refueling boom) through situational simulation (such as crisis response or convoy driver training) to full motion simulations which train pilots or soldiers and law enforcement in scenarios that are too dangerous to train in actual equipment using live ordinance.

Computer games from simple arcade to massively multiplayer online game and training programs such as flight and driving simulators. Entertainment environments such as motion simulators that immerse the riders/players in a virtual digital environment enhanced by motion, visual and aural cues. Reality simulators, such as one of the Virunga Mountains in Rwanda that takes you on a trip through the jungle to meet a tribe of mountain gorillas. Or training versions such as one which simulates taking a ride through human arteries and the heart to witness the buildup of plaque and thus learn about cholesterol and health.

In parallel with scientist, artists like Knowbotic Research, Donna Cox, Rebecca Allen, Robbie Cooper, Maurice Benayoun, Char Davies, and Jeffrey Shaw use the potential of immersive virtual reality to create physiologic or symbolic experiences and situations.

Other examples of immersion technology include physical environment / immersive space with surrounding digital projections and sound such as the CAVE, and the use of virtual reality headsets for viewing movies, with head-tracking and computer control of the image presented, so that the viewer appears to be inside the scene. The next generation is VIRTSIM, which achieves total immersion through motion capture and wireless head mounted displays for teams of up to thirteen immersants enabling natural movement through space and interaction in both the virtual and physical space simultaneously.

Use in Medical Care

New fields of studies linked to the immersive virtual reality emerges every day. Researchers see a great potential in virtual reality tests serving as complementary interview methods in psychiatric care. Immersive virtual reality have in studies also been used as an educational tool in which the visualization of psychotic states have been used to get increased understanding of patients with similar symptoms. New treatment methods are available for schizophrenia and other newly developed research areas where immersive virtual reality is expected to achieve melioration is in education of surgical procedures, rehabilitation program from injuries and surgeries and reduction of phantom limb pain.

Detrimental Effects

Simulation sickness, or simulator sickness, is a condition where a person exhibits symptoms similar to motion sickness caused by playing computer/simulation/video games (Oculus Rift is working to solve simulator sickness).

Motion sickness due to virtual reality is very similar to simulation sickness and motion sickness due to films. In virtual reality, however, the effect is made more acute as all external reference points are blocked from vision, the simulated images are three-dimensional and in some cases stereo sound that may also give a sense of motion. Studies have shown that exposure to rotational motions in a virtual environment can cause significant increases in nausea and other symptoms of motion sickness.

Other behavioural changes such as stress, addiction, isolation and mood changes are also discussed to be side-effects caused by immersive virtual reality.

References

- Mark J. P. Wolf (2008), The video game explosion: a history from PONG to PlayStation and beyond, p. 39, ABC-CLIO, ISBN 0-313-33868-X
- Jordan, Tim. Cyberpower: The Culture and Politics of Cyberspace and the Internet. Routledge, 1999. ISBN 0-415-17078-8

- Rollings, Andrew; Ernest Adams (2003). Andrew Rollings and Ernest Adams on Game Design. New Riders Publishing. pp. 395–415. ISBN 1-59273-001-9.

- Pečiva, J. 2007. Active Transactions in Collaborative Virtual Environments. PhD Thesis, Brno, Czech Republic, FIT VUT, ISBN 978-80-214-3549-0

- Timothy Murray, Derrick de Kerckhove, Oliver Grau, Kristine Stiles, Jean-Baptiste Barrière, Dominique Moulon, Maurice Benayoun Open Art, Nouvelles éditions Scala, 2011, French version, ISBN 978-2-35988-046-5

- Geary, James (2002). The body electric: an anatomy of the new bionic senses. Rutgers University Press. p. 130. ISBN 0-8135-3194-2.

- Damer, Bruce. Avatars: Exploring and Building Virtual Worlds on the Internet. Peachpit Press, 1997. ISBN 0-201-68840-9

- Gregoire, Carolyn (14 January 2015). "People Can Predict Your Personality From Your Online Avatar". The Huffington Post. Retrieved 17 January 2015.

- "US Patent 3919691 - Tactile man-machine communication system". USPTO. 11 November 1975. Retrieved 29 December 2015.

- "Apple-klokka ble egentlig designet i Norge for 20 år siden". Teknisk Ukeblad digi.no. (Norwegian language). 30 March 2015.

- Daniel, B. "Motion Cueing in the Chalmers Driving Simulator: An Optimization-Based Control Approach" (PDF). Chalmers University. Retrieved 14 April 2014.

- Campbell, Mikey (2013-02-19). "Apple awarded patent for more accurate haptic feedback system". Apple Insider. Retrieved 3 April 2013.

3

Tools and Technologies used in Virtual Reality

Without technology one is unable to experience virtual reality, this chapter introduces the reader to technology like virtual reality headset, head-mounted display, EyeTap, head-up display, helmet-mounted display, virtual retinal display, MotionParallax3D, Leonar3Do etc. These state-of-the-art technologies give users a heightened and configurable digital reality.

Virtual Reality Headset

A virtual reality headset provides immersive virtual reality for the wearer. VR headsets are widely used with computer games but they are also used in other applications, including simulators and trainers. They comprise a stereoscopic head-mounted display (providing separate images for each eye), stereo sound, and head motion tracking sensors (which may include gyroscopes, accelerometers, structured light systems, etc.). Some VR headsets also have eye tracking sensors and gaming controllers.

The Oculus Rift development kit headset, showing the stereoscopic lens along with the control box.

History

An early VR headset, the Forte VFX1, was announced at CES in 1994. The VFX-1 has stereoscopic displays, 3-axis head-tracking, and stereo headphones. Sony, another pioneer, released the Glasstron in 1997, which has an optional positional sensor, allowing the wearer to view the surroundings, with the perspective moving as his head moves, giving a deep sense of immersion. These VR headsets gave MechWarrior 2 players a new visual perspective of seeing the battlefield from inside the cockpit of their craft. However, these early headsets failed commercially due to their limited technology and were described by John Carmack as like "looking through toilet paper tubes".

The Forte VFX1 headset from 1994.

In 2012, a crowdfunding campaign began for a VR headset known as Oculus Rift; the project was led by several prominent video game developers, including John Carmack who later became the company's CTO. In March 2014, the project's parent company Oculus VR was acquired by Facebook for US$2 billion. The final consumer-oriented release of Oculus Rift began shipping on 28 March 2016.

In March 2014, Sony demonstrated a prototype headset for PlayStation 4, which was later named PlayStation VR. In 2014, Valve Corporation demonstrated some headset prototypes, which lead to a partnership with HTC to produce the Vive, which focuses on "room scale" VR environments that users can naturally navigate within and interact with. The Vive was planned for a release in April 2016. and PlayStation VR later in 2016.

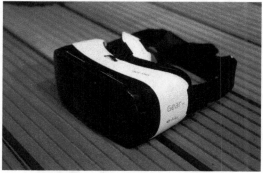

Samsung Gear VR, a VR headset designed exclusively for use with Samsung Galaxy smartphones.

Virtual reality headsets and viewers have also been designed for smartphones. Unlike headsets with integrated displays, these units are essentially enclosures which a smartphone can be inserted into. VR content is viewed from the screen of the device itself through lenses acting as a stereoscope, rather than using dedicated internal displays. Google released a series of specifications and associated DIY kits for virtual reality viewers known as Google Cardboard; these viewers are designed to be constructed using low-cost materials. Samsung Electronics parterned with Oculus VR to co-develop the Samsung Gear VR (which is exclusively compatible with Samsung Galaxy devices), while LG Electronics developed a headset with dedicated displays for its LG G5 smartphone known as LG 360 VR.

Constraints

Latency Requirements

Virtual reality headsets have significantly higher requirements for latency—the time it takes from a change in input to have a visual effect—than ordinary video games. If the system is too sluggish to react to head movement, then it can cause the user to experience virtual reality sickness, a kind of motion sickness. According to a Valve engineer, the ideal latency would be 7-15 milliseconds. A major component of this latency is the refresh rate of the display, which has driven the adoption of displays with a refresh rate from 90 Hz (Oculus Rift and HTC Vive) to 120 Hz (PlayStation VR).

The graphics processing unit (GPU) also needs to be more powerful to render frames more frequently. Oculus cited the limited processing power of Xbox One and PlayStation 4 as the reason why they are targeting the PC gaming market with their first devices.

Asynchronous Reprojection/Time Warp

A common way to reduce the perceived latency or compensate for a lower frame rate, is to take an (older) rendered frame and morph it according to the most recent head tracking data just before presenting the image on the screens. This is called asynchronous reprojection or "asynchronous time warp" in Oculus jargon.

PlayStation VR synthesizes "in-between frames" in such manner, so games that render at 60 fps natively result in 120 updates per second. SteamVR (HTC Vive) will also use "interleaved reprojection" for games that cannot keep up with its 90 Hz refresh rate, dropping down to 45 fps.

The simplest technique is applying only projective transformation to the images for each eye (simulating rotation of the eye). The downsides are that this approach cannot take into account the translation (changes in position) of the head. And the rotation can only happen around the axis of the eyeball, instead of the neck, which is the true axis for head rotation. When applied multiple times to a single frame, this causes "positional judder", because position is not updated with every frame.

A more complex technique is positional time warp, which uses pixel depth information from the Z-buffer to morph the scene into a different perspective. This produces other artifacts because it has no information about faces that are hidden due to occlusion and cannot compensate for position-dependent effects like reflections and specular lighting. While it gets rid of the positional judder, judder still presents itself in animations, as timewarped frames are effectively frozen. Support for positional time warp was added to the Oculus SDK in May 2015.

Resolution and Display Quality

Because virtual reality headsets stretch a single display across a wide field of view (up to 110° for some devices according to manufacturers), the magnification factor makes flaws in display technology much more apparent. One issue is the so-called screen-door effect, where the gaps between rows and columns of pixels become visible, kind of like looking through a screen door. This was especially noticeable in earlier prototypes and development kits, which had lower resolutions than the retail versions.

Lenses

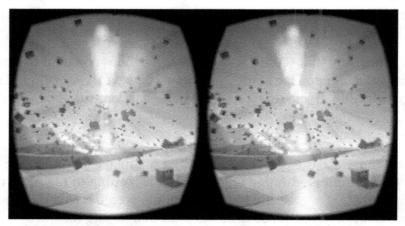

Image captured from an Oculus Rift DK2, showing compensation for lens distortion and chromatic aberration.

The lenses of the headset are responsible for mapping the up-close display to a wide field of view, while also providing a more comfortable distant point of focus. One challenge with this is providing consistency of focus: because eyes are free to turn within the headset, it's important to avoid having to refocus to prevent eye strain.

The lens introduce distortion and chromatic aberration, which are corrected in software.

Medicine

Medical Training

Virtual reality headsets are being currently used as means to train medical students for surgery. It allows them to perform essential procedures in a virtual, controlled environment. Students perform surgeries on virtual patients, which allows them to acquire the skills needed to perform surgeries on real patients. It also allows the students to revisit the surgeries from the perspective of the lead surgeon.

Traditionally, students had to participate in surgeries and often they would miss essential parts. But, now surgeons have been recording surgical procedures and students are now able to watch whole surgeries again from the perspective of lead surgeons with the use of VR headsets, without missing essential parts. Students can also pause, rewind, and fast forward surgeries.

Head-Mounted Display

A head-mounted display (or *helmet-mounted display*, for aviation applications), both abbreviated HMD, is a display device, worn on the head or as part of a helmet, that has a small display optic in front of one (monocular HMD) or each eye (binocular HMD).

There is also an optical head-mounted display (OHMD), which is a wearable display that can reflect projected images and allows a user to see through it.

A binocular head-mounted display (HMD).

A professional head-mounted display (HMD).

A HTC Vive headset.

Overview

A typical HMD has one or two small displays, with lenses and semi-transparent mirrors embedded in eyeglasses (also termed *data glasses*), a visor, or a helmet. The display units are miniaturised and may include cathode ray tubes (CRT), liquid crystal displays (LCDs), liquid crystal on silicon (LCos), or organic light-emitting diodes (OLED). Some vendors employ multiple micro-displays to increase total resolution and field of view.

Types

HMDs differ in whether they can display only computer-generated imagery (CGI), or only live imagery from the physical world, or a combination.

- Most HMDs display only a computer-generated image, sometimes referred to as a virtual image.

- Some HMDs allow a CGI to be superimposed on a real-world view. This is sometimes referred to as augmented reality or mixed reality. Combining real-world view with CGI can be done by projecting the CGI through a partially reflective mirror and viewing the real world directly. This method is often called *optical see-through*. Combining real-world view with CGI can also be done electronically by accepting video from a camera and mixing it electronically with CGI. This method is often called *video see-through*.

Optical HMD

An optical head-mounted display uses an optical mixer which is made of partly silvered mirrors. It can reflect artificial images, and let real images cross the lens, and let a user look through it.

Various methods have existed for see-through HMD's, most of which can be summarized into two main families based on *curved mirrors* or *waveguides*. Curved mirrors have been used by Laster Technologies, and by Vuzix in their Star 1200 product. Various waveguide methods have existed for years. These include diffraction optics, holographic optics, polarized optics, and reflective optics.

Applications

Major HMD applications include military, government (fire, police, etc.), and civilian-commercial (medicine, video gaming, sports, etc.).

Aviation and Tactical, Ground

Ruggedized HMDs are increasingly being integrated into the cockpits of modern helicopters and fighter aircraft. These are usually fully integrated with the pilot's flying helmet and may include protective visors, night vision devices, and displays of other symbology.

Military, police, and firefighters use HMDs to display tactical information such as maps or thermal imaging data while viewing a real scene. Recent applications have included the use of HMD for paratroopers. In 2005, the Liteye HMD was introduced for ground combat troops as a rugged, waterproof lightweight display that clips into a standard US PVS-14 military helmet mount. The self-contained color monocular organic light-emitting diode (OLED) display replaces the NVG tube and connects to a mobile computing device. The LE has see-through ability and can be used as a standard HMD or for augmented reality applications. The design is optimized to provide high definition data under all lighting conditions, in covered or see-through modes of operation. The LE has a low power consumption, operating on four AA batteries for 35 hours or receiving power via standard Universal Serial Bus (USB) connection.

The Defense Advanced Research Projects Agency (DARPA) continues to fund research in augmented reality HMDs as part of the Persistent Close Air Support (PCAS) Program. Vuzix is currently working on a system for PCAS that will use holographic waveguides to produce see-through augmented reality glasses that are only a few millimeters thick.

Engineering

Engineers and scientists use HMDs to provide stereoscopic views of computer-aided design (CAD) schematics. These systems are also used in the maintenance of complex systems, as they can give a technician a simulated *x-ray vision* by combining computer graphics such as system diagrams and imagery with the technician's natural vision.

Medicine and Research

There are also applications in surgery, wherein a combination of radiographic data (X-ray computed tomography (CAT) scans, and magnetic resonance imaging (MRI) imaging) is combined with the surgeon's natural view of the operation, and anesthesia, where the patient vital signs are within the anesthesiologist's field of view at all times.

Research universities often use HMDs to conduct studies related to vision, balance, cognition and neuroscience.

An eye tracking HMD with LED illuminators and cameras to measure eye movements

As of 2010, the use of predictive visual tracking measurement to identify mild traumatic brain injury was being studied. In visual tracking tests, a HMD unit with eye tracking ability shows an object moving in a regular pattern. People without brain injury are able to track the moving object with *smooth pursuit eye movements* and correct trajectory. The test requires both attention and working memory which are difficult functions for people with mild traumatic brain injury. The question being studied, is whether results for people with brain injury will show visual-tracking gaze errors relative to the moving target.

Gaming and Video

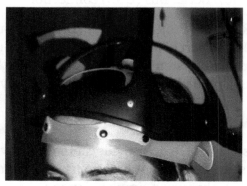

Disney HMD mount

Low cost HMD devices are available for use with 3D games and entertainment applications.

One of the first commercially available HMDs was the Forte VFX1 which was announced at Consumer Electronics Show (CES) in 1994. The VFX-1 had stereoscopic displays, 3-axis head-tracking, and stereo headphones.

Another pioneer in this field was Sony, which released the Glasstron in 1997. It had as an optional accessory a positional sensor which permitted the user to view the surroundings, with the perspective moving as the head moved, providing a deep sense of immersion. One novel application of this technology was in the game MechWarrior 2, which permitted users of the Sony Glasstron or Virtual I/O's iGlasses to adopt a new visual perspective from inside the cockpit of the craft, using their own eyes as visual and seeing the battlefield through their craft's own cockpit.

Sony has released the *Personal 3D Viewer* (or HMZ-T1), a fully surround-sound headset for 3D gaming and movies.

Sensics demonstrated at CES 2012 a gaming and entertainment goggle that included an on-board Android processor and hand tracking to facilitate natural interaction.

As of 2013, many brands of video glasses can be connected to video and DSLR cameras, making them applicable as a new age monitor. As a result of the glasses ability to block out ambient light, filmmakers and photographers are able to see clearer presentations of their live images.

The Oculus Rift is an upcoming virtual reality (VR) head-mounted display created by Palmer Luckey that the company Oculus VR is developing for virtual reality simulations and video games.

The HTC Vive is an upcoming virtual reality head-mounted display. The headset is produced by a collaboration between Valve and HTC, with its defining feature being precision room-scale tracking, and high-precision motion controllers.

The PlayStation VR is the only virtual reality headset coming out for gaming consoles, for the PlayStation 4.

Sports

A HMD system has been developed for Formula One drivers by Kopin Corp. and the BMW Group. According to BMW, *"The HMD is part of an advanced telemetry system approved for installation by the Formula One racing committee... to communicate to the driver wirelessly from the heart of the race pit."* The HMD will display critical race data while allowing the driver to continue focussing on the track. Pit crews control the data and messages sent to their drivers through two-way radio.

Recon Instruments released on 3 November 2011 two head mounted displays for ski goggles, MOD and MOD Live, the latter based on an Android operating system.

Training and Simulation

A key application for HMDs is training and simulation, allowing to virtually place a trainee in a situation that is either too expensive or too dangerous to replicate in real-life. Training with HMDs covers a wide range of applications from driving, welding and spray painting, flight and vehicle simulators, dismounted soldier training, medical procedure training, and more. However, a number of unwanted symptoms have been caused by prolonged use of certain types of head-mounted displays, and these issues must be resolved before optimal training and simulation is feasible.

Paratrooper training with an HMD

Performance parameters

- Ability to show stereoscopic imagery. A binocular HMD has the potential to display a different image to each eye. This can be used to show stereoscopic images. It should be borne in mind that so-called 'Optical Infinity' is generally taken by flight surgeons and display experts as about 9 metres. This is the distance at which, given the average human eye rangefinder "baseline" (distance between the eyes or Interpupillary distance (IPD)) of between 2.5 and 3 inches (6 and 8 cm), the angle of an object at that distance becomes essentially the same from each eye. At smaller ranges the perspective from each eye is significantly different and the expense of generating two different visual channels through the *computer-generated imagery* (CGI) system becomes worthwhile.

- Interpupillary distance (IPD). This is the distance between the two eyes, measured at the pupils, and is important in designing head-mounted displays.

- Field of view (FOV) – Humans have an FOV of around 180°, but most HMDs offer far less than this. Typically, a greater field of view results in a greater sense of immersion and better situational awareness. Most people do not have a good feel for what a particular quoted FOV would look like (e.g., 25°) so often manufacturers will quote an apparent screen size. Most people sit about 60 cm away from their monitors and have quite a good feel about screen sizes at that distance. To convert the manufacturer's apparent screen size to a desktop monitor position, divide the screen size by the distance in feet, then multiply by 2. Consumer-level HMDs typically offer a FOV of about 30-40° whereas professional HMDs offer a field of view of 60° to 150°.

- Resolution – HMDs usually mention either the total number of pixels or the number of pixels per degree. Listing the total number of pixels (e.g., 1600×1200 pixels per eye) is borrowed from how the specifications of computer monitors are presented. However, the pixel density, usually specified in pixels per degree or in arcminutes per pixel, is also used to determine visual acuity. 60 pixels/° (1 arcmin/pixel) is usually referred to as eye limiting resolution, above which increased resolution is not noticed by people with normal vision. HMDs typically offer 10 to 20 pixels/°, though advances in micro-displays help increase this number.

- Binocular overlap – measures the area that is common to both eyes. Binocular overlap is the basis for the sense of depth and stereo, allowing humans to sense which objects are near and which objects are far. Humans have a binocular overlap of about 100° (50° to the left of the nose and 50° to the right). The larger the binocular overlap offered by an HMD, the greater the sense of stereo. Overlap is sometimes specified in degrees (e.g., 74°) or as a percentage indicating how much of the visual field of each eye is common to the other eye.

- Distant focus (collimation). Optical methods may be used to present the images at a distant focus, which seems to improve the realism of images that in the real world would be at a distance.

- On-board processing and operating system. Some HMD vendors offer on-board operating systems such as Android, allowing applications to run locally on the HMD, and eliminating the need to be tethered to an external device to generate video. These are sometimes referred to as *smart goggles*.

Support of 3D Video Formats

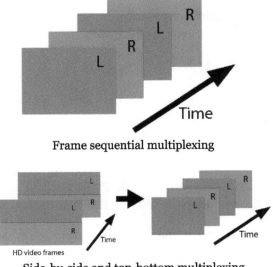

Frame sequential multiplexing

Side-by-side and top-bottom multiplexing

Depth perception inside an HMD requires different images for the left and right eyes. There are multiple ways to provide these separate images:

- Use dual video inputs, thereby providing a completely separate video signal to each eye

- Time-based multiplexing. Methods such as frame sequential combine two separate video signals into one signal by alternating the left and right images in successive frames.

- Side by side or top-bottom multiplexing. This method allocated half of the image to the left eye and the other half of the image to the right eye.

The advantage of dual video inputs is that it provides the maximum resolution for each image and the maximum frame rate for each eye. The disadvantage of dual video inputs is that it requires separate video outputs and cables from the device generating the content.

Time-based multiplexing preserves the full resolution per each image, but reduces the frame rate by half. For example, if the signal is presented at 60 Hz, each eye is receiving just 30 Hz updates. This may become an issue with accurately presenting fast-moving images.

Side-by-side and top-bottom multiplexing provide full-rate updates to each eye, but reduce the resolution presented to each eye. Many 3D broadcasts, such as ESPN, chose to provide side-by-side 3D which saves the need to allocate extra transmission bandwidth and is more suitable to fast-paced sports action relative to time-based multiplexing methods.

Not all HMDs provide depth perception. Some lower-end modules are essentially bi-ocular devices where both eyes are presented with the same image.

3D video players sometimes allow maximum compatibility with HMDs by providing the user with a choice of the 3D format to be used.

Peripherals

- The most rudimentary HMDs simply project an image or symbology on a wearer's visor or reticle. The image is not slaved to the real world, i.e., the image does not change based on the wearer's head position.

- More sophisticated HMDs incorporate a positioning system that tracks the wearer's head position and angle, so that the picture or symbology displayed is congruent with the outside world using see-through imagery.

- Head tracking – Slaving the imagery. Head-mounted displays may also be used with tracking sensors that detect changes of angle and orientation. When such data is available in the system computer, it can be used to generate the appropriate computer-generated imagery (CGI) for the angle-of-look at the particular time. This allows the user to *look around* a virtual reality environment simply by moving the head without the need for a separate controller to change the angle of the imagery. In radio-based systems (compared to wires), the wearer may move about within the tracking limits of the system.

- Eye tracking – Eye trackers measure the point of gaze, allowing a computer to sense where the user is looking. This information is useful in a variety of contexts such as user interface navigation : by sensing the user's gaze, a computer can change the information displayed on a screen, bring added details to attention, etc.

- Hand tracking – tracking hand movement from the perspective of the HMD allows natural interaction with content and a convenient game-play mechanism

EyeTap

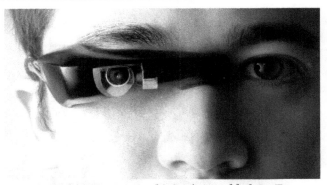

Man wearing a one-eyed injection-molded EyeTap

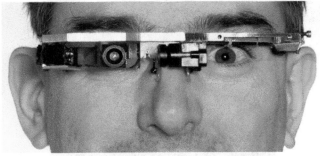

EyeTap inventor Steve Mann wearing a metal frame Laser EyeTap (computer-controlled laser light source run from "GlassEye" camera)

An EyeTap is a device that is worn in front of the eye that acts as a camera to record the scene available to the eye as well as a display to superimpose computer-generated imagery on the original scene available to the eye. This structure allows the user's eye to operate as both a monitor and a camera as the EyeTap intakes the world around it and augments the image the user sees allowing it to overlay computer-generated data over top of the normal world the user would perceive. The EyeTap is a hard technology to categorize under the three main headers for wearable computing (constancy, augmentation, mediation) for while it is in theory a constancy technology in nature it also has the ability to augment and mediate the reality the user perceives.

In order to capture what the eye is seeing as accurately as possible, an EyeTap uses a beam splitter to send the same scene (with reduced intensity) to both the eye and a camera. The camera then digitizes the reflected image of the scene and sends it to a computer. The computer processes the image and then sends it to a projector. The projector sends the image to the other side of the beam splitter so that this computer-generated image is reflected into the eye to be superimposed on the original scene. Stereo EyeTaps modify light passing through both eyes, but many research prototypes (mainly for reasons of ease of construction) only tap one eye.

EyeTap is also the name of an organization founded by inventor Steve Mann to develop and promote EyeTap-related technologies such as wearable computers.

Possible Uses

Inventor Steve Mann using weather-resistant EyeTap together with a hydraulophone

An EyeTap is somewhat like a head-up display (HUD). The important difference is that the scene available to the eye is also available to the computer that projects the head-up display. This enables the EyeTap to modify the computer generated scene in response to the natural scene. One use, for instance, would be a sports EyeTap: here the wearer, while in a stadium, would be able to follow a particular player in a field and have the EyeTap display statistics relevant to that player as a floating box above the player. Another practical use for the EyeTap would be in a construction yard as it would allow the user to reference the blueprints, especially in a 3D manner, to the current state of the building, display a list of current materials and their current locations as well perform basic measurements. Or, even in the business world, the EyeTap has great potential, for it would be capable of delivering to the user constant up to date information on the stock market, the user's corporation, and meeting statuses. On a more day-to-day basis some of Steve Mann's first uses for the technology was using it to keep track of names of people and places, his to-do lists, and keeping track of his other daily ordeals. The EyeTap Criteria are an attempt to define how close a real, practical device comes to such an ideal. EyeTaps could have great use in any field where the user would benefit from real-time interactive information that is largely visual in nature. This is sometimes referred to as *computer-mediated reality*, commonly known as *augmented reality*.

Eyetap has been explored as a potential tool for individuals with visual disabilities due to its abilities to direct visual information to parts of the retina that function well. As well, Eyetap's role in sousveillance has been explored by Mann, Jason Nolan and Barry Wellman.

Possible Side Effects

Users may find that they experience side effects such as headaches and difficulty sleeping if usage occurs shortly before sleep. Mann finds that due to his extensive use of the device that going without it can cause him to feel "nauseous, unsteady, naked" when he removes it.

Cyborglogs & EyeTaps

The EyeTap has applications in the world of cyborg logging, as it allows the user the ability to perform real-time visual capture of their daily lives from their own point of view. In this way, the EyeTap could be used to create a lifelong cyborg log or "glog" of the user's life and the events they participate in, potentially recording enough media to allow producers centuries in the future to present the user's life as interactive entertainment (or historical education) to consumers of that era.

History

Steve Mann created the first version of the EyeTap, which consisted of a computer in a backpack wired up to a camera and its viewfinder which in turn was rigged to a helmet. Ever since this first version, it has gone through multiple models as wearable computing evolves, allowing the EyeTap to shrink down to a smaller and less weighty version.

Currently the EyeTap consists of the eyepiece used to display the images, the keypad which the user can use to interface with the EyeTap and have it perform the desired tasks, a CPU which can be attached to most articles of clothing and in some cases even a Wi-Fi device so the user can access the Internet and online data.

Principle of Operation

The Eyetap functions by redirecting light from the user's eye using a diverter (the previously mentioned beam splitter) into a sensor. The sensor then processes the collected light rays and the data after having the computer image super-imposed on it is sent to the aremac, a display device capable of displaying data at any fitting depth. The output rays from the aremac are reflected off the diverter back into the eye of the user along with the original light rays.

A conceptual diagram of an EyeTap;

In these cases, the EyeTap views infrared light, as well as the overall design schematic of how the EyeTap manipulates lightrays.

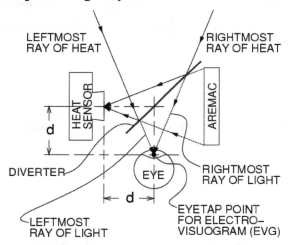

Components

CCD Cameras (Charge-coupled device) are the most common type of digital camera used today.

HUd (Video Gaming)

In video gaming, the HUD (head-up display) or Status Bar is the method by which information is visually relayed to the player as part of a game's user interface. It takes its name from the head-up displays used in modern aircraft.

The HUD is frequently used to simultaneously display several pieces of information including the main character's health, items, and an indication of game progression (such as score or level).

Shown on the HUD

The *SuperTuxKart* HUD displays the character's speed, position, and amount of nitro, while also displaying the map of the course in the lower-left corner.

While the information that is displayed on the HUD depends greatly on the game, there are many features that players recognize across many games. Most of them are static onscreen so that they stay visible during gameplay. Common features include:

- Health / lives – this might include the player's character and possibly other important characters, such as allies or bosses. Real-time strategy games usually show the health of every unit visible on screen. Also, in many (but not all) first- and third-person shooters, when the player is damaged, the screen (or part of it) flashes briefly (usually in red color, representing blood) and shows arrows or other similar images that point to the direction the threat came from, thus informing the player from which direction the enemies are attacking.

- Time – This may be a timer counting down the time limit or the time left until a specific event (including when to begin racing in the *Mario Kart* series). It may also be a timer counting up to records such as lap times in racing games, or the length of time a player can last in games based on survival. Many HUDS also use time displays to show the in-game time, such as the current time of day or year within the game. Some games may also display the real time.

- Weapons/ammunition – Most action games (first- and third-person shooters in particular) show what weapon is being used, and also how much ammunition is in it. Can show other available weapons, and objects like health packs, radios, etc.

- Capabilities – gameplay options that are often accessible by the player during gameplay, such as available weapons, items, or spells. This can include when the ability will become usable again, such as ammunition, magic points, or some other type of "charge up" timer. Icons and/or text may appear in the HUD to indicate other actions that are only available at certain times or in certain places, to show they are available to perform and which button performs it; for example the text "A – open door" may be displayed, but only when the character is near a door.

- Menus – Menus to exit, change options, delete files, change settings, etc.

- Game progression – the player's current score, money, lap, or level (as in stage or as in experience points). This might also include the character's current task or quest.

- Mini-map – a small map of the area that can act like a radar, showing the terrain, allies and/or enemies, locations like safe houses and shops, streets, etc.

- Speedometer/Tachometer – used in most games which feature drivable vehicles. Usually shown only when driving one of these.

- Context-sensitive information – shown only as it becomes important, such as tutorial messages, special one-off abilities, and speech subtitles.

- Reticle / cursor / crosshair – an indication of where the character is aiming or where the mouse pointer is. Pressing a key while pointing at an object or character with the cursor can issue actions like shooting, talking, picking up objects, manipulating switches, using computers, etc.

- Stealthometer – displays the awareness level of enemies to the player's presence (used in stealth games and some first person shooters).

- Compass / Quest Arrow - sometimes found in RPGs, first person shooters and driving games, they help guide the player toward his or her objective. An example is in the first-person shooter *BioShock*, which displays an arrow pointing the direction of the next objective on the top of the player's HUD. Sometimes the compass itself might not be a real compass, rather one that points toward the next location or goal. Another notable example is in the open-world driving game *Crazy Taxi*, which became the subject of a patent infringement lawsuit between Sega and Fox Interactive over similar game mechanics in *The Simpsons: Road Rage*.

There are also trends common among genres and platforms. Many online games show player names and a chat text box for talking to the other players. RTS games tend to have complex user interfaces, with context-sensitive panels and a full-overview minimap with fog of war.

How the HUD is

Typically this information is represented numerically, with the health level being a number from 0–100 (percent): 100 representing full health and 0 representing empty, no health or death. However, many other methods of visual representation can be used. For instance, certain games employ a "health bar" which empties as the player becomes hurt such as *Tekken*, *Street Fighter*, and many others.

Armour levels are also commonly monitored, either through a separate readout, or as part of the health system. For example, *Halo* uses one recharging shield bar, acting as the health level. When this is depleted the player can only take a few more hits before death. The same goes in *Destroy All Humans!*, but in the form of Crypto's shields. Traditionally, games used lives to represent health. Every time the main character was injured he would lose one of his limited lives. Another way to display the life in the HUD is demonstrated in *Gears of War*, where the characters life is displayed only when he is taking damage, in which case a red cog known as the Crimson Omen appears in the center of the screen. The more visible the Crimson Omen is, the more damage the player has sustained and the closer he is to death. This health system is known as the 'Red Ring' system.

There is also a lot of variance with regards to the display of other information. Some games permanently display all the weapons a character is currently carrying, others rely on a pull up weapon selector. Inventory or storage space may also be permanently overlaid over the screen, or accessed via a menu. Alternatively, only a limited number of items stored in the inventory might be displayed at once, with the rest being rotated into view using the [and] keys.

In order to maintain the suspension of disbelief, some games make the HUD look like a real HUD within the context of the game's world. Many first-person vehicle simulation games use this technique, showing instruments and displays that the driver of the vehicle would be expected to see. The displays in the helmet in the first-person adventure game *Metroid Prime* or *Star Wars: Republic Commando* also mimic the player's point of view. A similar method is used in *Tom Clancy's Ghost Recon Advanced Warfighter* and *Crysis*. In some of these circumstances where the player and character within the game are meant to see the same 'HUD' information, *Halo* for example, the term HMD (Helmet Mounted Display) would technically be more accurate. This is not to be confused with Head-Up Display.

Some games provide the player with an option to hide part or all of the HUD. This is usually used to create cleaner looking screenshots and videos, which can be essential to producing machinima. Certain games like *Pac-Man World* and *Super Mario Galaxy 2* even keep the HUD elements off-screen without any option. When this method is used, they will only appear when affected. In some games, they can temporarily be displayed all at once with the press of a button. In games where that method is not used, the only way to display them at once is by pausing the game.

A few games give players extensive control over their HUD, such as customizing position, size, color, and opacity. *World of Warcraft* is notable for allowing players to significantly modify and enhance the user interface through Lua scripting.

Despite the modern dominance of 3D graphics in games, HUDs are frequently rendered with a 2D look, often using sprites.

Reduction of Elements

Sometimes, for the sake of realism, information normally displayed in the HUD is instead disguised as part of the scenery or part of the vehicle in which the player is traveling. For example, when the player is driving a car that can sustain a certain number of hits, a smoke trail might appear when the car can take only two more hits, fire might appear from the car to indicate that the next hit will be fatal. Wounds and bloodstains may sometimes appear on injured characters who may also limp, stagger, slouch over or breathe heavily to indicate they are injured, a notable example being *Resident Evil 2*.

In rare cases, no HUD is used at all, leaving the player to interpret the auditory and visual cues in the gameworld. The elimination of elements has hardly become a trend in game development, but can be witnessed in several titles as of late. Some examples of games without HUDs are *Silent Hill 2, Jurassic Park: Trespasser, Ico, The Getaway, Fable III, Another World, Mirror's Edge, King Kong, Dead Space, Call of Cthulhu: Dark Corners of the Earth, Resident Evil,* and *Tomb Raider* (2013).

HUDs and Burn-in

Prolonged display (that stays on the screen in a fixed position, remaining static) of HUD elements on certain CRT-based screens may cause permanent damage in the form of burning into the inner coating of the television sets, which is impossible to repair. Players who pause their games for long hours without turning off their television or putting it on standby risk harming their TV sets. Plasma TV screens are also at risk, although the effects are usually not as permanent.

Burn-in can still happen on LCD monitors, but only when the same image is displayed for weeks.

Other Uses

The Sega Dreamcast, released in 1998, uses a VMU on many games as a HUD. A notable example is *Resident Evil 2, Resident Evil 3: Nemesis* and *Resident Evil Code: Veronica* all using the VMU to show a mini version of the HUD, which displays the protagonists health and ammo. This feature was resurrected with the introduction of the Nintendo Wii U, which uses the Wii U GamePad for some games as a HUD.

Helmet-Mounted Display

A helmet-mounted display (HMD) is a device used in some modern aircraft, especially combat aircraft. HMDs project information similar to that of head-up displays (HUD) on an aircrew's visor or reticle, thereby allowing them to obtain situation awareness and/or cue weapons systems to the direction his head is pointing. Applications which allow cuing of weapon systems are referred to as helmet-mounted sight and display (HMSD) or helmet-mounted sights (HMS). These devices were created first by South Africa, then the Soviet Union and followed by the United States.

Requirement

Aviation HMD designs serve these purposes:

- using the head angle as a pointer to direct air-to-air and air-to-ground weapons seekers or other sensors (e.g., radar, FLIR) to a target merely by pointing his head at the target and actuating a switch via HOTAS controls. In close combat prior to HMDs, the pilot had to align the aircraft to shoot at a target. HMDs allow the pilot to simply point his head at a target, designate it to weapon and shoot.

- displaying targeting and aircraft performance information (such as airspeed, altitude, target range, weapon seeker status, "g", etc.) to the pilot while "heads-up", eliminating the need to look inside the flightdeck.

- displaying sensor video for the purpose of:
  - verification that the chosen sensor has been cued to the right target or location without requiring the pilot to look inside the flightdeck
  - viewing outside terrain using sensor video in degraded visual conditions.

HMD systems, combined with High Off-Boresight (HOBS) weapons, results in the ability for aircrew to attack and destroy nearly any target seen by the pilot. These systems allow targets to be designated with minimal aircraft maneuvering, minimizing the time spent in the threat environment, and allowing greater lethality, survivability, and pilot situational awareness.

History

The first aircraft with simple HMD devices appeared for experimental purpose in the mid-1970s to aid in targeting heat seeking missiles. These rudimentary devices were better described as Helmet-Mounted Sights. Mirage F1AZ of the SAAF (South African Air Force) used a locally developed helmet-mounted sight. This enables the pilot to make bore attacks, without having to maneuver to the optimum firing position. South

Africa subsequently emerged as one of the pioneers and leaders in helmet-mounted sight technology. The SAAF was also the first air force to fly the helmet sight operationally. The US Navy's Visual Target Acquisition System (VTAS), made by Honeywell Corporation was a simple mechanical "ring and bead"–style sight fitted to the front of the pilot's helmet that was flown in the 1974–78 ACEVAL/AIMVAL on U.S. F-14 and F-15 fighters

VTAS received praise for its effectiveness in targeting off-boresight missiles, but the U.S. did not pursue fielding it except for integration into late-model Navy F-4 Phantoms equipped with the AIM-9 Sidewinder. HMDs were also introduced in helicopters during this time.

The first operational jet fighters with HMD (Mirage F1AZ) were fielded by the South African Air Force. After the South African system had been proven in combat, playing a role in downing Soviet aircraft over Angola, the Soviets embarked on a crash program to counter the technology. As a result, the MiG-29 was fielded in 1985 with an HMD and a high off-boresight weapon (R-73), giving them an advantage in close in maneuvering engagements.

Several nations responded with programs to counter the MiG-29/HMD/R-73 (and later Su-27) combination once its effectiveness was known, principally through access to former East German MiG-29s that were operated by the unified German Air Force.

The first successful HMD outside South Africa and the Soviet Union was the Israeli Air Force Elbit DASH series, fielded in conjunction with the Python 4, in the early 1990s. American and European fighter HMDs lagged behind, not becoming widely used until the late 1990s and early 2000s. The U.S.-UK-Germany responded initially with a combined ASRAAM effort. Technical difficulties led to the U.S. abandoning ASRAAM, instead funding development of the AIM-9X and the Joint Helmet-Mounted Cueing System in 1990.

Technology

While conceptually simple, implementation of aircraft HMDs is quite complex. There are many variables:

- precision - the angular error between the line-of-sight and the derived cue. The position of the *helmet* is what is used to point the missile, it thus must be calibrated and fit securely on the pilot's head. The line between the pilot's eye and the reticle on the visor is known as the line of sight (LOS) between the aircraft and the intended target. The user's eye must stay aligned with the sight – in other words, current HMDs cannot sense where the eye is looking, but can place a "pipper" between the eye and the target.

- latency or slew rate - how much lag there is between the helmet and the cue.

- field of regard - the angular range over which the sight can still produce a suitably accurate measurement.

- weight and balance - total helmet weight and its center of gravity, which are particularly important under high "g" maneuvers. Weight is the largest problem faced by fighter aircraft HMD designers. This is much less a concern for helicopter applications, making elaborate helicopter HMDs common.

- safety and flightdeck compatibility, including ejection seat compatibility.

- optical characteristics – calibration, sharpness, distant focus (or 'Collimation', a technique used to present the images at a distant focus, which improves the readability of images), monocular vs. binocular imagery, eye dominance, and binocular rivalry.

- durability and ability to handle day to day wear and tear.

- cost, including integration and training.

- fit and interfacing the aviator's head to the aircraft – head anthropometry and facial anatomy make helmet fitting a crucial factor in the aviator's ability to interface with the aircraft systems. Misalignment or helmet shift can cause an inaccurate picture.

Head Position Sensing

HMD designs must sense the elevation, azimuth and tilt of the pilot's head relative to the airframe with sufficient precision even under high "g" and during rapid head movement. Three basic methods are used in current HMD technology - optical, electromagnetic and sonic.

Hybrid Inertial Optical Tracking

Hybrid inertial tracking systems employs a sensitive Inertial Measurement Unit (IMU) and an optical sensor to provide reference to the aircraft. The optical sensor also constrains IMU drift. Hybrid trackers feature low latency and high accuracy. The *Thales Visionix Scorpion HMCS utilizes a tracker called the Hybrid Optical-based Inertial Tracker (HObIT).

Optical Tracking

Optical systems employ infrared emitters on the helmet (or flightdeck) infrared detectors in the flightdeck (or helmet), to measure the pilot's head position. The main limitations are restricted fields of regard and sensitivity to sunlight or other heat sources. The MiG-29/AA-11 Archer system uses this technology. The Cobra HMD as used on both the Eurofighter Typhoon and the JAS39 Gripen both employ the optical helmet tracker developed by Denel Optronics (now part of Zeiss Optronics).

Electromagnetic Tracking

Electromagnetic sensing designs use coils (in the helmet) placed in an alternating field (generated in the flightdeck) to produce alternating electrical voltages based on the movement of the helmet in multiple axes. This technique requires precise magnetic mapping of the flightdeck to account for ferrous and conductive materials in the seat, flightdeck sills and canopy to reduce angular errors in the measurement.

Sonic Tracking

Acoustic sensing designs use ultrasonic sensors to monitor the pilot's head position while being updated by computer software in multiple axes. Typical operating frequencies are in the 50 to 100 kHz range and can be made to carry audio sound information directly to the pilot's ears via subcarrier modulation of the sensong ultrasonic sensing signals.

Optics

Older HMDs typically employ a compact CRT embedded in the helmet, and suitable optics to display symbology on to the pilot's visor or reticle, focused at infinity. Modern HMDs have dispensed with the CRT in favor of micro-displays such as Liquid Crystal on Silicon (LCOS) or Liquid Crystal Display (LCD) along with a LED illuminator to generate the displayed image. Advanced HMDs can also project FLIR or NVG imagery. A recent improvement is the capability to display color symbols and video.

Major Systems

Systems are presented in rough chronological order of initial operating capability.

Integrated Helmet And Display Sight System (IHADSS)

IHADSS

In 1985, the U.S. Army fielded the AH-64 Apache and with it the Integrated Helmet and Display Sighting System (IHADSS), a new helmet concept in which the role of the helmet was expanded to provide a visually coupled interface between the aviator and the aircraft. The Honeywell M142 IHADSS is fitted with a 40° by 30° field of view, video-with-symbology monocular display. IR emitters allow a slewable thermographic camera sensor, mounted on the nose of the aircraft, to be slaved to the aviator's head movements. The display also enables Nap-of-the-earth night navigation. IHADSS is also used on the Italian Agusta A129 Mangusta.

ZSh-5 / Shchel-3UM

The Russian designed Shchel-3UM HMD design is fit to the ZSh-5 series helmet, and is used on the MiG-29 and Su-27 in conjunction with the R-73 (missile). The HMD/ Archer combination gave the MiG-29 and Su-27 a significantly improved close combat capability and quickly became the most widely deployed HMD in the world.

Display and Sight Helmet (DASH)

The Elbit Systems DASH III was the first modern Western HMD to achieve operational service. Development of the DASH began during the mid-1980s, when the IAF issued a requirement for F-15 and F-16 aircraft. The first design entered production around 1986, and the current GEN III helmet entered production during the early to mid-1990s. The current production variant is deployed on IDF F-15, and F-16 aircraft. Additionally, it has been certified on the F/A-18 and F-5. The DASH III has been exported and integrated into various legacy aircraft, including the MiG-21. It also forms the baseline technology for the US JHMCS.

The DASH GEN III is a wholly embedded design, where the complete optical and position sensing coil package is built within the helmet (either USAF standard HGU-55/P or the Israeli standard HGU-22/P) using a spherical visor to provide a collimated image to the pilot. A quick-disconnect wire powers the display and carries video drive signals to the helmet's Cathode Ray Tube (CRT). DASH is closely integrated with the aircraft's weapon system, via a MIL-STD-1553B bus.

Joint Helmet-Mounted Cueing System (JHMCS)

After the U.S. withdrawal from ASRAAM, the U.S. pursued and fielded JHMCS in conjunction with the Raytheon AIM-9X, in November 2003 with the 12th and 19th Fighter Squadrons at Elmendorf AFB, Alaska. The Navy conducted RDT&E on the F/A-18C as lead platform for JHMCS, but fielded it first on the F/A-18 Super Hornet E and F aircraft in 2003. The USAF is also integrating JHMCS into its F-15E, F-16, and F-22 aircraft.

JHMCS

JHMCS is a derivative of the DASH III and the Kaiser Agile Eye HMDs, and was developed by Vision Systems International (VSI), a joint venture company formed by Rockwell Collins and Elbit (Kaiser Electronics is now owned by Rockwell Collins). Boeing integrated the system into the F/A-18 and began low-rate initial production delivery in fiscal year 2002. JHMCS is employed in the F/A-18A++/C/D/E/F, F-15C/D/E, and F-16 Block 40/50 with a design that is 95% common to all platforms.

Unlike the DASH, which is integrated into the helmet itself, JHMCS assemblies attach to modified HGU-55/P, HGU-56/P or HGU-68/P helmets. JHMCS employs a newer, faster digital processing package, but retains the same type of electromagnetic position sensing as the DASH. The CRT package is more capable, but remains limited to monochrome presentation of calligraphic symbology. JHMCS provides support for raster scanned imagery to display FLIR/IRST pictures for night operations and provides collimated symbology and imagery to the pilot. The integration of the night-vision goggles with the JHMCS was a key requirement of the program.

When combined with the AIM-9X, an advanced short-range dogfight weapon that employs a Focal Plane Array seeker and a thrust vectoring tail control package, JHMCS allows effective target designation up to 80 degrees either side of the aircraft's nose. In March 2009, a successfully 'Lock on After Launch' firing of an ASRAAM at a target located behind the wing-line of the 'shooter' aircraft, was demonstrated by a Royal Australian Air Force (RAAF) F/A-18 using JHMCS.

Scorpion Helmet Mounted Cueing System (HMCS)

Thales Introduced the Scorpion Helmet-Mounted Cueing System to the military aviation market in 2008. Scorpion was the winner of the Helmet Mounted Integrated Targeting (HMIT) program in 2010. Scorpion has the distinction of being the first color HMD introduced. It was developed for targeting pod, gimbaled sensor or high off-boresight missile cueing mission scenarios. Unlike most HMDs, which require custom helmets, Scorpion was designed to be installed on standard issue HGU-55/P and HGU-

68/P helmets and is fully compatible with standard issue U.S. Pilot Flight Equipment without special fitting. It is also fully compatible with standard unmodified AN/AVS-9 Night Vision Goggles (NVG) and Panoramic Night Vision Goggles (PNVG).

Scorpion HMCS mounted on a HGU-55/P helmet with a clear visor

Scorpion uses a novel optical system featuring a light-guide optical element (LOE) which provides a compact color collimated image to the pilot. This allows the display to be positioned between the pilot's eyes and NVGs. The display can be positioned as the pilot wishes. Sophisticated software correction accommodates the display position, providing an accurate image to the pilot and allowing the Scorpion HMCS to be installed onto a pilot's existing helmet with no special fitting. A visor can be deployed in front of the display providing protection during ejection. The visor can be clear, glare, high contrast, gradient, or laser protective. An NVG mount can be installed in place of the visor during flight. Once installed, NVGs can be placed in front of the display, thus allowing the pilot to view both the display symbols as well as the NVG image simultaneously.

Scorpion has been deployed on the U.S. A-10C and F-16 Block 30 and F-22 aircraft. The first squadron to deploy into Afghanistan in early 2013 with the HMIT (Scorpion) system was the 74th Fighter Squadron.

The U.S. Army Common Helmet Mounted Display (CHMD) program was awarded to Raytheon in early 2013 and will implement a new display from Thales for the integration effort. CHMD is part of the Air Warrior program. The Thales CHMD features an upgraded LOE display with a larger field of view than the HMIT version. CHMD is designed to mount to a standard HGU-56/P Rotary Wing helmet.

Aselsan AVCI

Aselsan of Turkey is working to develop a similar system to the French TopOwl Helmet, called the AVCI Helmet Integrated Cueing System. The system will also be utilized into the T-129 Turkish Attack Helicopter.

TopOwl-F (Topsight/TopNight)

The French thrust vectoring Matra MICA (missile) for its Dassault Rafale and late-model Mirage 2000 fighters was accompanied by the Topsight HMD by Sextant Avionique. TopSight provides a 20 degree FoV for the pilot's right eye, and calligraphic symbology generated from target and aircraft parameters. Electromagnetic position sensing is employed. The Topsight helmet uses an integral embedded design, and its contoured shape is designed to provide the pilot with a wholly unobstructed field of view.

TopNight, a Topsight derivative, is designed specifically for adverse weather and night air to ground operations, employing more complex optics to project infrared imagery overlaid with symbology. The most recent version the Topsight has been designated TopOwl-F, and is qualified on the Mirage-2000-5 Mk2 and Mig-29K.

Eurofighter Helmet-Mounted Symbology System

HMSS

The Eurofighter Typhoon utilizes the Helmet-Mounted Symbology System (HMSS) developed by BAE Systems and Pilkington Optronics. It is capable of displaying both raster imagery and calligraphic symbology, with provisions for embedded NVGs. As with the DASH helmet, the system employs integrated position sensing to ensure that symbols representing outside-world entities move in line with the pilot's head movements.

Helmet-Mounted Display System

Vision Systems International (VSI; the Elbit Systems/Rockwell Collins joint venture) along with Helmet Integrated Systems, Ltd. developed the Helmet-Mounted Display System (HMDS) for the F-35 Joint Strike Fighter aircraft. In addition to standard HMD capabilities offered by other systems, HMDS fully utilizes the advanced avionics architecture of the F-35 and provides the pilot video with imagery in day or night conditions. Consequently, the F-35 is the first tactical fighter jet in 50 years to fly without a HUD. A

BAE Systems helmet was considered when HMDS development was experiencing significant problems, but these issues were eventually worked out. The Helmet-Mounted Display System was fully operational and ready for delivery in July 2014.

Helmet-Mounted Display System for the F-35 Lightning II Joint Strike Fighter

JedEyes TM

JedEyes TM is a new system recently introduced by Elbit Systems especially to meet Apache and other rotary wing platform requirements. The system is designed for day, night and brownout flight environments. JedEyes TM has a 70 x 40 degree FOV and 2250x1200 pixels resolution.

Cobra

Sweden's JAS 39 Gripen fighter utilizes the Cobra HMD, developed by BAE Systems, Denel Optronics of South Africa, and Saab. It has been exported to the South African Air Force.

Future Technology

- VSI is developing the QuadEyeTM Night Vision Cueing & Display (NVCD) for the U.S. Navy and U.S. Air Force, and is also producing the DASH Generation IV HMD.

- Eye tracking – Eye trackers measure the point of gaze relative to the direction of the head, allowing a computer to sense where the user is looking. These systems are not currently used in aircraft.

- Direct retinal projection – Systems that project information directly onto the wearer's retina with a low-powered laser (virtual retinal display) are also in experimentation.

Optical Head-Mounted Display

An optical head-mounted display (OHMD) is a wearable device that has the capability of reflecting projected images as well as allowing the user to see through it that is augmented reality.

A man controls Google Glass using the touchpad built into the side of the device

an optical head-mounted display concept

Types

Various techniques have existed for see-through HMDs. Most of these techniques can be summarized into two main families: "Curved Mirror" (or Curved Combiner) based and "Waveguide" or "Light-guide" based. The curved mirror technique has been used by Vuzix in their Star 1200 product, by Olympus, and by Laster Technologies. Various waveguide techniques have existed for some time. These techniques include diffraction optics, holographic optics, polarized optics, and reflective optics:

- Diffractive waveguide – slanted diffraction grating elements (nanometric 10E-9). Nokia technique now licensed to Vuzix.

- Holographic waveguide – 3 holographic optical elements (HOE) sandwiched together (RGB). Used by Sony and Konica Minolta.

- Polarized waveguide – 6 multilayer coated (25–35) polarized reflectors in glass sandwich. Developed by Lumus.

- Reflective waveguide – thick light guide with single semi reflective mirror. This technique is used by Epson in their Moverio product.

- "Clear-Vu" reflective waveguide – thin monolithic molded plastic w/ surface reflectors and conventional coatings developed by Optinvent and used in their ORA product.

- Switchable waveguide – developed by SBG Labs.

Input Devices

Head-mounted displays are not designed to be workstations, and traditional input devices such as keyboards do not support the concept of smart glasses. Input devices that lend themselves to mobility and/or hands-free use are good candidates, for example:

- Touchpad or buttons

- Compatible devices (e.g. smartphones or control unit)

- Speech recognition

- Gesture recognition

- Eye tracking

- Brain–computer interface

Notable Manufacturers

MicroOptical and MyVu

MicroOptical MV-1 was released in 2002

In June 1995, MicroOptical was founded by Dr. Mark Spitzer to develop advanced micro-optical devices reduced to the size of integrated circuits. The company was funded by the Defense Advanced Research Projects Agency through a contract with the U.S.

Army Soldier Systems Command for the development of optical micro-electrome-chanical systems (MEMS). In 1997, MicroOptical demonstrated the eyewear display in which the viewing optics were incorporated in the eyeglass lens. The eyeglasses display provided a 320x240 pixel resolution with 8 bit greyscale and a field of view of approximately 8 degrees (horizontal).

On 16 June 2003, MicroOptical announced the availability of the SV-6 PC Viewer, the first eyewear-mounted display specifically designed for use with mobile personal computers. It was small, ultra-lightweight and highly ergonomic and could connect to mobile computing devices via a VGA output. Its initial price tag was US$1995. In March 2007, MicroOptical changed its name to MyVu and at CES 2008 it demonstrated the Crystal 701, video eyewear which lets the user watch a large virtual screen from 6 feet away and It featured MyVu's patented SolidOptex® optical system, a VGA (640x480) resolution, a cables that allow the user to connect it to MP4 players, DVD players, camcorders, or gaming systems with composite video output and a battery that provides up to 4 hours of video viewing. In May 2008, the Crystal was launched at Amazon and Best Buy with the price tag of $300.

However, the company did not survive the 2008 recession, and in 2010 it was dissolved. Its assets, including patents, were sold to Foxconn which then formed subsidiary View Link Technology in Singapore, with the mission to establish a new line of wearable near-eye systems for industrial, medical, and consumer use. In August 2012, Mark Spitzer, formerly a principal scientist at Kopin Corporation and the founder and CEO of MicroOptical/MyVu, was hired by Google as a Director of Operations at Google X. In April 2013, Google acquired several of MicroOptical/MyVu patents from Foxconn, who is in contract with Google to manufacture the Google Glass in Santa Clara, California.

Sony

In 1997, Sony released the Glasstron, an HMD which included two LCD screens and two earphones for video and audio respectively. It also had a mechanical shutter to allow the display to become see-through.

At SID 2008, Sony unveiled a holographic-based see-through eyewear display that shows full-color video images at a transmissivity of 85% and a luminance of 2500 cd/m2. On 14 November 2012 Sony filed a patent for a binocular eyewear display which features a camera, battery packs, a 2D interface and customizable screens by allowing the user to move the lens several millimeters. This recent filing is a continuation on patents filed in 2008 and 2009.

IBM and Olympus

In September 1998, IBM Japan demonstrated a wearable PC. Its components included a lightweight monocular head-mounted display with a monochrome resolution, a headphones for sound and video, a controller / microphone for control and a control unit. It ran Windows 98 and featured a 233 MHz Pentium MMX, 64 MB of RAM, a 340 MB IBM MicroDrive and USB interface. It could be controlled by voice commands or through a hand-held tracker ball. It was intended to be marketed for maintenance, repair and system installation staff by allowing the user to call up information from reference manuals and reference books on the eye level display, keeping their hands free.

In December 1999, IBM Japan and Olympus Optical demonstrated the PC Eye-Trek, a wearable PC that comprises the IBM-developed small PC unit and a monocular, eyewear display developed by Olympus (in replacement of IBM's monochrome eyewear display). Olympus's eyewear display used a free-shaped prism and a high performance optical filter to allow it to be lightweight and an optical see-through. It featured a 0.47-inch reflective-field sequential LCD display with 800 x 600 full-color resolution supplied by Colorado Micro Display and gave the impression of looking at 10-inch screen from a distance of 20 inches. By using reflective-type LCD, the power consumption was kept to a minimal 1.6 watts. Independently. Olympus showed a prototype finger-set input device. In demonstration, the index finger movement was assigned as slow cursor movement, an index and middle finger together were assigned as quick cursor movement. When a finger bends quickly, the movement is interpreted as a "click". Combined with the PC Eye-Trek, a user can select an icon by just moving and tapping a finger in the air. In 2000, IBM launched the "Park Bench" TV commercial, which featured its vision for voice-activated wearable PCs.

At CEATEC 2010, NTT DoCoMo demonstrated the AR Walker, an augmented reality glasses which were developed by Olympus in 2008.

On 5 July 2012 Olympus announced the MEG4.0, a Monocular eyewear display that contains a QVGA (320 x 240) resolution display and can connect to devices through Bluetooth 2.1. No announcements regarding the launch date or the price were made.

Mirage Innovations and Nokia

In 1998, the Israeli company Mirage Innovations was founded by Yair David and Yariv Ben-Yehuda. In 2001, the company R&D team transferred multicolor still images by diffractive planar optics and developed monocular displays. In February 2001 the company started negotiating with Nokia to develop the technology for use in Nokia's mobile phones and other mobile devices, but in September 2003 Nokia broke off the discussions. In September 2007, Mirage discovered that Nokia had filed three patent applications with the U.S. Patent and Trademark Office for technology that Mirage developed by itself or helped Nokia develop. The company tried to settle the matter but Nokia responded by accusing the company of infringement. Following Nokia's threat, Mirage was unable to secure key financing and was shut down in early 2008.

At Nokia World 2009, Nokia Research Center demonstrated an optical see-through eyewear display. It included eye-tracking capabilities, thus allowing the user to navigate and control the glasses just but focusing on the images or looking up or down. On 21 October 2011, Vuzix announced that it has entered into a technology license agreement with Nokia to develop and produce see-through waveguide optics for use in eyewear displays based on Nokia's proprietary see-through (Exit Pupil Expanding) EPE optics technology. At CES 2012, Vuzix demonstrated the SMART Glasses, a see-through eyewear display technology based on integrated HD display engines and waveguide optics that were licensed from Nokia. Vuzix also announced plans for a line of both monocular and binocular SMART Glasses with integrated head tracking and options for multiple camera technologies for the commercial, industrial and consumer market.

DigiLens and SBG Labs

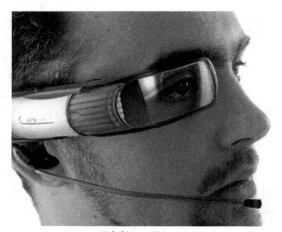

DigiLens DL40

In June 1997, DigiLens was founded by Jonathan D. Waldern with the mission to develop and market Switchable Bragg Grating nano-composite materials for the optical telecommunication and wireless microdisplay markets. On 11 January 2000, the company demonstrated the DL40, a compact, lightweight monocular eyewear display with a see-through and RGB color capabilities based on holographic polymer-dispersed liquid crystals technology. Later DigiLens changed its business model to focus its R&D on fibernet switching chips rather than HMDs. In October 2003, DigiLens was acquired by SBG Labs. Nowadays SBG Labs produces head-up displays based on their switchable waveguide technology for the United States Army and the People's Liberation Army. It also develops the VIRTUALITY HMEyetrack, a binocular see-through eyewear display.

Lumus

In 2000, the Israeli company Lumus was founded by Dr. Yaakov Amitai to develop and market its Light-guide Optical Element (LOE) technology for eyewear displays (see-through wearable displays). The LOE is a patented optical waveguide that makes use of multiple partial reflectors embedded in a single substrate to reflect a virtual image into the eye of the wearer. Specifically, the image is coupled into the LOE by a "Pod" (micro-display projector) that sits at the edge of the waveguide—in an eyeglass configuration, this is embedded in the temple of the glasses. The image travels through total internal reflection to the multiple array of partial reflectors and are reflected to the eye. While each partial reflector shows only a portion of the image,the optics are such that the wearer sees the combined array and perceives it as a single uniform image projected at infinity. The transparent display enables a virtual image to be seamlessly overlaid over the wearer's real world view. This is especially true when the source image comprises a black background with light color wording or symbology being displayed. Black is essentially see-through color, while lighter colored objects, symbols or characters appear to float in the wearer's line of sight. Conversely, full screen images like documents, internet pages, movies which are typically brighter colors can be displayed to look like a large virtual image floating a few meter's away from the wearer.

Lumus DK-40 Development Kit

After years of R&D and building its patent portfolio, the company started officially selling product in 2008 with the PD-18: a top-down, transparent monocular display with SVGA resolution 32 degree FoV, and full color. The PD-18 and its derivative, the PD-14, were aimed at professional and military markets. In 2010 Lumus' technology received high level validation when the US Air Force selected Gentex's Scorpion Helmet Mounted Cueing System (which employs the Lumus PD-14), with Raytheon as the primary contractor, for the HMIT program for A-10 and F-16 Aircraft. This display and contract win marked the first time a full color HMD was selected for combat aviation. Subsequently, Lumus' display as part of Thales Visionix's (formerly Gentex)Helmet Mounted Cueing System has been selected for the CHMDS / Air Soldier program. Once the roll out has been completed on this program, Lumus displays will represent the majority of HMDs deployed in the worldwide combat aviation market.

Lumus also has been working behind the scenes for years with a handful of Tier 1 consumer electronics manufacturers and tech companies. The company aims to be the Intel or the Qualcomm of the wearable display market—selling its optical engine modules as OEM components, while the Tier 1 companies will make the final products. Lumus is very quiet on its activities in this space citing confidentiality limitations, and barring rare trade show appearances (CES 2014,2012,2008, 2007, and a couple SID shows) the company exerts minimal marketing effort. Furthermore, Lumus' sparse website only shows a portion of its offerings to the consumer market. Other products or optical engine modules it makes for OEM customers will remain veiled until such customers launch their Lumus-based products.

MicroVision

In 2002, Microvision launched the Nomad Personal Display System, a head-worn, monochrome red, see-through virtual retinal display and in March 2004 it introduced the Nomad Expert Technician System, which was about 40% smaller, lighter, and costs less to manufacture than the prior version. However, following the poor ergonomics and eye strain of its products, the company decided to discount the product line in 2006.

The company continued to research and develop wearable displays and sought to develop a lightweight, see-through eyewear display, using its PicoP display engine and special optics that would embedded into fashionable glasses.

Penny

In February 2005, the Swedish company Penny was founded by Erik Lundström based on his own research at KTH and University of Stockholm where a first prototype was presented year 2000. The technology is patented by Erik Lundström with Penny as the owner.

Development of C Wear Interactive Glasses began in Jan 2006, the first proof of concept prototype of the C Wear Interactive Glasses BM10 was released for beta testing in January 2009 and sold as a 0-series to the market 4 months later. It was developed to significantly improve the use of information in a mobile environment for users with the need of Augmented Reality (AR) data without the ability to use hands or users having their hands occupied.

On 4 April 2009, the company announced that it signed a contract with BAE Systems Hagglunds in which the companies will jointly work on the integration of the Interactive Glasses BM10 in the BAE Systems Hägglunds products. BAE Systems Hägglunds tested the glasses in its tanks.

In September 2010, the development of the next version BM20 was initiated and the first 0 series was planned to be released in December 2012. In October 2011, the company introduced the C Wear Interactive Glasses BM20 during the Innovative Sweden event at Stanford University in Silicon Valley. The first complete series manufactured of the C Wear Interactive Glasses are to be released during 2014.

The C Wear Interactive Glasses BM20 comprises a see-through retina projection unit with an 873 x 500 full-color resolution OLED display with diagonal field of view of 47 degrees giving the impression of a ~70-inch display at 2 meters. The transparency enables the image to be shown in the user direct line of sight. Navigation in the user interface is performed by a head tracking device based on 3D MEMS gyros and click commands by a soft sensor applied toward the user's own jawbone muscle. By pressing the jaw together the user "clicks".

In September 2013, Fraunhofer Institute announced that Penny and C Wear Interactive Glasses has been chosen as one of the partners in the LIAA project with aims creating and implementing a framework that enables humans and robots to truly work together in assembly tasks.

Brother Industries

At Expo 2005, Brother Industries demonstrated a stationary-type of its Imaging Display, a projection technology that focuses light, of an intensity harmless to the eyes, onto the retina and then moves the light at high speed to create afterimages that give the user the impression of viewing a 16 square inch screen from a distance of 1 meter. The company developed the system by applying optical system technologies based on their laser printing technology, and piezoelectric technologies based on their ink-jet printing technology. It was developed in order to enable users to read documents such as operation manuals at the narrow spaces, or to be hands-free when they want to use both hands.

In 2008, Brother succeeded in developing a spectacle-type wearable RID prototype that's able to show SVGA resolution (800×600) with a 60 Hz frame rate and weights only 350 g. On 21 July 2010, it announced the AiRScouter and exhibited the device at "Brother World JAPAN 2010" in Tokyo on 15 September. On 24 August 2011, it announced the commercialization of the AiRScouter.

On 17 October 2011, NEC announced in Japan the Tele Scouter, a device that is based on the AirScouter.

Konica Minolta

At CEATEC 2006, Konica Minolta displayed a prototype of lightweight, holographic-based see-through eyewear display which uses a prism with thickness of 3.5 mm and a holographic element to reduce the weight of the display to 27 grams. Possible applications under consideration included giving workers access to an instruction manual or allowing commuters to watch a video while riding a train.

Optinvent

In February 2007, the French company Optinvent was founded by Kayvan Mirza and Khaled Sarayeddine, with the mission to design and market optical projection systems that use microdisplays or electronic display slides, based on the Projection Optics work developed within the Thomson Group. The company sought to develop and market see-through eyewear displays, pico projectors, head-up displays, professional camera viewfinders, flight simulators and rear and front projection TVs, based on its unique optical technologies (Clear-Vu optics, Nano-Beam module and Slim-Chin Optical Engine). In September 2009, the company revealed that it is developing a small, lightweight optical see-through eyewear display based on its Clear-Vu technology at the cost of less than $200 per unit. The eyewear display was scheduled for release by the end of 2010 by Japanese maker.

At Augmented World Expo 2013, Optinvent demonstrated a prototype of their ORA see-through mobile AR display platform. The demonstrator included a monocular see-through display with the patented "Flip-Vu" feature allowing two positions for the virtual image. The display can be positioned directly in the wearer's field of vision or below it. One position is the "AR mode" whereby the image is directly superimposed on the wearers central field of vision; then by flipping the display down (mechanically), the wearer can have a "dashboard mode" whereby the virtual display is below the wearer's field of vision. This gives the possibility of having both true AR and a "glance at" capability in one device. A developer's version of the device running Android 4.1 Jelly Bean called the ORA-S including an SDK was said to be released soon and will include bluetooth and Wi-Fi connectivity, a nine axis orientation sensor, a camera, a microphone, loudspeaker, and battery in the form of photochromic sunglasses.

Optical Research Associates

At the SPIE Optics + Photonics 2010 conference, the Engineering Services team at Optical Research Associates (ORA) demonstrated an optical see-through eyewear display with a 20-degree full diagonal field of view, 432 x 240 panel resolution and a distortion correction via an electronic warper. The company was said to be seeking partners to commercialize the device. On 7 October 2010, Synopsys announced that it acquires Optical Research Associates.

Augmented Vision

In November 2007, the University of Arizona's 3DVIS Lab (3D Visualization and Imaging System Lab), led by director Dr. Hong Hua, developed a polarized head-mounted projection display where the polarization states of the light are deliberately manipulated to maximize the luminous transfer efficiency. It comprises a pair of high-resolution ferroelectric liquid-crystal-on-silicon (FLCOS) microdisplays that help to further improve theoverall light efficiency and image quality and have much higher optical efficiency than a transmissive-type LCD.

On 19 April 2010, Augmented Vision Inc was founded by Drs. Chunyu Gao and Hong Hua to develop optical see-through eyewear displays based on the freeform optical waveguide technology which is a thin, see-through optical assembly that enables the design of a lightweight eyewear displays that look like conventional glasses and offer a high-quality video display along with unobtrusive see-through vision to the real world.

In September 2011, the company was awarded an Army Phase I SBIR to develop an oc-clusion-capable optical see-through eyewear display and in April 2012 it was invited for an Army Phase II SBIR proposal submission. In May 2012, the company successfully designed the eyewear display and in June it passed the DCAA auditing for government contracting.

Vuzix

At CES 2011, Vuzix unveild the Raptyr, a see through AR glasses prototype which use holographic optics to let the user see a virtual 70-inch screen from a distance of 10-feet. The Raptyr, which have won CES Innovation Award, feature a 6-megapixel camera, a microphone, headphones and a motion tracking system. It could be plugged into a PC, smart phone, or gaming system. Additionally, the lenses can electronically darken to compensate for brighter or darker environments.

On 18 May 2011, Vuzix announced the STAR 1200 a see-through AR-enabled binocular glasses which is aimed for wide variety of industrial, commercial, defense and some consumer applications. It features a native 16:9 format that offers full color WVGA (852 x 480) which provide a video viewing experience similar to a 60-inch flat panel television viewed from 10-feet along with a 6 degrees of freedom (DOF) motion track-ing sensors and a built in camera for tracking and recognizing the real world. It was released in August 2011 for $4999.

On 13 November 2012, Vuzix announced the Smart Glasses M100. This device features a 16:9 WQVGA (428x240-pixel) resolution projector that projects a 4-inch display as if it were 14 inches away from the user's face. It has an OMAP4430 at 1 GHz processor, 1 GB of RAM, 4 GB of internal storage and runs on Android 4.0 Ice Cream Sandwich, although it can also be hosted on iOS software or other compatible devices. Its camera can shoot 720p HD video and there is a gyroscope, accelerometer and integrated com-pass for accurate head-tracking features. On the audio side, the M100 has an earpiece and a noise-canceling microphone. Also included are Bluetooth, Wi-Fi 802.11b/g/n and a microSD card slot. The Vuzix M100 is expected to cost under $500 and is sched-uled for commercial release by late 2013. The m100 was officially released in December 2012 for $1000: double the original announced price.

On January 3 2015 Intel invested $25M into Vuzix in exchange taking a 30% share in the company. This investment by Intel coupled with the technology and processing horsepower they can bring will surely lead to dramatic reduction in product size and increase in processing horsepower.

Atheer Labs

At D11 Conference 2013, the startup company Atheer Labs unveild its 3D augmented reality glasses prototype. The prototype included binocular lens, 3D images support, a rechargeable battery, WiFi, Bluetooth 4.0, accelerometer, gyro and an IR. User could interact with the device by voice commands and the mounted camera allowed the users to interact naturally with the device with gestures.

On 19 December 2013, Atheer Labs started an Indiegogo campaign to raise funds for their augmented reality systems. They raised $214,407 of their $100,000 goal. They offered two flavors of their system: the Atheer Developer Kit and the Atheer One. Both systems were augmented reality transparent eyewear display systems that contained cameras for tracking as well as a depth sensor primarily for tracking of hand gestures. The stand-alone Atheer Developer Kit was priced at $850 while the Atheer One which is intended to be connected to an Android phone or tablet was priced at $500. A SDK was made available to work with the Android OS.

On 27 June 2014 Atheer cancelled all orders for their Developer Kit and the Atheer One.

On 5 of December 2014, Atheer begins marketing mobile smart glasses for enterprise and industrial applications including oil, medical, construction and other field services. Atheer is shipping the AiR (Augmented interactive Reality) Smart Glasses platform developer kit, the AiR DK2, to select customers. AiR Smart Glasses are mobile 3D augmented reality see through smart glasses with patented, touch-free gesture control that is designed to improve productivity for those who work in the field and/or with their hands.

The Atheer AiR platform consists of the Atheer AiR Smart Glasses and the Atheer AiR OS based on Android 4.2. Featuring the Qualcomm Snapdragon CPU, the platform includes binocular lens, 3D imaging support, a rechargeable battery, WiFi, Bluetooth 4.0, an accelerometer, gyro, magnetometer, an ambient light sensor and IR. External Ports include USB, HDMI Out, DC Power In, an Earphone/Microphone stereo jack and includes internal storage as well as MicroSD support.

Epson

By the end of 2009, Epson began the development of an eyewear display that would deliver a big-screen experience to people on the go. Thus, it was intended to be small, lightweight and comfortable to be convenient for travelers and optical see-through so that viewers could see their surroundings while watching multimedia content. On 9 November 2011, it announced in Japan the Moverio BT-100, a 3D-enabled optical see-through eyewear display which features 0.52-inch displays with 960×540 resolution that give the impression of viewing a 3D virtual 80-inch display from a distance 5 m. It is powered by Android 2.2 and packs Wi-Fi IEEE 802.11b/g/n (direct access to YouTube and a web browser) and microUSB. The Moverio was shipped to Japanese stores on 25 November and was expected to initially sell 10,000 units. In March 2012 Epson launched the Moverio in the United States.

On 6 January 2014, Epson announced the development of the Moverio BT-200 Mobile Viewer. In addition to being 60% lighter, and having prescription inserts, it also introduces motion tracking, a camera, and more powerful (1.2 GHz) CPU. In addition to content consumption, the new Moverio is being promoted for use with full augmented reality.

Meta

In December 2012, Meta was founded by Meron Gribetz, based on the work of a Columbia University team that began in 2011. On 17 May 2013, the company launched a Kickstarter campaign to raise funds to manufacture the Meta 1, an augmented reality wearable display that is based on Epson's Moverio BT-100. Meta's outward-facing camera captures gestures allowing users to interact with virtual games, architectural renderings and other 3D objects by using their hands. To get one of the first-generation devices required a pledge of $650 or more to the Kickstarter campaign. The Kickstarter campaign was successful in raising $194,444, topping its pledged goal of $100,000.

The highly anticipated Meta 1 shipped out around the world in January 2015 after many updates, tweaks and refinements. Meta's system leverages Unity, as the 3D environment, and has put their SDK in the hands of talented hackers and developers at prestigious hackathons in order to see the system in action.

Meta has also announced the Meta Pro, with 40 degree field of view, attached Intel i5 computer, and many other enhancements, with a price of $3,650. The delivery date for the Meta Pro has not yet been announced, but details can be requested at the Meta website.

The Meta website lists Prof. Steve Mann, the father of wearable computing as its Chief Scientist, alongside Columbia University's Prof. Steven Feiner as its lead advisor and co-founders CTO Raymond Lo and COO Ben Sand.

GlassUp

In 2012, the Italian company GlassUp was founded by Francesco Giartosio and Gianluigi Tregnaghi to develop and market its augmented reality eyewear display. Initially, the project started in June 2011, when Francesco and his team saw an augmented reality glasses concept video. Following it, the team researched the eyewear display market and in September 2011 it sought and hired Gianluigi Tregnaghi, the biggest field expert in Italy, who developed optical systems for airplane pilots' helmets. In the summer of 2012, the team thought it found the solution that would hit the mark, and patented it.

At CeBIT 2013, the company showcased its project to turn a pair of glasses into a head-mounted secondary display for the smartphone. The prototype device featured a projector that beams images onto the glass panel baked into the right-side lens as well as a yellow-and-black, 320 x 240 resolution display. The company planned to release two versions, one with Bluetooth 4.0 and one with Bluetooth 3.1 to ensure a wide range of compatibility with Android and iOS devices, and aimed to have finished versions ready for the Augmented World Expo in June 2013.

At the same time, the company planned to start Kickstarter campaign to generate the funds necessary for a pre-sale, priced at $399 / €299. It spent two months setting up a company in the US, opening a bank account, an Amazon account, getting a tax number and seeking a local resident. At the end, it came out that Kickstarter does not accept the eyeglasses category anymore. On 9 June 2013 GlassUp started an Indiegogo campaign to raise funds and as of 18 August the campaign has raised $105,641 of its pledged goal of $150,000.

Laster Technologies

In January 2005, the French company Laster Technologies was founded by a group of experts in optics and image processing at CNRS (Centre Nacional de la Recherche Scientifique). The company's patented EnhancedView technology uses a unique optoelectronic device based on a semi-reflective diopter with a mathematically calculated curve enabling the reflection of a virtual collimated image directly into the wearer's field of view. The use of EnhancedView technology, coupled with an OLED micro-screen provides a 40 ° x 30 ° (H x V) field of vision with a resolution of 800 x 600 pixels or more. This is equivalent to viewing a floating screen of 90 cm diagonal at a distance of one meter. It is the result of an intensive collaborative development work with the Institut d'Optique and the University of Paris-Sud over several years.

In September 2006, the company won a research grant for the development of a prototype demonstrator for augmented reality in French Museums. It worked on this project with four partners: INRIA, Cité des Sciences et de l'Industrie, the Pierre-and-Marie-Curie University and Naska films. In July 2009, the company presented the augmented reality experience "Observe the Earth in 3D" at the inauguration of the permanent exhibition Explora, "Objective : Earth" at the Cité des Sciences et de l'Industrie. A projected video of Earth globe was placed at the center of a semi-circular table. Visitors are placed around the table and wear Laster glasses which allows them to see the Earth globe and overlay of virtual satellites around the Earth.

Innovega

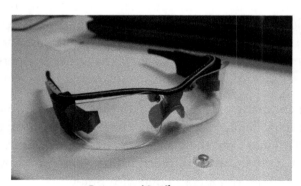

Innovega iOptik system

In June 2008, Innovega was co-founded by the former MicroVision employees: Randall Sprague, Steve Willey and Jerome Legerton. The company developed the iOptik eyewear display. It comprises a pair of contact lens which refocus polarized light to the pupil and allows the wearer to focus on an image that is as near as 1.25 cm to the eye, thus enabling displays to be built into normal-looking glasses without the bulky optics. In April 2012, the company signed a contract to deliver a fully functioning prototype to the Pentagon's research laboratory, DARPA. At CES 2013, the company demonstrated a prototype of its eyewear display that features a field of view of 60 degrees or more. It also claimed that a field of view of nearly 120 degrees is already in the works. The first version of Innovega's glasses are designed for military use, but it's planning a consumer version by 2014 or 2015.

Fraunhofer COMEDD

At SID 2012, the German institute Fraunhofer COMEDD presented for the first time an evaluation kit of its OLED-based eyewear display which enables the user to test the technology and develop applications The institute successfully developed OLED-on-silicon microchips, which are display and camera at the same time, and can be integrated into eyeglasses with an appropriate optical construction. At the moment the eyewear display can be offered with a bright red shining OLED display, but the scientists of Fraunhofer COMEDD are currently working on the possibility to provide the information in full-color so that people can experience whole film sequences. Fraunhofer COMEDD is working in partnership with Fraunhofer IOSB who is developing the eye-tracking capabilities for the eyewear and Trivisio who is responsible for the eyewear design.

The Technology Partnership (TTP)

On 10 September 2012, TTP announced that it developed an eyewear that looks like conventional glasses and use transparent, curved lenses that do not obstruct the wearer's field of view. The technology works by using an embedded low-power, miniature projector optics to project a light at an angle of approximately 45° towards the lens that contains an embedded grating structure to redirect the light into the eye, as well as performing a number of other optical functions such as astigmatic compensation. It also invented a very high speed switchable fast focus lens technology that can be used to create a true 3D experience. The September 2012 prototype can only show a monochrome, 640 x 480 image, not a moving video, but the hardware to do that is expected to be ready in the next model. An electrodes mounted at the temple of the eyewear can measure an electronic signals in the muscles to figure out which way the eyes are looking and that is translated into UI. The company is not planning to manufacture its display or eye-tracking technology, but instead hopes to license it to third parties. It is currently in negotiation with a California-based company.

Telepathy

In January 2013, the Japanese company Telepathy was founded by the augmented reality entrepreneur Takahito Iguchi. At SXSW 2013 the company unveiled the Telepathy One, an eyewear display that consists of a small micro projector to create a virtual 5-inch screen that appears to float in front of the wearer's eye and a built-in micro camera. It uses an OS built off Linux and can connect to other devices via Bluetooth. It allows users to receive e-mails, check updates on social networks, and even share whatever scene the user is looking at with his friends. A Consumer version is expected to hit the US before the 2013 Christmas season.

Oculon Optoelectronics

Founded in March 2004, the Taiwanese company Oculon Optoelectronics is a well-experienced optoelectronics company that has been engaged in the design and the development of head mounted display (HMD) and a series of light-weighted portable display products. At Computex Taipei 2013 the company demonstrated a prototype of its Oculon Smart Glasses, an eyewear display which is expected to compete the Google Glass with better screen, longer battery life and less than half the price. The prototype carries a 640 x 480-pixel resolution, but the final version will have a 720p display. Images appear translucent, making them easy to see through. It will be offered in two versions – monocular and binocular – while the Google Glass only offers a monocular version. Among Oculon's features will be speech recognition, gesture control and the ability to connect to a Bluetooth control pad for navigation. The company expects to go into mass production of the Oculon by late 2013 and is hoping to hit an MSRP of $500. As an OEM, Oculon will not release the Smart Glasses on its own, but instead will sell it to a variety of vendors who will take the device to market under their own brands. Consumer versions are expected to be released by late 2013.

Fujitsu

At MWC 2013, Fujitsu showcased the Laser Head Set (LHS), a headset display that uses a laser to project a high-resolution video onto a clear mirror in front of your eye which bounces it back into the retina. It provides a field of view of 40 degrees and produces a translucent image, letting the user to look through the projected image to see his surrounding. It was developed in collaboration with the University of Tokyo and QD Laser Inc. By Mobile World Congress 2014, Fujitsu plans to debut the Laser Eye Wear (LEW), based on the same technology that is condensed into a pair of normal-looking glasses.

Baidu

On 1 April 2013, an article at Sina Tech reported that the Chinese search giant Baidu is allegedly testing Baidu Eye, a monocular eyewear display which features a miniature LCD display, camera for taking pictures, bone conduction technology, and some sort of facial recognition search. It has been in development for several years by a team under the direction of Baidu's chief product designer Sun Yun-feng. The company intends to develop a wearable device industry standards and to license it to manufacturers. Based on its cloud ecosystem, it plans to launch an application store so developers can create apps for the device. It also cooperation with Qualcomm, to use its latest power control chip to reduce the power consumption and by that to extend the battery life time to 12 hours or more. This device is fully functional by voice commands. It was at first thought to be an April Fools' Day joke, but on 3 April its existence was confirmed to Mashable by Baidu's director of international communications, Kaiser Kuo. A working prototype has been built.

Microsoft

In May 2011, Microsoft filed patents for an optically see-through eyewear display with augmented reality capabilities. The patent describes how it could augment the wearer's view by using the device. For instance, it could be used at a baseball game to show up statistics and details of characters in a play or at a opera house to show the lyrics next to the opera singer as an alternative to displays placed at the side of the stage. It also states that the eyewear display could be operated by a wrist-worn computer, voice-commands or by flicking the eyes to a certain spot. In 2012, a two years old 56-page roadmap document by Microsoft appeared on Scribd. It revealed that Microsoft's Innovation Center in Foraleza, Brazil is developing the code-named Fortaleza, an eyewear display that appears to be Wi-Fi and 4G-enabled and incorporates augmented reality. It also revealed plans to make the it capable of syncing with Microsoft's Xbox One and the Kinect. No concrete release date was given, but the document suggests sometime in 2014 at earliest. The document was removed at the request of Covington & Burling LLP, an international law firm that represents Microsoft. The file has since found a home on multiple hosting services and websites, but soon afterwards Microsoft sent takedown notice to sites that were hosting the document, including Dropbox. Ihned.cz, a technology site based in the Czech Republic, received a notice from Alan Radford, Internet Investigator on behalf of Microsoft for hosting the document. In 2014, Microsoft revealed the device, naming it HoloLens. In 2015,6 October event Microsoft demonstrated the demo of HoloLens and made its developer edition available at $3000.

LAFORGE Optical

In March 2013, the boston-startup LAFORGE Optical was founded by five former and current students of the Rochester Institute of Technology, with the intention to design and market an eyewear with an embedded heads-up display system. In December 2013, the company launched pre-order sales of its Icis eyewear on the company's official website for $220. The Icis will ship in mid-2016.

Toshiba

At Ceatec trade show, Toshiba unveild the Toshiba Glass, a prototype of pair of glasses with a tiny, lightweight projector which displays an image. Toshiba Glass was jointly created by Yamamoto Kogaku Co. which makes glasses under the Swans brand.

Ashkelon Eyewear Technologies

In November 2013, Ashkelon Eyewear Technologies Ltd was founded by the Israeli celebrity inventor Benny Goldstein, with the intention to develop and bring to market a very low cost wearable heads up display. Their first product, the Ashkelon Visor, is launching for around $20 and should arrive at consumers hands somewhere in the middle of 2015.

Other Manufacturers

Other manufacturers include:

- Recon Instruments
- Rockwell Collins
- BAE Systems
- Silicon Micro Display
- Shimadzu
- TDK
- SA Photonics
- ODALab
- Virtual Vision Inc / eMagin
- nVision Industries
- NVIS
- Liteye Systems
- Trivisio
- i-O Display Systems
- Cinoptics

Recent Developments

2012

- On 17 April 2012, Oakley's CEO Colin Baden stated that the company has been working on a way to project information directly onto lenses since 1997, and has 600 patents related to the technology, many of which apply to optical specifications.

- On 18 June 2012, Canon announced the MR (Mixed Reality) System which simultaneously merges virtual objects with the real world at full scale and in 3D. Unlike the Google Glass, the MR System is aimed for professional use with a price tag for the headset and accompanying system is $125,000, with $25,000 in expected annual maintenance.

2013

- At MWC 2013, the Japanese company Brilliant Service introduced the Viking OS, an operating system for HMD's which was written in Objective-C and relies on gesture control as a primary form of input. It includes a facial recognition system and was demonstrated on a revamp version of Vuzix STAR 1200XL glasses ($4,999) which combined a generic RGB camera and a PMD CamBoard nano depth camera.

- At Maker Faire 2013, the startup company Technical Illusions unveiled castAR augmented reality glasses which are well equipped for an AR experience: infrared LEDs on the surface detect the motion of an interactive infrared wand, and a set of coils at its base are used to detect RFID chip loaded objects placed on top of it; it uses dual projectors at a framerate of 120 Hz and a retroreflective screen providing a 3D image that can be seen from all directions by the user; a camera sitting on top of the prototype glasses is incorporated for position detection, thus the virtual image changes accordingly as a user walks around the CastAR surface.

Market structure

Analytics company IHS has estimated that the shipments of smart glasses may rise from just 50,000 units in 2012 to as high as 6.6 million units in 2016. According to a survey of more than 4,600 U.S. adults conducted by Forrester Research, around 12 percent of respondents are willing to wear Google Glass or other similar device if it offers a service that piques their interest. Business Insider's BI Intelligence expects an annual sales of 21 million Google Glass units by 2018.

According to reliable reports, Samsung and Microsoft are expected to develop their own version of Google Glass within six months with a price range of $200 to $500. Samsung has reportedly bought lenses from Lumus, a company based in Israel. Another source says Microsoft is negotiating with Vuzix.

In 2006, Apple filed patent for its own HMD device.

In July 2013, APX Labs founder and CEO Brian Ballard stated that he knows of 25-30 hardware companies who are working on their own versions of smart glasses, some of which APX is working with.

Comparison of Various OHMDs Technologies

Combiner technology	Size	Eye box	FOV	Other	Example
Flat combiner 45 degrees	Thick	Medium	Medium	Traditional design	Vuzix, Google Glass
Curved combiner	Thick	Large	Large	Classical bug-eye design	Many products (see through and occlusion)
Phase conjugate material	Thick	Medium	Medium	Very bulky	OdaLab
Buried Fresnel combiner	Thin	Large	Medium	Parasitic diffraction effects	The Technology Partnership (TTP)
Cascaded prism/mirror combiner	Variable	Medium to Large	Medium	Louver effects	Lumus, Optinvent
Free form TIR combiner	Medium	Large	Medium	Bulky glass combiner	Canon, Verizon & Kopin (see through and occlusion)
Diffractive combiner with EPE	Very thin	Very large	Medium	Haze effects, parasitic effects, difficult to replicate	Nokia / Vuzix
Holographic waveguide combiner	Very thin	Medium to Large in H	Medium	Requires volume holographic materials	Sony
Holographic light guide combiner	Medium	Small in V	Medium	Requires volume holographic materials	Konica Minolta
Combo diffuser/contact lens	Thin (glasses)	Very large	Very large	Requires contact lens + glasses	Innovega & EPFL
Tapered opaque light guide	Medium	Small	Small	Image can be relocated	Olympus

Virtual Retinal Display

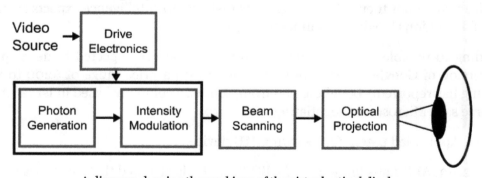

A diagram showing the workings of the virtual retinal display

A virtual retinal display (VRD), also known as a retinal scan display (RSD) or retinal projector (RP), is a display technology that draws a raster display (like a television)

directly onto the retina of the eye. The user sees what appears to be a conventional display floating in space in front of them.

History

In the past similar systems have been made by projecting a defocused image directly in front of the user's eye on a small "screen", normally in the form of large glasses. The user focused their eyes on the background, where the screen appeared to be floating. The disadvantage of these systems was the limited area covered by the "screen", the high weight of the small televisions used to project the display, and the fact that the image would appear focused only if the user was focusing at a particular "depth". Limited brightness made them useful only in indoor settings as well.

Only recently a number of developments have made a true VRD system practical. In particular the development of high-brightness LEDs have made the displays bright enough to be used during the day, and adaptive optics have allowed systems to dynamically correct for irregularities in the eye (although this is not always needed). The result is a high-resolution screenless display with excellent color gamut and brightness, far better than the best television technologies.

The VRD was invented by Kazuo Yoshinaka of Nippon Electric Co. in 1986. Later work at the University of Washington in the Human Interface Technology Lab resulted in a similar system in 1991. Most of the research into VRDs to date has been in combination with various virtual reality systems. In this role VRDs have the potential advantage of being much smaller than existing television-based systems. They share some of the same disadvantages however, requiring some sort of optics to send the image into the eye, typically similar to the sunglasses system used with previous technologies. It also can be used as part of a wearable computer system.

A Washington-based startup, MicroVision, Inc., has sought to commercialize VRD. Founded in 1993, MicroVision's early development work was financed by US government defense contracts and resulted in the prototype Head-Mounted Display, **Nomad**.

The first aftermarket automotive Head-Up Display using this direct-to-eye retinal scanning method was designed by Pioneer Corporation. In 2012, Pioneer's **AR-HUD** was launched in Japan. AR-HUD's core technology involves a laser beam scanning display developed by MicroVision, Inc.

MotionParallax3D

The MotionParallax3D displays are a class of virtual reality devices that create the illusion of volumetric objects by displaying a projection of a virtual object generated to match the viewer's position relative to the screen.

Principles

MotionParallax3D displays contain one or more flat or curved screens. These screens have different sizes, shapes, and mutual disposition depending on the form factor of the device. The projections of virtual objects are formed so that the virtual image the user sees looks exactly the same as the image that would be seen if the virtual object actually existed. In order to display the correct projections of virtual objects, the virtual reality system requires the current coordinates of the observer's eyes.

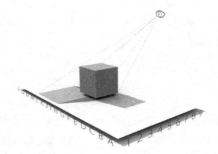

The general principal of making a projection with MotionParallax3D displays

The image of the object the user sees

The projection of a virtual object displayed on the screen

In contrast with stereo displays involving only binocular vision, the MotionParallax3D displays utilize one of the most important principles of human spatial perception—motion parallax. Motion parallax is a displacement of the parts of the image relative to each other with the angular velocity proportional to the distance difference between the parts of the image and a viewer when the relative position of the viewer and the observed object changes. The MotionParallax3D displays use this mechanism of perceiving volume by constantly changing the image displayed based on the current coordinates of the user's eyes. Due to this, the virtual objects are shifted relative to each other and relative to the visible real objects according to the laws and principles applying to the real world's objects. It allows the brain to build the a holistic view of the world containing both real and virtual objects with indistinguishable behavior. Most MotionParallax3D displays are based on stereo displays and display separate images to the left and right eyes. This gives a substantial advantage in building a complete system of virtual reality, but is not necessary for the perception of volume since the motion parallax mechanism alone is enough for the brain to perceive virtual objects as having a definite shape, volume, and a distance from the user's eyes.

Tracking Systems

To make the image projection display correctly, the system requires up-to-date and exact coordinates of the user's eyes. The MotionParallax3D displays get these coordinates from the head-tracking systems.

The tracking systems for MotionParallax3D displays can be based on different principles:

- Optical:
    - o Based on active markers (NettleBox)
    - o Based on passive markers (EON ICube)
    - o Based on face, eye, head contour etc. recognition (Amazon Fire Phone)
- Ultrasonic (RUCAP UM-5)
- Electromagnetic
- Mechanical
- Mixed, combining several tracking mechanisms e.g. using gyroscopes and accelerometers in addition to optical markers.

Quality Indicators

The quality of MotionParallax3D displays, which is mostly based on how realistically a virtual image can be displayed, is determined by a combination of three main characteristics:

- Stereoscopic separation quality (if it is done)
- Rendering quality
- Geometric accuracy of the projection.

Stereoscopic separation quality decreases due to ghosting – a phenomenon where each eye, in addition to the image intended for it, perceives the image intended for the other eye. Ghosting can be caused by different factors, e.g. luminophore afterglow in plasma screens or the incomplete matching of the polarization direction during polarization stereoscopic separation.

Rendering quality is generally not a problem for modern MotionParallax3D displays, however, the high detalization of rendering and the use of special effects allow psychological mechanisms for volume perception such as texture gradient, shading, etc. and they help increase the reality of the perception.

The *geometric accuracy of the projection* of 3D-scenes is the most important indicator of MotionParallax3D display quality. It is influenced by the accuracy of the head-tracking and the interval between the moment when the tracking starts and the moment when the image is displayed. Tracking accuracy affects the accuracy of the projection. The architecture and geometry of the tracking devices, quality of calibration, and the integrated value of inaccuracy, which is affected by noise, can all contribute to a reduction in projection correctness. The interval between when the user's head-tracking starts, and when the image is displayed, is the primary cause of geometric incorrectness of 3D-scenes projection in MotionParallax3D systems. Latency occurs because operations such as head-tracking, rendering and displaying the projection require time.

"If large amounts of latency are present in the VR system, users may still be able to perform tasks, but it will be by the much less rewarding means of using their head as a controller, rather than accepting that their head is naturally moving around in a stable virtual world." John Carmack

"When it comes to VR and AR, latency is fundamental – if you don't have low enough latency, it's impossible to deliver good experiences, by which I mean virtual objects that your eyes and brain accept as real. By "real," I don't mean that you can't tell they're virtual by looking at them, but rather that your perception of them as part of the world as you move your eyes, head, and body is indistinguishable from your perception of real objects. The key to this is that virtual objects have to stay in very nearly the same perceived real-world locations as you move; that is, they have to register as being in almost exactly the right position all the time. Being right 99 percent of the time is no good, because the occasional mis-registration is precisely the sort of thing your visual system is designed to detect, and will stick out like a sore thumb.

Assuming accurate, consistent tracking (and that's a big if, as I'll explain one of these days), the enemy of virtual registration is latency. If too much time elapses between the time your head starts to turn and the time the image is redrawn to account for the new pose, the virtual image will drift far enough so that it has clearly wobbled (in VR), or so that is obviously no longer aligned with the same real-world features (in AR)." Michael Abrash

Modern MotionParallax3D displays use head-tracking forecast technology that compensates for the delay partially, but the accuracy and the forecast horizon are highly dependent on the quality of the initial data (accuracy) and also the quantity of the data-sets with the user's position coordinates that the system receives per time unit.

The peculiarity of visual perception is that the brain interprets the latency of virtual object images not as latency but as a distortion of the geometry of virtual objects. In this case, the dissonance between the information the user receives from the visual perception and the vestibular apparatus can cause symptoms of virtual reality sickness which include nausea, headache, and ophthalmalgia (eye pain). Higher quality Motion-Parallax3D displays reduce the chances of these symptoms occurring. However, even in case of a perfect MotionParallax3D display, the symptoms of cybersickness can occur in susceptible individuals due to the dissonance of the focusing and convergence visual mechanisms; if a virtual object is located at a considerable distance from the surface on which the projected image is displayed, an attempt to fix the eyes and focus on the nearby virtual objects can lead to the opposite result.

"Perceiving latency in the response to head motion is also one of the primary causes of simulator sickness." John Carmack

The Place of MotionParallax3D displays among VR systems

NettleBox virtual reality display

Currently all widely used computer virtual reality devices can be divided into two classes:

- MotionParallax3D displays

- HMD (head-mounted display) displays.

In addition to these two classes there are other more exotic variants: e.g. the CastAR system, under development, in which the projection of the correct image onto a surface is achieved by placing the projectors directly on the glasses. However such devices are not so widespread at the moment and exist only as prototypes.

Head-mounted displays usually isolate users from the real world, whereas MotionParallax3D displays allow users to keep their orientation in the environment. This also imposes restrictions on MotionParallax3D displays; since the user sees both real and virtual objects, it is necessary to make their behavior identical which is achieved by reducing latency to an acceptable level (no more than 20 ms).

Implementations

Because MotionParallax3D displays are a tracking system connected to devices that form and display the images, there are a lot of form factors with disparities in size: from the smartphones to the virtual reality rooms to full immersion systems. Below are the most common representatives of each class.

EON ICube Mobile

CAVE Crayoland

Amazon Fire Phone

- Stereo 3D: not present

- Tracking system : optical, tracking of the user's eyes position

The ZSpace virtual reality system

- Stereo 3D: passive stereo

- Tracking system: optical, tracking of passive markers

The NettleBox virtual reality system

- Stereo 3D: Active 3D

- Tracking system: optical, tracking of active markers

EON ICube CAVE

- Stereo 3D: Active 3D

- Tracking system: optical, tracking of the passive markers position

Leonar3Do

Leonar3Do is an integrated software and hardware platform, which is capable of creating an entire three-dimensional virtual reality environment. It enables the transformation of the traditional configuration of desktop computers (or other devices) into an interactive complete three-dimensional work environment. By using this virtual reality kit, creation, manipulation and analysis of three-dimensional objects are feasible in a real three-dimensional space. The solutions, products, and applications based on Leonar3Do platform are developed and marketed by Leonar3Do International Inc. (founded by the inventor of Leonar3Do, Daniel Rátai, Budapest, Hungary).

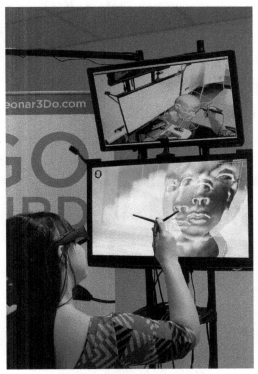

LeoCapture in use

About the Technology and Structure

Leonar3Do has the following main hardware components:

- The so-called "bird", which is the spatial input device. This device replaces the traditional mouse, which was originally

developed for the 2D flat dimension of desktop computers. The bird has six degrees of freedom; thanks to this feature, the user of Leonar3Do can not only grab and move the entire space or the object but rotation is also possible.

- Three-dimensional glasses with built-in infra LEDs which enables the detection of the eyeglasses' position.

- The three sensors which should be placed on the top of the display.

- The central panel which enables the bi-directional communication.

The three sensors' task is to track the position of both the 3D glasses and the input device (bird) and send this information to the central unit. The central unit transmits the received data to the computer and the Leonar3Do system software which generates, manages and displays the virtual reality environment produced in accordance with the data processed. The result is a complete 3D virtual reality environment. The user perceives the virtual object from any angle, as if it were real. Leonar3Do also has a complete software development kit, which allows the development, in the generally known programming language, of new applications, based on the Leonar3Do platform. By Leonar3Do's modeling software, users can give physical attributes to virtual objects like changeable mass, gravity, impeccability, and rebounding.

Versions of Leonar3Do and additional Applications

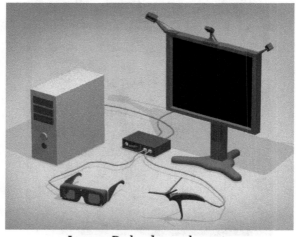

Leonar3Do hardware elements

Leonar3Do Hardware Kit

This box contains the following components:

- central panel

- 3D glasses

- bird (the spatial input device)

- the 3 sensors

- AVC (Analog Video Controller)

- DVC (Digital Video Controller)

- Leonar3Do Software and Operating Instructions DVD

Further solutions and software applications are available, based on Leonar3Do platform:

Products and industrial solutions

- Vimensio: This solution was also built on the Leonar3Do platform, and its main target is primary, secondary, and higher education.

  By using Vimensio, users can create

  virtual reality environments, simulations or develop new 3D VR (virtual reality) applications for effective studying. Vimensio contains the above mentioned Leonar3Do hardware elements and the Vimensio educational software.

  Vimensio Edit: Gives users the ability to create their own three-dimensional educational applications, without the usage of programming languages.

  Vimensio Play: A cross-platform application system which allows the presentation of the already created three-dimensional content.

- Leonar3Do for 3D Designers and Artists: It offers an interactive and intuitive way of 3D VR modeling. This solution contains the LeoWorld, and the Leo-Brush software (details below); also, an Autodesk Maya plug-in has been already developed for the Leonar3Do platform. Small changes can be carried out more precisely by manipulating the vertex, polygon, and face surfaces. The so-called BOX MODELING character building is also feasible in the spatial space. The hardware kit is also included.

- Leopoly: Leopoly was also built on the Leonar3Do platform, and its main target is online co-creation, sculpting and sharing 3D models.

Software Applications

Software applications require a 3D monitor and a Leonar3Do Professional Edition Kit or a Vimensio Kit, including the Leonar3Do system software and the hardware elements.

- LeoWorld: A 3D VR (virtual reality) animation and modeling software. It enables real time polygon optimisation, lightning modification, and 3D coloring. The software forms the geometry of the object in real-time as the polygons are rearranged. Users can also give physical attributes to the 3D virtual objects like changeable mass, gravity, impeccability, and rebounding.

- LeoCapture: With the help of this software, the 3D VR work process, which has been carried out by the user, can be captured in 3D, and represented (even in real-time) in the flat 2D environment without a 3D camera and 3D player. The software creates the accurate video clips with the help of a traditional web camera.

- LeoConf Software: LeoConf is the multi-user version of Leonar3Do. This means that the picture which is displayed by any Leonar3Do application, is also can be projected in real time to the audience. LeoConf is suitable to create 3D demonstrations or presentations for masses of people, just like in a 3D cinema.

- LeoBrush: LeoBrush is-an air-brush simulator software. The software application transforms the monitor into a canvas, and the bird can be used as a 3D air-brush. The user can save the completed creation in various file types.

- LeoGomoku: This is the 3D virtual reality version of the so-called "Tic Tac Toe" game.

- SDK Software: Application development software, which enables the development of new, Leonar3Do-based software in a C++ or OpenGL working environment. It includes the application programming surface, the sample files, the source code, and one year of developer support.

- Autodesk Maya plug-in: Leonar3Do International has developed a 3D plug-in for the Autodesk Maya software. The plug-in allows the viewing of the processing objects in real time 3D without rendering. Subtle changes can be carried out precisely by manipulating the vertex, polygon, and face surfaces. The so-called BOX MODELING character building is also feasible in the spatial space.

- Unity game engine plug-in: The plug-in for Unity game engine, allows the user to develop a unique 3D VR game.

- Vimensio software: The Vimensio software has been developed for educational use. It has the aforementioned Leonar3Do features. In addition, it has an integrated application builder software, with which the users are able to create their own educational content. Vimensio also offers built-in, preconstructed educational content. With the help of this software, teaching, studying, and demonstrating is made possible in a 3D virtual reality environment.

Services

Personalized services are also available. (e.g. trainings, development support, etc.)

History of Leonar3Do

Even in his childhood, Daniel Rátai was already interested in the construction of spatial 3D drawing. He wanted to break with the 2D drawing and modeling method in which all designing methods are rooted. This motivation has led to the creation of the first edition of Leonar3Do, which won him the second prize of National High School Competition in Innovation (2004). In 2005, the Hungarian Association for Innovation asked Daniel to represent Hungary at the final of Intel International Science and Engineering Fair (Intel ISEF) (May 2005, Arizona, PX). Daniel Rátai and the Leonar3Do project was awarded six first prizes at the fair (details below). In the same year Daniel founded 3D For All Ltd. (the present Leonar3Do International Inc.) as a family business. The development team and the entire company succeeded by 2010 to turn Daniel Rátai's invention into a finished 3D virtual reality product. In 2011, venture capital was invested into the business by PortfoLion, enabling the company to make further developments and to start the mass-production of Leonar3Do virtual reality kit.

Awards

- 2005: International Science and Engineering Fair (Arizona, Phoenix May 2005, Intel–ISEF)

The inventor, Daniel Rátai, and his Leonar3Do project was awarded with the following six first prizes:

1. First Place: IEEE Computer Society Award

2. First Place: Computer Science Award - Presented by Intel Foundation

3. First Place: Patent and Trademark Office Society Award

4. Best of Category: Computer Science - Presented by Intel Foundation

5. Intel Foundation Achievement Award

6. Seaborg SIYSS Award.

In the same year, a planetoid was named after Daniel by Massachusetts Institute of Technology Lincoln Laboratory. In addition, he won the György Oláh Young Scientist Award.

- 2008: Spring: Daniel Rátai was awarded by the Prime Minister with the Youth of March state award, for his innovative activity.

September: The Tech Award (San Jose, Tech Museum of Innovation) In the category of education, the Leonar3Do project was awarded to be among the five most significant innovations of the world. This Tech Award was the first to be was won by a Hungarian project.

- 2009: Pannon Role Model Award

December: Patronage was taken over the Leonar3Do education project, by the Conference of Hungarian Rectors.

- 2010: The Intelius International Entrepreneurship Award was won by the Leonar3Do, at Kairos Society Global Summit, the New York Stock Exchange.

- 2011: February: The Man of the Year - The Hope of the Future Award (by Blikk magazine)

December: Hungarian Heritage award

- 2012: Las Vegas: Leonar3Do was awarded with the "Best of CES" award, by Vanquard Marketing, at (Consumer Electronics Show).

In December, Leonar3Do inventor Dániel Rátai received the Docler Holding New Generation Gábor Dénes prize in the Hungarian Parliament.

References

- Howard, Ian P. Perceiving in Depth, Volume 3: Other Mechanisms of Depth Perception (Oxford Psychology Series). Oxford University Press. pp. 84–122. ISBN 978-0-19-976416-7.

- "CastAR will return $1M in Kickstarter money and postpone augmented reality glasses shipments". Venture Beat. Retrieved 31 May 2016.

- Rousseau, Rémi (2014-08-13). "Virtual surgery gets real: What the Oculus Rift could mean for the future of medicine". Medium. Retrieved 2016-04-12.

- "Russian virtual reality platform Fibrum to measure itself against Google's Daydream". East-West Digital News. Retrieved 2016-07-27.

- Nagata, Kazuaki (9 October 2014). "Toshiba Glass sets sights on less obtrusive wearable tech". The Japan times. Retrieved 25 March 2016.

- Steven Millward (3 September 2014). "Here's Baidu Eye, the Google Glass rival from China's top search engine". Tech In Asia. Retrieved 9 September 2014.

- "IFA 2014: Samsung Galaxy Note 4, Note Edge, Gear VR and Gear S hands-on". GSMArena.com. Retrieved 2015-11-24.

- "Cyborg genius claims he's the next step in human evolution". The Jamaica Observer. 3 September 2009. Retrieved 24 February 2013.

4

Virtual Reality Therapy: An Overview

Due to its immense potential, virtual reality has become the choice of technology in a method of psychotherapy called virtual reality therapy (VRT) or virtual reality exposure therapy (VRET). This application of virtual reality in therapy enables the clinician to control and stimulate the exposure of the patient to triggers and triggering levels. This chapter examines this novel use of virtual reality in psychotherapy and in telerehabilitation and helps the reader consider the possibilities that exist for virtual reality in the sphere of medicine and therapeutics.

Virtual Reality Therapy

Virtual reality therapy (VRT), also known as virtual reality immersion therapy (VRIT), simulation for therapy (SFT), virtual reality exposure therapy (VRET), and computerized CBT (CCBT), is a method of psychotherapy that uses virtual reality technology to treat patients with anxiety disorders and phobias where it has proven very effective. It is now one of the primary treatments for PTSD. New technology also allows for the treatment of addictions and other conditions including those caused by lesions (Lamson, ext. ref. 2, pp. 108–111).

Description

Virtual reality therapy (VRT) uses specially programmed computers, visual immersion devices and artificially created environments to give the patient a simulated experience that can be used to diagnose and treat psychological conditions that cause difficulties for patients. In many environmental phobias, reaction to the perceived hazards, such as heights, speaking in public, flying, close spaces, are usually triggered by visual and auditory stimuli. In VR-based therapies, the virtual world is a means of providing artificial, controlled stimuli in the context of treatment, and with a therapist able to monitor the patient's reaction. Unlike traditional cognitive behavior therapy, VR-based treatment may involve adjusting the virtual environment, such as for example adding controlled intensity smells or adding and adjusting vibrations, and allow the clinician to determine the triggers and triggering levels for each patient's reaction. VR-based therapy systems may allow replaying virtual scenes, with or without adjustment, to habituate the patient to such environments. Therapists who apply virtual reality exposure therapy, just as those who apply in-vivo exposure therapy, can take one of two approaches concerning the intensity of exposure. The first approach is called flooding, which refers to the most intense approach where stimuli that produce the most anxiety are presented first. For soldiers who have developed PTSD from combat, this could mean first exposing them to a virtual reality scene of their fellow troops being shot or injured followed by less stressful stimuli such as only the sounds of war. On the other hand, what is referred to as graded-exposure takes a more relaxed approach in which the least distressing stimuli are introduced first. VR-exposure, as compared to in-vivo exposure has the advantage of providing the patient a vivid experience, without the associated risks or costs. VRT has great promise since it historically produces a "cure" about 90% of the time at about half the cost of traditional cognitive behavior therapy authority, and is especially promising as a treatment for PTSD where there are simply not enough psychologists and psychiatrists to treat all the veterans with anxiety disorders diagnosed as related to their military service.

History

Virtual reality therapy (VRT) was pioneered and originally termed by Max North documented by the first known publication (Virtual Environment and Psychological Disorders, Max M. North, and Sarah M. North, Electronic Journal of Virtual Culture, 2,4, July 1994), his doctoral VRT dissertation completion in 1995 (began in 1992), and followed with the first known published VRT book in 1996 (Virtual Reality Therapy, an Innovative Paradigm, Max M. North, Sarah M. North, and Joseph R. Coble, 1996. IPI Press. ISBN 1-880930-08-0). His pioneered virtual reality technology work began as early as 1992 as a research faculty at Clark Atlanta University and supported by funding from U.S. Army Research Laboratory.

An early exploration in 1993–1994 of VRT was done by Ralph Lamson a USC graduate then at Kaiser Permanente Psychiatry Group. Lamson began publishing his work in 1993. As a psychologist, he was most concerned with the medical and therapeutic aspects, that is, how to treat people using the technology, rather than the apparatus, which was obtained from Division, Inc. *Psychology Today* reported in 1994 that these 1993–1994 treatments were successful in about 90% of Lamson's virtual psychotherapy patients. Lamson wrote in 1993 a book entitled *Virtual Therapy* which was published in 1997 directed primarily to the detailed explanation of the anatomical, medical and therapeutic basis for the success of VRT. In 1994–1995, he had solved his own acrophobia in a test use of a third party VR simulation and then set up a 40 patient test funded by Kaiser Permanente. Shortly thereafter, in 1994–1995, Larry Hodges, then a computer scientist at Georgia Tech active in VR, began studying VRT in cooperation with Max North who had reported anomalous behavior in flying carpet simulation VR studies and attributed such to phobic response of unknown nature. Hodges tried to hire Lamson without success in 1994 and instead began working with Barbara Rothbaum, a psychologist at Emory University to test VRT in controlled group tests, experiencing about 70% success among 50% of subjects completing the testing program.

In 2005, Skip Rizzo of USC's Institute for Creative Technologies, with research funding from the Office of Naval Research (ONR), started validating a tool he created using assets from the game *Full Spectrum Warrior* for the treatment of posttraumatic stress disorder. *Virtual Iraq* was subsequently evaluated and improved under ONR funding and is supported by Virtually Better, Inc. They also support applications of VR-based therapy for aerophobia, acrophobia, glossophobia, and substance abuse. *Virtual Iraq* proved successful in normalization of over 70% of PTSD sufferers, and that has now become a standard accepted treatment by the Anxiety and Depression Association of America. However, the VA has continued to emphasize traditional prolonged exposure therapy as the treatment of choice, and VR-based therapies have gained only limited adoption, despite active promotion by DOD. This is interesting in view of VRT having much lower cost and apparently higher success rates, and a $12-million ONR funded study is currently underway to definitively compare the efficacy of the two methods, PET and VRT. Military labs have subsequently set up dozens of VRT labs and treatment centers for treating both PTSD and a variety of other medical conditions. The use of VRT has thus become a mainstream psychiatric treatment for anxiety disorders and is finding increasing use in the treatment of other cognitive disorders associated with various medical conditions such as addiction, depression and insomnia.

Efficacy

Randomized, tightly controlled, acrophobia treatment trials at Kaiser Permanente pro-vided >90% effectiveness, conducted in 1993–94. Of 40 patients treated, 38 showed marked reduction in phobic reaction to heights and self-reported reaching their goals. Research found that VRT allows patients to achieve victory over virtual height situations they could not confront in real life, and that gradually increasing the height and danger in a virtual environment produced increasing victories and greater self-confidence in the patient that they could actually confront the situation in real life. "Virtual therapy interventions empower people. The simulation technology of virtual reality lends itself to mastery oriented treatment ... Rather than coping with threats, phobics manage progressively more threatening aspects in a computer gener-ated environment ... The range of applications can be extended by enhancing the real-ness and interactivity so that actions elicit reactions from the environments in which individuals immerse themselves".

Another study examined the effectiveness of virtual reality therapy in treating military combat personnel recently returning from the current conflicts in Iraq and Afghani-stan. Rauch, Eftekhari and Ruzek conducted a study with a sample of 42 combat ser-vicemen who were already diagnosed with chronic PTSD (post-traumatic stress disor-der). These combat servicemen were prescreened using several different diagnostic self-reports including the PTSD military checklist, a screening tool used by the military in the determination of the intensity of the diagnosis of PTSD by measuring the pres-ence of PTSD symptoms. Although 22 of the servicemen dropped out of the study, the results of the study concerning the 20 remaining servicemen still has merit.

The servicemen were given the same diagnostic tests after the study which consisted of multiple sessions of virtual reality exposure and virtual reality exposure therapy. The servicemen showed much improvement in the diagnostic scores, signaling a decrease of symptoms of PTSD. Likewise, a three-month follow-up diagnostic screening was also administered after the initial sessions that were undergone by the servicemen. The results of this study showed that 15 of the 20 participants no longer met diagnostic criteria for PTSD and improved their PTSD military checklist score by 50% for the assessment following the study. Even though only 17 of the 20 participants participated in the 3-month follow-up screening, 13 of the 17 still did not meet the criteria for PTSD and maintained their 50% improvement in the PTSD military checklist score. These results show promising effects and help to validate virtual reality therapy as an efficacious mode of therapy for the treatment of PTSD (McLay, et al., 2012).

Continued Development

Larry Hodges, formerly of Georgia Tech and now Clemson University and Barbara Rothbaum of Emory University, have done extensive work in VRT, and also have several patents and founded a company, Virtually Better, Inc.

In the United States, the United States Department of Defense (DOD) continues funding of VRT research and is actively using VRT in treatment of PTSD.

Current Applications

There are VRT or computerized CBT (CCBT) sessions, some immersive and some not, in which the user interacts with computer software (either on a PC, or sometimes via a voice-activated phone service), instead of face to face with a therapist. For people who are embarrassed by their phobias or feeling depressed and withdrawn, the prospect of having to speak to someone about their innermost problems can be unpleasant. In this respect, VRT/CCBT either in a VR lab or online, is an option. With the huge number of PTSD sufferers and the shortage of available mental health professional, VRT is expanding. New VR therapy sessions are even being done via the well known VR provider Second Life.

In February 2006 the UK's National Institute of Health and Clinical Excellence (NICE) recommended that VRT be made available for use within the NHS across England and Wales, for patients presenting with mild/moderate depression, rather than immediately opting for antidepressant medication. Some areas have developed, or are trialing.

There are a number of providers currently offering VERT. Some offer interactive communication with therapists and live feedback has shown to improve the result of online VRT/CCBT.

At Auckland University in New Zealand, a team led by Dr. Sally Merry have been developing a computerized CBT fantasy "serious" game to help tackle depression amongst adolescents. The game has a number of features to help combat depression, where the user takes on a role of a character who travels through a fantasy world, combating "literal" negative thoughts and learning techniques to manage their depression.

In 2011, three researchers at York University proposed an affordable virtual reality exposure therapy (VRET) system for the treatment of phobias that could be set up at home.

Treatment for Lesions

Virtual reality therapy has two promising potential benefits for treatment of hemispatial neglect patients. These include improvement of diagnostic techniques and as a supplement to rehabilitation techniques.

Current diagnostic techniques usually involve pen and paper tests like the line bisection test. Though these tests have provided relatively accurate diagnostic results, advances in virtual reality therapy (VRT) have proven these tests to not be completely thorough. Dvorkin et al. used a camera system that immersed the patient into a virtual reality world and required the patient to grasp or move object in the world, through tracking of arm and hand movements. These techniques revealed that pen and paper tests provide relatively accurate qualitative diagnoses of hemispatial neglect patients, but VRT provided accurate mapping into a 3-dimensional space, revealing areas of space that were thought to be neglected but which patients had at least some awareness. Patients were also re-tested 10 months from initial measurements, during which each went through regular rehabilitation therapy, and most showed measurably less neglect on virtual reality testing whereas no measurable improvements were shown in the line bisection test.

Virtual reality therapy has also proven to be effective in rehabilitation of lesion patients suffering from neglect. A study was conducted with 24 individuals suffering from hemispatial neglect. A control group of 12 individuals underwent conventional rehabilitation therapy including visual scanning training, while the virtual reality group (VR) were immersed in 3 virtual worlds, each with a specific task. The programs consisted of

1. "Bird and Ball" in which a patient touches a flying ball with his or her hand and turns it into a bird

2. "Coconut," in which a patient catches a coconut falling from a tree while moving around

3. "Container" in which a patient moves a box carried in a container to the opposite side.

Each of the patients of VR went through 3 weeks, 5 days a week, of 30-minute intervals emerged in these programs. The controls went through the equivalent time in traditional rehabilitation therapies. Each patient took the star cancellation test, line bisection test, and Catherine Bergego Scale (CBS) 24 hours before and after the three-week treatment to assess the severity of unilateral spatial neglect. The VR group showed a higher increase in the star cancellation test and CBS scores after treatment than the control group ($p<0.05$), but both groups did not show any difference in the line bisection test and K-MBI before and after treatment. These results suggest that virtual reality programs can be more effective then conventional rehabilitation and thus should be further researched.

Advantages

The preference of virtual reality exposure therapy over in-vivo exposure therapy is often debated, but there are many obvious advantages of virtual reality exposure therapy that make it more desirable. For example, the proximity between the client and therapist can cause problems when in-vivo therapy is used and transportation is not reliable for the client or it is impractical for them to travel as far as needed. However, virtual reality exposure therapy can be done from anywhere in the world if given the necessary tools. Going along with the idea of unavailable transportation and proximity, there are many individuals who require therapy but due to various forms of immobilizations (paralysis, extreme obesity, etc..) they can not physically be moved to where the therapy is conducted. Again, because virtual reality exposure therapy can be conducted anywhere in the world, those with mobility issues will no longer be discriminated against. Another major advantage is fewer ethical concerns than in-vivo exposure therapy. Once again, considering the idea of close proximity no longer being a requirement, this decreases the chances of inappropriate client-therapist relations taking place.

Concerns

There are a few ethical concerns concerning the use and development of using virtual reality simulation for helping clients/patients with mental health issues. One example of these concerns is the potential side effects and aftereffects of virtual reality exposure. Some of these side effects and aftereffects could include cybersickness (a type of motion sickness caused by the virtual reality experience), perceptual-motor disturbances, flashbacks, and generally lowered arousal (Rizzo, Schultheis, & Rothbaum, 2003). If severe and widespread enough, these effects should be mitigated via various methods by those therapists using virtual reality. Another ethical issue of some concern is how virtual reality is use by clinicians in that clinicians should be certified to use virtual reality for their clients/patients. Due to the relative newness of virtual reality exposure, there may not be many clinicians who have experience with the nuances of virtual reality exposure and the therapy that virtual reality exposure is meant to be used for. According to Rizzo et al. (2003), virtual reality technology should only be used as a tool for qualified clinicians instead of being used to further one's practice or garner an attraction for new clients/patients. Another ethical issue is the issue of who is developing the virtual reality and thus benefiting from its sale? In terms of the development of virtual reality technology, some firms double as out-patient clinics. For example, The Virtually Better virtual reality exposure therapy system originates from an outpatient clinic that uses the technology as well as other like therapies such as cognitive behavioral therapy and exposure therapy (Virtually Better Inc., 2013). Another non-scientific agenda being explored with VRET is that of the concern of the overall mental health of military personnel by the United States Department of Defense. In 2011, the Department of Defense gave researchers at Emory University School of Medicine, New York-Presbyterian/Weill Cornell Medical Center and University of Southern California an $11-million grant to conduct research on the two different types of exposure therapy, traditional and virtual reality, with a drug in order to treat PTSD. Another concern when applying virtual reality exposure therapy is the idea of "over-exposure" that can take place "in the name of science." Due to the relatively short time that virtual reality exposure therapy has been used and studied, it is very possible that researchers/therapists could choose to take advantage of patients in order to gain more insight regarding the efficacy of the therapy. Also, the therapist may choose to over-expose clients in order to determine exactly how much aversive stimuli an individual can withstand and still see progress.

Virtual Reality in Telerehabilitation

Virtual reality in telerehabilitation is a method used first in the training of musculoskeletal patients using asynchronous patient data uploading, and an internet video link. Subsequently, therapists using virtual reality-based telerehabilitation prescribe exercise routines via the web which are then accessed and executed by patients through a web browser. Therapists then monitor the patient's progress via the web and modify the therapy asynchronously without real-time interaction or training.

Background

The computer technology that allows development three-dimensional virtual environments consists of both hardware and software. The current popular, technical, and scientific interest in virtual environments is inspired, in large part, by the advent and availability of increasingly powerful and affordable visually oriented, interactive, graphical display systems and techniques lacking only sense and sensibility.

The term "virtualized reality" (VR) was coined and introduced in a paper by Kanade. The traditional virtual reality world is typically constructed using simplistic, artificially created computer-aided design (CAD) models. VR starts with the real-world scene and virtualizes it. Virtual reality is a practical, affordable technology for the practice of clinical medicine, and modern, high-fidelity virtual reality systems have practical applications in areas ranging from psychiatry to surgical planning and telemedicine. Through VR's capacity to allow the creation and control of dynamic 3-dimensional, ecologically valid stimulus environments within which behavioral response can be recorded and measured, it offers clinical assessment and rehabilitation options not available with traditional methods.

Application

The value of VR systems for the investigation and rehabilitation of cognitive and perceptual impairments and current and potential applications of VR technology address six neurorehabilitation issues. Korean researchers developed and assessed the value of a new rehabilitation training system to improve postural balance control by combining virtual reality technology with an unfixed bicycle. The system was effective as a training device; in addition, the technology might have a wider applicability to the rehabilitation field.

Tracy and Lathan investigated the relationship between motor tasks and participants' spatial abilities by training participants within a VR based simulator and then observing their ability to transfer training from the simulator to the real world. The study demonstrated that subjects with lower spatial abilities achieved significant positive transfer from a simulator based training task to a similar real world robotic operation task.

Virtual environments were applied to assess the training of inexperienced powered wheelchair users and demonstrated that the two virtual environments represent a potentially useful means of assessing and training novice powered wheelchair users. A recently completed project at the University of Strathclyde has resulted in the development of a wheelchair motion platform which, in conjunction with a virtual reality facility, can be used to address issues of accessibility in the built environment.

Many cases have applied virtual reality technology to telemedicine and telerehabilitation service development. Because telemedicine focuses principally on transmitting medical information, VR has potential to enhance the practice. State of the art of VR-based telemedicine applications is used in remote or augmented surgery as well as in surgical training, both of which are critically dependent on eye–hand coordination. Recently, however, different researchers have tried to use virtual environments in medical visualization and for assessment and rehabilitation in neuropsychology.

Case studies for VR applications were conducted that were internet deliverable and they identified technical, practical, and user challenges of remote VR treatment programs. To improve understanding of deficits in autism and in left visual-spatial neglect, Trepagnier et al. investigated face gaze behavior in autism and right hemisphere stroke, using virtual reality and gaze sensing technology.

An at-home stroke telerehabilitation service was developed using virtual reality haptics. Researchers from Rutgers University and Stanford University developed a virtual reality-based orthopedic telerehabilitation system.

The use of virtual reality technologies in the rehabilitation of patients with vestibular system disorders and in the provision of remote medical consultation for those patients. He stated that an appropriately designed VR experience could greatly increase the rate of adaptation in these patients.

References

- Haworth, M. Brandon; Baljko, Melanie; Faloutsos, Petros (2012-01-01). "PhoVR: A Virtual Reality System to Treat Phobias". Proceedings of the 11th ACM SIGGRAPH International Conference on Virtual-Reality Continuum and Its Applications in Industry. VRCAI '12. New York, NY, USA: ACM: 171–174. doi:10.1145/2407516.2407560. ISBN 9781450318259.

- Westwood, James D.; Helene M. Hoffman, Randy S. Haluck, Greg T. Mogel, R. Phillips, Richard A. Robb, K.G. Vosburgh (2005). Medicine Meets Virtual Reality 13: The Magical Next Becomes The Medical Now. IOS Press. p. 294. ISBN 1-58603-498-7.

- Tracey, M. R.; C. E. Lathan (2001). "The interaction of spatial ability and motor learning in the transfer of training from a simulator to a real task". Studies in Health Technology and Informatics. 81: 521–7. ISBN 1-58603-143-0. PMID 11317801.

- Rydmark, M.; J. Boeren and R. Pasher; Pascher, R (2002). "Stroke rehabilitation at home using virtual reality, haptics and telemedicine". Studies in Health Technology and Informatics. 85: 434–7. ISBN 1-58603-203-8. PMID 15458128.

- Viirre, E. (1996). "Vestibular telemedicine and rehabilitation". Studies in Health Technology and Informatics. 29: 299–305. ISBN 90-5199-250-5. PMID 10163763.

- Johanna S. Kaplan; David F. Tolin (6 September 2011). "Exposure Therapy for Anxiety Disorders". psychiatrictimes.com. Retrieved 20 October 2015.

- Zoroya, Gregg (23 April 2012). "Veterans' mental health treatment not as timely as contended". USATODAY.COM. Retrieved 20 October 2015.

- Lamson, Ralph J. "CyberEdge Information Services: CEJ Archive, Virtual Therapy of Anxiety Disorders". cyberedge.com. Retrieved 20 October 2015.

- "Dr. Ralph Lamson, PHD - San Rafael, CA - Substance Abuse Counseling - Healthgrades.com". Healthgrades. Retrieved 20 October 2015.

- "Virtual Therapy: Prevention and Treatment of Psychiatric Conditions by Immersion in Virtual Reality Environments: Ralph Lamson: 9782553006319: Amazon.com: Books". amazon.com. Retrieved 20 October 2015.

- "Evaluating Virtual Reality Therapy for Treating Acute Post Traumatic Stress Disorder - Office of Naval Research". www.onr.navy.mil. Retrieved 2015-11-15.

- Marilyn Flynn and Skip Rizzo: Treating Post Traumatic Stress with Virtual Reality. YouTube. 23 August 2010. Retrieved 20 October 2015.

5

Applications of Virtual Reality

Virtual reality simulation helps formulate and create real-life scenarios with no liability and hence has found application in diverse fields like disaster management, pilot training, recreation of locations, enhancing amusement park experience etc. This chapter illustrates these applications by the use of examples like advanced disaster management simulator, flight simulator, Unmanned Aircraft System Simulation, VR Coaster, Virtual tour and Google Street View.

Advanced Disaster Management Simulator

The ADMS (advanced disaster management simulator) is an emergency and disaster management training simulation system designed to train incident commanders, first responders, and incident command teams in a real-time, interactive virtual reality(VR) environment. ADMS was first introduced by Environmental Tectonics Corporation (ETC-C:US) in 1992. The development of ADMS was in response to the crash of British Airtours Flight 28M at the Manchester airport in 1985, in which 55 people died. Following the accident research indicated that first responder training should include realistic scenarios. The first ADMS system was produced for the UK Ministry of Defence, and delivered to Royal Air Force's (RAF) Manston Facility. Since its inception, ADMS has evolved into a modular, expandable disaster simulation platform, with systems in use worldwide.

History

Virtual Reality and Emergency Management Training

The successful use of virtual reality simulation in disaster management training initiatives is a popular area for research. It has been found that when trainees are able to participate, both verbally and physically in a training exercise, retention is 90%, in great contrast to a 10% retention rate of what they hear, and 50% retention rate of what they see and hear.

Traditionally classroom lectures, tabletop exercises and live-training drills have been utilized for training. While these teaching methodologies are effective, virtual reality simulation seems to have bridged the gap between them. Virtual reality offers the opportunity to create an emergency situation that could not otherwise be experienced due to safety, cost and environmental factors. From a safety standpoint, training in a synthetic environment allows the student to experiment while carrying out dangerous actions, and offers the ability to repeat the exercise until the trainee feels confident and prepared for real-life incidents.

Technology

The ADMS relies on a physics engine and built in artificial intelligence to provide realistic, 3D emergency situations. The Disaster scenarios include algorithms which take into account: type of threat, time of day, precipitation, wind, visibility, condition of casualties, terrain, and traffic and bystander behavior ADMS training exercises are unscripted and open-ended, requiring interactive decision making and participation from the users to affect the outcome of the training exercise. The development, escalation, or resolution of the situation is determined by the trainees' decisions and the use of intelligent resources they command.

ADMS is a networked framework and a family of applications which may be run on a single station or as a multi-user system with several networked stations giving independent access to several viewpoints and control interfaces within the same environment and scenario. ADMS projects its simulations using panoramic high-definition multimedia interface, visual displays and directional sound. The simulation engine includes key models including: artificial intelligence, physics, logic, and messaging and applications comprising a visual engine, sound engine, messaging daemon and graphical user interface.

Environments

ADMS environments are developed in either geo-typical or geo-specific environments. Geo-specific environments are created using exact 3D modeling of the specified location, and can include buildings, streets, vehicles, terrain and people, specific airports or schools, or entire cities.

Products and Applications

- ADMS-COMMAND Designed for training incident commanders in a diverse range of emergency scenarios, ranging from car accidents to low-frequency, high casualty situations, either in single or multi-agency operations. Trainees make decisions and give verbal commands, enabling the real-time action of the simulator. The system can be expanded to include additional simulation elements, including vehicle controls and cabs, and 180 degree immersive visual displays.

- ADMS-DRIVE Designed to train, assess and recertify drivers in safe and effective driving procedures. It is also utilized as a training platform to train emergency responders to drive under stressful situations, and by airport snow removal teams to train in snow removal operations during winter conditions.

ADMS-DRIVE immerses the user in a realistic, virtual environment in which dynamic elements such as traffic, signal lights, people and weather create a realistic and challenging representation of the situation.

- ADMS-ARFF Designed as an aircraft rescue and firefighting vehicle simulator which focuses on correct turret operation, driving and communication, vehicle positioning, firefighting with turrets and Command and Control. The trainee uses controls and joysticks to maneuver the vehicle in an airport environment and deals with airplane disaster.

- ADMS-HRET HRET (High-reach extendable turret) is intended to be a training aid for operators to become familiar with, and enhance the skills necessary for actual hands on operation of the Rosenbauer HRET. HRET is a portable desktop system that comes with a console that includes a real HRET-joystick and relevant switches. Trainees can drive to the scene, train various external and internal fire scenarios, and penetrate the aircraft by using the piercing device.

- ADMS-BART The behavioral assessment research tool (BART) was developed initially for the Netherlands Institute for Safety, Research Department. BART focuses on human behavior and the effect it has in a real-life incident. ADMS-BART creates an environment where virtual human subjects act as they would in a live situation. This system made it possible to use virtual reality for studying virtual behaviors in fires, allowing for changes in the live environment to mitigate the damages in the event of a live incident.

- ADMS-US Is a standardized simulation system, programmed with ten (10) geo-typical situation environments which resemble Anytown USA. ADMS-US is a portable, laptop based simulator which is utilized for either individual or multi-agency training who do not require geo-specific capabilities.

Compliance

On January 27, 2009, the U.S. Army Program Executive Office for Simulation, Training and Instrumentation (PEO STRI) awarded ETC STOC II eligibility for the ADMS. STOC II is an ID/IQ (Indefinite Delivery/Indefinite Quantity) contract vehicle with a ceiling of $17.5 billion over a period of 10 years. All branches of the military are eligible to utilize STOC II to quickly obtain simulation and training solutions from a panel of pre-qualified companies. The purpose of this contract vehicle was to provide an efficient method for the U.S. military and its coalition service members to acquire what they need.

Additionally, ADMS was designed to be NIMS compliant. The National Incident Management System has developed a unified approach to allow governmental agencies to work in unison with the private sector with the common goal of preparing for, preventing, responding to, recovering from, and mitigating the effects of incidents of any cause, size, location, or complexity.

Flight Simulator

A military Flight simulator at Payerne air base, Switzerland

A flight simulator is a device that artificially re-creates aircraft flight and the environment in which it flies, for pilot training, design, or other purposes. It includes replicating the equations that govern how aircraft fly, how they react to applications of flight controls, the effects of other aircraft systems, and how the aircraft reacts to external factors such as air density, turbulence, wind shear, cloud, precipitation, etc. Flight simulation is used for a variety of reasons, including flight training (mainly of pilots), the design and development of the aircraft itself, and research into aircraft characteristics and control handling qualities.

History of flight Simulation

World War I (1914–18)

An area of training was for air gunnery handled by the pilot or a specialist air gunner. Firing at a moving target requires aiming ahead of the target (which involves the so-called lead angle) to allow for the time the bullets require to reach the vicinity of the target. This is sometimes also called "deflection shooting" and requires skill and practice. During World War I, some ground-based simulators were developed to teach this skill to new pilots.

The 1920s and 1930s

The best-known early flight simulation device was the Link Trainer, produced by Edwin Link in Binghamton, New York, USA, which he started building in 1927. He later patented his design, which was first available for sale in 1929. The Link Trainer was a basic metal frame flight simulator usually painted in its well-known blue color. Some of these early war era flight simulators still exist, but it is becoming increasingly difficult to find working examples.

Link Trainer

The Link family firm in Binghamton manufactured player pianos and organs, and Ed Link was therefore familiar with such components as leather bellows and reed switches. He was also a pilot, but dissatisfied with the amount of real flight training that was available, he decided to build a ground-based device to provide such training without the restrictions of weather and the availability of aircraft and flight instructors. His design had a pneumatic motion platform driven by inflatable bellows which provided pitch and roll cues. A vacuum motor similar to those used in player pianos rotated the platform, providing yaw cues. A generic replica cockpit with working instruments was mounted on the motion platform. When the cockpit was covered, pilots could practice flying by instruments in a safe environment. The motion platform gave the pilot cues as to real angular motion in pitch (nose up and down), roll (wing up or down) and yaw (nose left and right).

Initially, aviation flight schools showed little interest in the "Link Trainer". Link also demonstrated his trainer to the U.S. Army Air Force (USAAF), but with no result. However, the situation changed in 1934 when the Army Air Force was given a government contract to fly the postal mail. This included having to fly in bad weather as well as good, for which the USAAF had not previously carried out much training. During the first weeks of the mail service, nearly a dozen Army pilots were killed. The Army Air Force hierarchy remembered Ed Link and his trainer. Link flew in to meet them at Newark Field in New Jersey, and they were impressed by his ability to arrive on a day with poor visibility, due to practice on his training device. The result was that the USAAF purchased six Link Trainers, and this can be said to mark the start of the world flight simulation industry.

World War II (1939–1945)

The principal pilot trainer used during World War II was the Link Trainer. Some 10,000 were produced to train 500,000 new pilots from allied nations, many in the USA and Canada because many pilots were trained in those countries before returning to Europe or the Pacific to fly combat missions. Almost all US Army Air Force pilots were trained in a Link Trainer.

A Link Trainer at Freeman Field, Seymour, Indiana, 1943

A different type of World War II trainer was used for navigating at night by the stars. The Celestial Navigation Trainer of 1941 was 13.7 m (45 ft) high and capable of accommodating the navigation team of a bomber crew. It enabled sextants to be used for taking "star shots" from a projected display of the night sky.

1945 to the 1960s

In 1954 United Airlines bought four flight simulators at a cost of $3 million from Curtiss-Wright that were similar to the earlier models, with the addition of visuals, sound and movement. This was the first of today's modern flight simulators for commercial aircraft.

Types of Flight Training Devices in Service

Training for Pilots

Cockpit of a twinjet flight simulator.

Rudder control system trainer for a Grumman S-2 Tracker

Several different devices are utilized in modern flight training. Cockpit Procedures Trainer (CPT) are used to practice basic cockpit procedures, such as processing emergency checklists, and for cockpit familiarization. Certain aircraft systems may or may not be simulated. The aerodynamic model is usually extremely generic if present at all.

Technology

Motion

Statistically significant assessments of skill transfer based on training on a simulator and leading to handling an actual aircraft are difficult to make, particularly where motion cues are concerned. Large samples of pilot opinion are required and many subjective opinions tend to be aired, particularly by pilots not used to making objective assessments and responding to a structured test schedule. For many years, it was believed that 6 DOF motion-based simulation gave the pilot closer fidelity to flight control operations and aircraft responses to control inputs and external forces and gave a better training outcome for students than non-motion-based simulation. This is described as "handling fidelity", which can be assessed by test flight standards such as the numerical Cooper-Harper rating scale for handling qualities. Recent scientific studies have shown that the use of technology such as vibration or dynamic seats within flight simulators can be equally as effective in the delivery of training as large and expensive 6-DOF FFS devices.

Qualification and approval

Procedure

When a manufacturer wishes to have an ATD model approved, a document that contains the specifications for the model line and that proves compliance with the appropriate regulations is submitted to the FAA. Once this document, called a Qualification

Approval Guide (QAG), has been approved, all future devices conforming to the QAG are automatically approved and individual evaluation is neither required nor available.

Flight Simulator "Levels" and other Categories

The following levels of qualification are currently being granted for both airplane and helicopter FSTD:

US Federal Aviation Administration (FAA)

Flight Training Devices (FTD)

- FAA FTD Level 4 - Similar to a Cockpit Procedures Trainer (CPT), but for helicopters only. This level does not require an aerodynamic model, but accurate systems modeling is required.

- FAA FTD Level 5 - Aerodynamic programming and systems modeling is required, but it may represent a family of aircraft rather than only one specific model.

- FAA FTD Level 6 - Aircraft-model-specific aerodynamic programming, control feel, and physical cockpit are required.

- FAA FTD Level 7 - Model specific, helicopter only. All applicable aerodynamics, flight controls, and systems must be modeled. A vibration system must be supplied. This is the first level to require a visual system.

Full Flight Simulators (FFS)

- FAA FFS Level A - A motion system is required with at least three degrees of freedom. Airplanes only.

- FAA FFS Level B - Requires three axis motion and a higher-fidelity aerodynamic model than does Level A. The lowest level of helicopter flight simulator.

- FAA FFS Level C - Requires a motion platform with all six degrees of freedom. Also lower transport delay (latency) over levels A & B. The visual system must have an outside-world horizontal field of view of at least 75 degrees for each pilot.

- FAA FFS Level D - The highest level of FFS qualification currently available. Requirements are for Level C with additions. The motion platform must have all six degrees of freedom, and the visual system must have an outside-world horizontal field of view of at least 150 degrees, with a Collimated (distant focus) display. Realistic sounds in the cockpit are required, as well as a number of special motion and visual effects.

European Aviation Safety Agency (EASA, ex JAA)

Flight Navigation and Procedures Trainer (FNPT)

- EASA FNPT Level I

- EASA FNPT Level II

- EASA FNPT Level III

- MCC - Not a true "level" of qualification, but an add-on that allows any level of FNPT to be used for Multi Crew Coordination training.

Flight Training Devices (FTD)

- EASA FTD Level 1

- EASA FTD Level 2

- EASA FTD Level 3 - Helicopter only.

Full Flight Simulators (FFS)

- EASA FFS Level A

- EASA FFS Level B

- EASA FFS Level C

- EASA FFS Level D

Modern High-end Flight Simulators

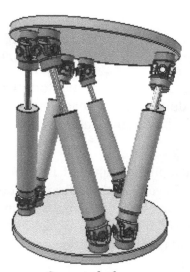

Stewart platform

Vertical Motion Simulator (VMS) at NASA/Ames

The largest flight simulator in the world is the Vertical Motion Simulator (VMS) at NASA Ames Research Center in "Silicon Valley" south of San Francisco. This has a very large-throw motion system with 60 feet (+/- 30 ft) of vertical movement (heave). The heave system supports a horizontal beam on which are mounted 40 ft rails, allowing lateral movement of a simulator cab of +/- 20 feet. A conventional 6-degree of freedom hexapod platform is mounted on the 40 ft beam, and an interchangeable cabin is mounted on the platform. This design permits quick switching of different aircraft cabins. Simulations have ranged from blimps, commercial and military aircraft to the Space Shuttle. In the case of the Space Shuttle, the large Vertical Motion Simulator was used to investigate a longitudinal pilot-induced oscillation (PIO) that occurred on an early Shuttle flight just before landing. After identification of the problem on the VMS, it was used to try different longitudinal control algorithms and recommend the best for use in the Shuttle program.

Disorientation Training

AMST Systemtechnik GmbH (AMST) of Austria and Environmental Tectonics Corporation (ETC) of Philadelphia, US, manufacture a range of simulators for disorientation training, that have full freedom in yaw. The most complex of these devices is the Desdemona simulator at the TNO Research Institute in The Netherlands, manufactured by AMST. This large simulator has a gimballed cockpit mounted on a framework which adds vertical motion. The framework is mounted on rails attached to a rotating platform. The rails allow the simulator cab to be positioned at different radii from the centre of rotation and this gives a sustained G capability up to about 3.5.

Unmanned Aircraft System Simulation

Unmanned aircraft system simulation focuses on training pilots (or operators) to control an unmanned aircraft or its payload from a control station. Flight simulation involves a device that artificially re-creates aircraft flight and the environment in which it flies for pilot training, design, or other purposes. It includes replicating the equations that govern how aircraft fly, how they react to applications of flight controls, the effects of other aircraft systems, and how the aircraft reacts to external factors such as air density, turbulence, wind shear, cloud, precipitation, etc.

Manned simulation is used for a variety of reasons, including flight training (mainly of pilots), the design and development of the aircraft itself, and research into aircraft characteristics and control handling qualities. Unlike manned simulation, unmanned aircraft system (UAS) simulation does not involve a pilot aboard the training device.

Unmanned Aircraft System (UAS) Simulation Training

Manned flight simulators employ various types of hardware and software, depending on the modeling detail and realism that is required for the role in which they are to be employed. Designs range from PC laptop-based models of aircraft systems (called Part Task Trainers or PTTs), to replica cockpits for initial familiarization, to highly realistic simulations of the cockpit, flight controls and aircraft systems for more complete pilot training.

The use of unmanned systems by defense forces globally has grown substantially over the past decade, and is only expected to continue to grow significantly. In addition, unmanned systems will be used increasingly for commercial applications such as remote inspection of pipelines and hydroelectric installations, surveillance of forest fires, observation of critical natural resources, assessing natural disasters and a range of other applications. This increase in the use of UAS capabilities results in the need to have more highly skilled UAS pilots, sensor operators, and mission commanders.

An unmanned aerial vehicle (UAV), commonly known as a drone and referred to as a Remotely Piloted Aircraft (RPA) by the International Civil Aviation Organization (ICAO), is an aircraft without a human pilot aboard. Its flight is controlled either autonomously by onboard computers or by the remote control of a pilot on the ground or in another vehicle. The typical launch and recovery method of an unmanned aircraft is by the function of an automatic system or an external operator on the ground. Historically, UAVs were simple remotely piloted aircraft, but autonomous control is increasingly being employed. A UAS is composed of the UAV, itself, as well as associated launch, recovery, and control hardware and software.

UAVs are usually deployed for military and special operation applications, but are also used in a small but growing number of civil applications, such as policing and firefighting, and nonmilitary security work such as surveillance of pipelines. UAVs are often preferred for missions that are too "dull, dirty or dangerous" for manned aircraft.

UAS Simulation Training allows UAV operators to train in real-time to operate UAVs in a virtual environment that is realistic and accurate, but without the risks and constraints of a real flight. UAS simulation includes:

- Simulated UAVS: The system allows training on both helicopter and fixed wing UAVs.

- Training with the actual ground station: The system uses real data generated by the actual UAV autopilot to provide an extremely realistic simulation.

- The virtual world in which the UAV flies is modeled in 3D with photo textures, and contains all the necessary features to simulate a mission in operational conditions.

- Payload simulation: The system generates real-time video to simulate the payload output in both visible and IR modes. This video is piped to the actual video station as in the real system.

- Simulation features: Multilingual interface, VCR type controls (replay forward / backward), Simulated weather functions, display options (flight panel, UAV trajectory), display of telemetry data.

UAS Simulation Training combines an open architecture with commercial-off-the-shelf hardware and simulation software that helps the use of proprietary designs to provide a comprehensive, platform-agnostic training system. Customers benefit from greater flexibility for evolution, networking, distributed mission training and combination within an integrated training environment. UAS is a solution that optimizes operational readiness while minimizing the use of live assets to train and prepare the integrated mission team for operations. The comprehensive solution also prepares the integrated mission team (pilot, payload specialist, and commanding officer) in platform operating procedures, data interpretation and analysis, and team interaction.

UAS Training in the United States Armed Forces

Potential Air Force UAS pilots and sensor operators attend three and a half months of specialized training courses, most of which is simulated. In simulated training for the Predator, operators use a manual control stick, rudder system and monitor system that is the same as the live simulator. The Air Force's primary UAS training bases are at Holloman Air Force Base, NM, Cannon AFB, NM, Ellsworth AFB, SD, and Whiteman AFB, MO, but will take initial flight training in Pueblo, CO.

Army soldiers receive training on smaller, easier to maneuver UAS, such as the Raven and Puma, from master trainers. Master trainers are selected from bases around the world and are given instruction at Ft. Benning, GA. These master trainers then train units at their home base. Army operators for larger UAS, such as the Shadow and Gray Eagle, conduct training in Ft. Huachuca, AZ because of its remote location. These operators are UAS fight specialist for a single specific model. This is due to the different capabilities and functions of each air craft. Training is a combination of live and simulated training to teach new operators. Training is easily simulated because it is almost the same experience as live training in the aircraft that is operated by a Ground Control Station (GCS).

The standard for the Navy was to use pilots who have completed at least one piloting tour before allowing training in operating a UAS. With the advancement and economy of simulators, the Navy is beginning to train enlisted personnel with flight experience to become operators. Capt. Patrick Smith, a Fire Scout program manager was quoted to state, "Ideally, we take [potential operators] from the SH-60 [SeaHawk] community and add them to the five-week program, mainly simulator-based." The Navy conducts

UAS training in Ft. Huachuca, AZ for live simulation or military installations near Patuxent River, MD for the Fire Scouts.

In 2014, Marines that complete the Basic School Officer course in Quantico, V.A., will have taken training in small UAS (Raven and Puma). UAS are not widely used in the Marines, but as the UAS become smaller and more mobile, they will become more integrated in mission resources. Marines recently started to receive training from the Group I (under 20 pounds) UAS Training and Logistics Support Activity in Camp Lejeune, N.C.

UAS in inventory for each branch of service:

- Air Force: MQ-1 Predator, MQ-9 Reaper, and RQ-4 Global Hawk.

- Army: RQ-11 Raven, RQ-7 Shadow, RQ-5 Hunter, MQ-1C Gray Eagle and RQ-20 Puma.

- Navy: BAMS, Firescout/VTUAV, STUAS, Scan Eagle, and UCASS UAS. The UCASS is scheduled to be replaced by the UCLASS in fiscal year 2015.

- Marine Corps: RQ-7 Shadow and STUAS.

UAS Training in Domestic/Civil Sectors

Firefighters, police, miners, and weather researchers are now using UAVs (commonly referred to as drones), which were first used in military sectors. The drones used by police and firefighters are the same type of drones; however, they are used for different purposes. UAVs have gone beyond the human capacity of lifting heavy loads, performing daring photography amidst a heavy storm, and digitizing images that can be converted into 3D maps.

Weather researchers use different drones to help predict weather, photograph storms and measure temperature. Drones are very essential for weather crews in predicting wind speed and temperature, wind direction, air temperature and pressure (Aerosonde Mark 4). Other drones are used for taking images of storm systems, even inside the storm itself. Like the Mark 4, NASA's Global Hawk is used to measure air temperature, wind speed, and pressure, but unlike the Mark 4, it can take images of the storm system.

In mining, drones help miners with tasks such as inspection and maintenance, carrying heavy equipment, and even carrying out tasks 24 hours a day/7 days a week. The mining industry uses drones such as Responder and Serenity to assist mining crews with maintenance, inspection, and imagery. Some drones within the mining industry assist workers with photography of the sediments to be mined so it can be calculated in terms of volume for removal and the stockpile of sediment graded by workers.

In police forces, drones are used for bomb detonation, response to incidents, pursuing criminals in the air, and determining a suspect's location using high tech camera systems (Viking 400-S). Other uses for drones in police sectors are to record incidents, create maps of the incidents in 3D models, and then later send them to officers' smart phones (Sensefly eBee). Other drones, such as the Kaman drop supplies and equipment for officers, as well as transport officers to and back from the crime scene. The E300 is used to stop criminals and record an incident.

Firefighters use the same drones, but for different purposes. For example, ELIMCO's E300 is used to put out fires, the Viking 400-S uses a camera to photograph incidents, then later transmits the images back to firefighting personnel for mapping the incidents electronically. The Information Processing Systems' MCV, like the E300 is used for putting out wildfires and man-made fires. The eBee, like its police variant takes photographs with a 16 MP camera, which is used to create 3D models of maps through integrating technology from Google Maps. It is later sent to firefighting personnel smart phones. The Kaman, like its police variant, is used to supply firefighters and victims of fires, and to provide medical assistance. The Defikopter sends defibrillators to victims of heart attack. To locate a victim, it uses a GPS system.

UAS Training in Higher Education

There are two primary roles or purposes for UAS in higher education:

- Training and certification of UAS operators

- UAS-related research

Specific UAS Applications by School

At the University of North Dakota (UND) Bachelor of Science in Aeronautics program, simulators are used for both operator certification and research purposes. For operator certification, UND uses Original Equipment Manufacturer (OEM) simulators specific to a particular vehicle (e.g., ScanEagle, MQ-8, etc.). Actual qualification training is on hold until the Federal Aviation Administration (FAA) puts standards in place for the use of UAS in United States airspace. However, students can learn basic operation principles and how UAS will function in national airspace. UND also conducts research funded by the Air Force Research Laboratory on task loading of UAS operators. This research compares single operators versus multi-operator crews and full auto-piloted systems versus remotely piloted systems.

Embry-Riddle Aeronautical University in Daytona Beach, FL uses simulators in an undergraduate UAS operator program awarding a Bacehlor of Science degree in Unmanned Aircraft Systems Science. Primarily, this program trains UAS operators, but it also serves a research role to test the application of UAS in national airspace.

Several other schools offer non-engineering based UAS undergraduate programs, of which simulators are an integral part. Some examples include:

- Indiana State University: Minor in Unmanned Systems

- Kansas State University – Salina: Bachelor of Science in Unmanned Aircraft Systems

- Oklahoma State University: UAS option for MS or PhD degrees in Mechanical and Aerospace Engineering

Agent based Modeling and Simulation of UAS

UAV Simulators generally focus on low-level flight control and coordination by using complex physics-based models that are geared towards accuracy. These simulators requires domain expertise and complex knowledge to build, learn and operate the simulator itself. Alternate simulators are being developed such as Agent Based Modeling and Simulation for UAS, especially by military.

Agent based modeling and simulation of UAV focuses on specialized issues such as coordination and planning. For example, the CoUAV. simulator focuses on cooperative search and MAS-Planes focuses on request servicing by decentralized coordination. Agent based simulation has also been used for UAV flight dynamic simulation modeling.

Agent based modeling and simulation has been used for managing missions for UAS. The authors used Codarra Avatar for their experiments. Codarra Avatar is a lightweight UAV which has been specifically built for small-scale reconnaissance and surveillance missions. This UAV can be assembled and disassembled very quickly and transported in a backpack. However, in becoming an autonomous UAV, the Codarra Avatar faces challenges of flight time, flight range, durability, limited computational power, limited sensory data, and flight regulations and restrictions. The authors developed Agent-Flight Control System Architecture (FCS) to combat the issues faced with the UAV.

FCS has an agent that sits at the top of a control tree, receives data at regular intervals, and issues high level waypoint commands. The agent is designed in JACK, an agent-oriented programming language. The behavior of agents defined using JACK are structured around the BDI (Belief, Desire, Intentions) theory of agency. The mission Management System is designed using the OODA (Observe, Orient, Decide, Act) Approach that was developed by Colonel John Boyd. Authors conducted successful tests in Melbourne, Australia, using an FCS Architecture on the Codarra Avatar UAV.

VR Coaster

A VR Coaster is a special kind of amusement park ride attraction, consisting of a roller coaster facility or ride that can be experienced with virtual reality headsets. The term

VR Coaster derives from the abbreviation of virtual reality and roller coaster. The first publicly operated VR Coasters have been opened in late 2015. Since then, several theme parks all over the world have been adapting this technology to extend their existing coaster facilities.

A train of Superman – The Ride Virtual Reality Coaster at the Six Flags New England theme park. Riders are wearing Gear VR virtual reality headsets.

Background and History

While virtual reality roller coaster simulations quickly became quite popular after the appearance of the Oculus Rift, it showed that dizziness and motion sickness, known as Virtual reality sickness, would be a major problem. This was caused by the offset between the simulated motion in VR and the lack of real motion, as the inner Sense of balance wouldn't feel the appropriate forces and turns. In order to test if this could be overcome by synchronizing VR movement to real motion, a research group of the University of Applied Sciences, Kaiserslautern, led by Prof. Dipl.-Des. Thomas Wagner, together with roller coaster manufacturer Mack Rides and Europa-Park, has been conducting experiments on actual roller coaster facilities in early 2014. It showed that, with a precise synchronization, not only the nausea would disappear, but also a new kind of attraction was created (as, for the first time, this setup allowed for a simulation ride to feature continuous g-forces, zero gravity and drops (or so called Air-time).

Still, the technical setup of the 2014 experiments was not feasible yet for a permanent installation. Most of all, mounting a computer on a coaster train would not have worked due to the continuous heavy vibrations; also the usual cable connection of a classical VR headset like the Oculus Rift would have meant a serious safety hazard. Wagner and his team could eventually overcome these problems by deploying so called mobile VR headsets like the Samsung Gear VR, where the entire image generation happens directly inside of the actual headset. The very first VR Coaster installations have been opened to the public in late 2015, starting at Europa-Park, Germany, followed by Canada's Wonderland and Universal Studios Japan, all of them developed by the startup company with the same name, VR Coaster GmbH & Co. KG, which originated from Wagners research group. As of June 2016, 17 theme parks worldwide are operating VR Coasters (list). The latest installations can be found in Six Flags parks, themed with Superman content from the DC Comics universe.

Technical Solutions

Key to a comfortable VR experience on an actual moving ride attraction is a precise synchronization of the virtual ride animation. To achieve this, the coaster train is equipped with special hardware that monitors the position of the train in the track layout and then wirelessly transmits this information to the headsets of the riders. This is also crucial, as the VR experience needs to run in absolute tracking mode (unlike relative tracking when used at home, where the VR view automatically rotates with a virtual vehicle), so without a precise tracking solution, curves and turns would not be in the right place. In other words, a virtual cockpit must always turn and travel in exactly the same direction as the real coaster car, which would not be possible without an automated synchronization. Still, as the human sense of balance can't detect absolute velocities but only acceleration and turns, speed and dimensions can be altered in VR. Even curves can be bent to different angles, as long as the relative direction of the turn is preserved (clockwise or counterclockwise).

Experience

As virtual reality allows for several modifications and extensions of the actual track layout, the size of the VR track can be much larger than the real one. This of course means that speeds can be much faster and heights much taller, as these aspects also grow with the increased dimensions. Most of all, there is no need to show an actual track or rails (which would give away what element comes next), other than for dramaturgical reasons. As the rider is totally immersed in the VR world, one can even be tricked by giving hints on a wrong track direction and then e.g. have a giant creature grabbing the virtual cockpit and carrying it into a different direction (which turns out to be the actual direction of the rails). Also, the effect of physical track elements like block brakes can be utilized in the VR experience for dramatic elements like crashing through a virtual barrier or building Riders report after their first VR Coaster ride that it is unlike anything they have ever experienced before.

Virtual Tour

A virtual tour is a simulation of an existing location, usually composed of a sequence of videos or still images. It may also use other multimedia elements such as sound effects, music, narration, and text. It is distinguished from the use of live television to affect tele-tourism.

The phrase "virtual tour" is often used to describe a variety of videos and photographic-based media. Panorama indicates an unbroken view, since a panorama can be either a series of photographs or panning video footage. However, the phrases "panoramic tour" and "virtual tour" have mostly been associated with virtual tours created using still cameras. Such virtual tours are made up of a number of shots taken from a single vantage point. The camera and lens are rotated around what is referred to as a no parallax point (the exact point at the back of the lens where the light converges).

A video tour is a full motion video of a location. Unlike the virtual tour's static wrap-around feel, a video tour is a linear walk-through of a location. Using a video camera, the location is filmed at a walking pace while moving continuously from one point to another throughout the subject location.

History

The origin of the term 'virtual tour' dates to 1994. The first example of a virtual tour was a museum visitor interpretive tour, consisting of 'walk-through' of a 3D reconstruction of Dudley Castle in England as it was in 1550. This consisted of a computer controlled laserdisc based system designed by British-based engineer Colin Johnson.

One of the first users of a virtual tour was Queen Elizabeth II, when she officially opened the visitor centre in June 1994. Because the Queen's officials had requested titles, descriptions and instructions of all activities, the system was named and described as: "Virtual Tour, being a cross between Virtual Reality and Royal Tour." Details of the original project can be viewed online. The system was featured in a conference held by the British Museum in November 1994 and in a subsequent technical paper.

Methods of Creation

Stitching Photographs

There are three popular ways of "stitching" virtual tours together.

1.) Rectilinear stitching. This involves the rotation of a digital camera, typically in the portrait (up and down) position and centered directly over the tripod. As the operator manually rotates the camera clockwise, the camera stops or clicks into a detent at regular intervals, such as every 30° of rotation. The rotator can be adjusted by changing the position of "detent ring or bolt," into another slot, to alter the interval of rotation: 40°, 60°, 90° etc.

If a given camera lens supports a wider view, one could select a larger detent value (for example, 60° instead of 30°). With a larger detent interval, fewer images are needed to capture a complete panoramic scene. The photographer may only need to take 6 shots as opposed to 10 shots to capture the same panorama. The combination of a precision rotator and a digital camera allows the photographer to take rectangular "slices" of any scene (indoors or outdoors). With a typical point and shoot digital camera, the photographer will snap 8, 10, 12 or 14 slices of a scene. Using specialized "photo stitching" software, the operator then assembles the "slices" into a single rectangular image, typically 4,500 pixels to 6,000 pixels wide. This technique, while extremely time consuming, has remained popular even through today as the required equipment, rotator heads and software are relatively inexpensive and easy to learn. A stitched panoramic view is also called "cylindrical"—as the resulting stitched panorama allows panning in a complete 360°, but offers a limited vertical field of about 50° degrees above or below the horizon line.

2.) Spherical stitching. This method requires the use of a "Fisheye lens" lens equipped digital SLR camera. The 2-shot fish eye camera system was made popular by IPiX in the mid-1990s and a two-shot rotator head that rotated and locked into 0° and 180° positions only. The camera was an Olympus or Nikon CoolPix camera and the lenses used were the Nikon FC-E8 or FC-E9 fish-eye lens. The IPiX 360 camera system enabled photographers to capture a full 360 X 360 floor to ceiling view of any scene with just 4 shots as opposed to the more time consuming 8, 10, or 12-shot rectilinear produced panoramas described above. This type of virtual tour required more expensive virtual tour camera equipment including (for example) a Sigma 8mm f/3.5 lens which allowed photographers to set their rotator heads to 90° and capture a complete virtual tour of any scene in just 4 shots (0°, 90°, 180°, 270°).

3.) Cubical stitching. This technique was one of the first forms of immersive, floor to ceiling virtual tours. Apple Computer pioneered this with the release of Apple's QuickTime VR in the early 1990s. Free utility software such as Cubic Converter and others allowed photographers to stitch and convert their panoramas into a "cube" like box to achieve a complete 360 X 360 view. Today, this technique is considered rather "old school," and spherical stitching has become more mainstream for producing these types of tours.

4) One-shot optics: Using one-shot panoramic optics one can create quick and easy panoramic videos and images such as the type used on the iPhone.

While programs such as Adobe Photoshop have new features that allow users to stitch images together, they only support "rectilinear" types of stitching. Photoshop cannot produce them as quickly or accurately as stitching software programs can such as Autodesk Stitcher. This is because there is sophisticated math and camera-lens profiles that are needed to create the desired panorama image which is based on your camera's depth of field (FOV) and the type of lens used. Cameras such as the Nikon D3 or D700 have a full frame digital SLR cameras, whereas the Nikon D90 or Canon T2i (Rebel line of Digital EOS cameras) have a smaller sensor. When full frame digital SLR cameras are used with a fish eye lens such as a Sigma 8mm F/3.5, a full circular image is captured. This allows you to shoot 2 or 3 shots per view to create a 360 X 360 stitched panoramic image. When used with a non full frame digital SLR camera like the Nikon

D90 or Canon digital Rebel and similar cameras, 4-shots are required with the camera in the portrait position. The resulting image will have the left and right sides cropped off each of the 4 images and each of the four corners, creating a rounded image.

Video-based Virtual Tours

With the expansion of video on the internet, video-based virtual tours are growing in popularity. Video cameras are used to pan and walk-through real subject properties. The benefit of this method is that the point of view is constantly changing throughout a pan. However, capturing high-quality video requires significantly more technical skill and equipment than taking digital still pictures. Video also eliminates viewer control of the tour. Therefore, the tour is the same for all viewers and subject matter is chosen by the videographer. Editing digital video requires proficiency with video editing software and has higher computer hardware requirements. Also, displaying video over the internet requires more bandwidth. Due to these difficulties, the task of creating video-based tours is often left to professionals.

Recently different groups have been using Google's system to provide access to private areas, which were previously unavailable to the general public.

Specialized Software

Various software products can be used to create media rich virtual tours, and some examples include methods developed by MOVES Institute at the Naval Postgraduate School. Additionally web-based software allows users to upload any JPEG spherical image or cylindrical image and create HD (High Definition) virtual tours.

Applications

Virtual tours are used extensively for universities and in the real estate industry. Virtual tours can allow a user to view an environment while on-line. Currently a variety of industries use such technology to help market their services and product. Over the last few years the quality and accessibility of virtual tours has improved considerably, with some websites allowing the user to navigate the tours by clicking on maps or integrated floor plans.

Web-based or Online

For most business purposes, a virtual tour must be accessible from everywhere. The major solution is a web-based virtual tour. In addition, a rich and useful virtual tour is not just a series of panoramic pictures. A better experience can be obtained by viewing a variety of materials such as that obtained from videos, texts, and still pictures in an interactive web content. There are many ways to gather data in a mixed web content, such as using rich content builders (Java applet or Adobe Flash being two examples) or a Web content management system.

Flash-based tours are becoming very popular today. A study done by the PEW Research Group showed that more than 5 million Americans watched virtual tours every day in 2004. PEW's research data which showed that Americans watching virtual tours rose from 54 million people in 2004 to 72 million people by August 2006, a two-year increase of 18 million.

Thanks in part to the recent explosion of many Internet devices, such as Apple's iPad, iPhone and other tablet computing platforms powered entirely by Google's Android 3 operating systems such as Motorola's Xoom, it can be predicted that consumption of virtual tour content, through the use of Adobe Flash and HTML5/CSS3 driven virtual tours will only increase over time.

Real Estate

Virtual tours are very popular in the real estate industry. Several types of such tours exist, including simple options such as interactive floor plans, and more sophisticated options such as full-service virtual tours. An interactive floor plan shows photographs of a property with the aid of a floor plan and arrows to indicate where each photograph was taken. Clicking on arrows shows the user where the camera was and which way the camera was pointing. Full service virtual tours are usually created by a professional photographer who will visit the property being sold, take several photos, and run them through stitching software. Matterport offers 3D camera services to create virtual tours. Full service virtual tours are usually more expensive than interactive floor plans because of the expense of the photographer, higher-end equipment used, such as a digital SLR camera, and specialized software. Real estate virtual tours are typically linked to the listing in the Multiple Listing Service.

Floored and Archilogic are two startups that offer the possibility of uploading a floor plan and turn it into a 3D model with proprietary algorithms. This allows potential homeowners to take a virtual tour of a home has not been built yet with a VR headset.

Virtual Walks

Virtual walk videos are documentary motion pictures shot as the camera continuously moves forward through an urban or natural area. The effect is to allow viewers to experience the sights they would see and the sounds they would hear were they actually traveling along a particular route at the same pace as the camera. Virtual walks based on real-world photography typically do not require the use of virtual reality goggles or headsets of the kind used by gamers.

Virtual Walks vs. Conventional Travel Videos

In realistically simulating the experience of moving through space, virtual walks—or virtual runs or bicycle rides—differ from conventional travel videos, which typically consist of a sequence of mostly static camera setups along a particular route or within a given area. The advantage of the conventional travel video is that one or more narrators or on-screen guides can provide insights into the geographical, historical, political, military, cultural, geological, or architectural aspects of the area. In terms of places visited, such a video will show the viewer sites A, D, G, and I. In comparison, the virtual walk will transport the viewer in continuous steps from site A to site B, from site D to site E, and so on. What the virtual walk video lacks in depth of coverage provided by a knowledgeable guide, it therefore makes up in sensory immediacy, as the viewer has the sensation of constantly moving forward. Many viewers of virtual walk videos report an immersive visual experience that they declare is the next-best thing to "being there."

Virtual walks appeal to those who want to experience the sights and sounds of particular places in the country or the world but who may not have the time or the financial or physical resources to actually travel there. They also appeal to treadmill or elliptical trainer users, for whom walking or running while watching these videos enhances the reality of the experience (and, at a minimum, reduce the boredom of the exercise).

DVD and Online Walks

A number of companies sell or rent virtual walk videos on DVDs or as downloads. An even greater variety of virtual walks is available online, mainly via YouTube. Typing the name of almost any major city plus "walk," "walking" or "virtual walk" will yield a multitude of results, though many of these videos, shot without the use of a Steadicam, are difficult to watch, due to the constant up and down motion of the image. (Exceptions include "Walking in Camden, London," "Paris, France: A Walking Travel Tour," and "Walking in Beijing Old Town.") The Dutch photographer and videographer Colijn Kees has produced hundreds of virtual walks, all shot with a Steadicam and high definition camera. Many of these virtual walks focus on cities of the Far East and central Asia, though a fair number are set in Russian and European cities, particularly Amsterdam.

Virtual Walk Techniques in Fiction Films

Some feature-length narrative motion pictures have made use of the virtual walk technique for dramatic purposes. These include the opening sequences of Orson Welles' *A Touch of Evil* and Robert Altman's *The Player*, the famous tracking shot through the Copacabana in Martin Scorcese's *Goodfellas*, Alexander Sokurov's *Russian Ark* (which consists of a single 96-minute Steadicam take), and, more recently Alfonso Cuarón's long tracking shots in *Gravity*, and almost the entire narrative structure of Alejandro Gonzáles Iñárrito's *Birdman*.

Google Street View

Google Street View is a technology featured in Google Maps and Google Earth that provides panoramic views from positions along many streets in the world. It was launched in 2007 in several cities in the United States, and has since expanded to include cities and rural areas worldwide. Streets with Street View imagery available are shown as blue lines on Google Maps.

Google Street View displays panoramas of stitched images. Most photography is done by car, but some is done by trekker, tricycle, walking, boat, snowmobile, and underwater apparatus.

History and Features

Street View had its inception in 2001 with The Stanford CityBlock Project, a Google-sponsored Stanford University research project. The project ended in June 2006, and its technology was folded into StreetView.

- 2007: Launched on 25 May in the United States using Immersive Media technology.

- 2008: In May Google announces that it was testing face-blurring technology on its photos of the busy streets of Manhattan. The technology uses a computer algorithm to search Google's image database for faces and blurs them. Street View integrated into Google Earth 4.3, the Maps application on the Apple iPhone, and the Maps application for S60 3rd Edition. In November, the drag and drop Pegman icon is introduced as the primary user interface element for connecting from Maps's 2D view into Street View's 3D view. When Pegman is dropped onto a particular set of coordinates in Google Maps for which Street View data is available, Street View opens and takes over the whole map window.

- 2009: Introduction of full-screen option. Smart Navigation introduced allowing users to navigate around the panoramas by double-clicking with their cursor on any place or object they want to see.

- 2010: Indoor views of businesses available. Google invites users to contribute panoramas of their own using gadgets with Android 4.2. Google highlights user-contributed panoramas with blue circle icons on Maps. The company also created a website to highlight places in the world where one can find them.

- 2013: Business interior views are shown as small orange circles. Businesses such as shops, cafés and other premises can pay a photographer to take panoramic images of the interior of their premises which are then included in Street View. Google sets up program to let third parties borrow the Street View Trekker (a backpack mounted camera) and contribute imagery to Google Maps.

- 2014: Street-level imagery from the past can now be seen, if available for a given street view.

- 2015: A partnership was announced between Street View and the environmental monitoring company Aclima. Cars began carrying sensors to detect pollutants such as nitrogen dioxide, ozone, and particulate matter. In October, support for Google Cardboard was announced allowing users to explore street view in 360 degree virtual reality.

Implementation

Street View is available as a component of Google Maps, as a web application, and as a mobile application for Android and iOS. Originally, Google Maps used Adobe Flash for Street View. Google overhauled Google Maps in 2013. The newer version uses JavaScript extensively and has a JavaScript application programming interface. The new Google Maps and Street View are slower than the old version. A user can switch to the old version of Google Maps, which is especially useful when Google Maps is more sluggish than usual.

Data Capturing Equipment

Taken in Oct 2010, a Google Maps Camera Car showcased on Google campus in Mountain View, California

A Google car takes a selfie in a street mirror in Nagiso, Nagano, Japan

- Cameras: Street View imagery has come from several generations of camera systems developed in-house. The cameras contain no mechanical parts, including the shutter, instead using CMOS sensors and an electronic rolling shutter. Widely deployed versions are:

   o R2: the earliest photos were captured with a ring of eight 11-megapixel CCD sensors with commercial photographic wide-angle lenses.

- o R5: uses a ring of eight 5-megapixel CMOS sensors with custom low-flare lenses, plus a fisheye lens on top to capture upper levels of buildings.

- o R7: uses 15 of the same sensors and lenses as R5, but no fish-eye.

- Positioning: recorded photographs must be associated with accurate positioning. This is done via a Global Positioning System, wheel speed sensor, and inertial navigation sensor data.

- Laser range scanners from Sick AG for the measuring of up to 50 meters 180° in the front of the vehicle. These are used for recording the actual dimensions of the space being photographed.

- Vehicles: data recording equipment is usually mounted on the roof of a car. A Trike (tricycle) was developed to record pedestrian routes including Stonehenge, and other UNESCO World Heritage sites. In 2010 a snowmobile-based system captured the 2010 Winter Olympics sites. Trolleys have been used to shoot the insides of museums, and in Venice the narrow roads were photographed with backpack-mounted cameras, and canals were photographed from boats.

Pegman

As noted above, the drag-and-drop Pegman icon is the primary user interface element used by Google to connect Maps to Street View. His name comes from his resemblance to a clothespeg. When not in use, Pegman sits atop the Google Maps zoom controls. Occasionally Pegman "dresses up" for special events or is joined by peg friends in Google Maps. When dragged into Street View near Area 51, he becomes a flying saucer. When viewing older views, the Pegman in the minimap changes to Doc Brown from *Back to the Future*.

Pegman has occasionally appeared as a costumed character at Google events, such as the launch of Street View in France in 2008.

Privacy Concerns

Google Street View will blur houses for any user who makes a request, in addition to the automatic blurring of faces and licence plates. Privacy advocates have objected to the Google Street View, pointing to views found to show men leaving strip clubs, protesters at an abortion clinic, sunbathers in bikinis, and people engaging in activities visible from public property in which they do not wish to be seen publicly. Another concern is the height of the cameras, and in at least two countries, Japan and Switzerland, Google has had to lower the height of its cameras so as to not peer over fences and hedges. The service also allows users themselves to flag inappropriate or sensitive imagery for Google to review and remove. Police Scotland received an apology for wasting police time in

2014 from a local business owner in Edinburgh who in 2012 had staged a fake murder for the Google camera car by lying in the road "while his colleague stood over him with a pickaxe handle". In May 2010, it was revealed that Google had collected and stored payload data from unencrypted Wi-Fi connections as part of Street View. German authorities are considering legal action while the Foreign Minister said "I will do all I can to prevent it." Australian police have also been ordered to investigate.

The concerns have led to Google not providing or suspending the service in countries around the world.

- Austria: Google Street View was banned in Austria because Google was found to collect Wifi data unauthorized in 2010. After the ban was lifted rules were set up for how Street View can operate legally in Austria. Google has yet to resume service. Officially it welcomed the new guidelines but has ruled out operating under them. As of 2016 Google Street View is still unavailable.

- Australia: In 2010, Google Street View ceased operations in Australia, following months of investigations from Australian authorities. However, this cessation has since ended, with Google announcing plans to continue production on May 4, 2011 and subsequently releasing updated Street View imagery for Australian towns and cities on July 27, 2011.

- Germany: In 2011, Google stopped taking Street View images in Germany.

- India: In 2011, Google stopped taking street images in India, after receiving a letter from the local authorities.

- Canada: Street View cars had been spotted as early as September 2007, in Montréal, though service for Canada was delayed while attempting to settle with the Canadian government over its privacy laws.

Third-party Use of Images

Fine-art photographers have selected images for use in their own work. Although the images may be pixelated, the colours muddy, and the perspective warped, the photographs have been published in book form and exhibited in art galleries, such as the work of Jon Rafman at the Saatchi Gallery, London.

In his personal appreciation of Street View material, Rafman sees images which evoke the "gritty urban life" depicted in American street photography and the images commissioned by the Farm Security Administration. He also invokes the "decisive moment" esthetic of Henri Cartier-Bresson "as if I were a photojournalist responding instantaneously to an emerging event".

Michael Wolf won an honourable mention in Daily Life in the 2011 World Press Photo competition for some of his work using Google Street View.

Mishka Henner was short-listed for the 2013 Deutsche Börse Photography Prize in November 2012 for his series 'No Man's Land', which depicts sex workers at rural roadside locations.

Swedish programmer Anton Wallén developed a game called GeoGuessr, which places players into a Google Street View and has them guess its location.

Coverage

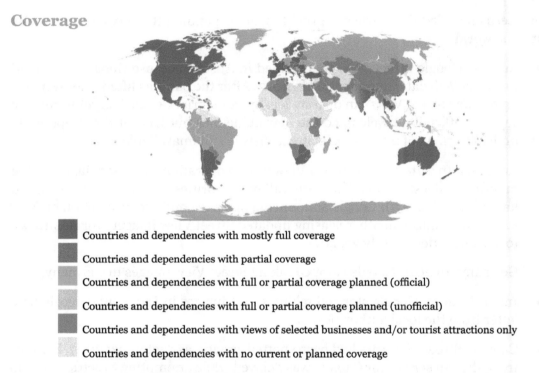

■ Countries and dependencies with mostly full coverage

■ Countries and dependencies with partial coverage

■ Countries and dependencies with full or partial coverage planned (official)

■ Countries and dependencies with full or partial coverage planned (unofficial)

■ Countries and dependencies with views of selected businesses and/or tourist attractions only

■ Countries and dependencies with no current or planned coverage

In June 2012, Google announced that it has captured 20 petabytes of data for Street View, comprising photos taken along 5 million miles of roads, covering 39 countries and about 3,000 cities. Coverage includes much of North and South America, from Cambridge Bay, Nunavut to Half Moon Island in the South Shetland Islands. Maps also include panoramic views taken under water such as in West Nusa Tenggara underwater coral, in the Grand Canyon, inside museums, and Liwa Desert in United Arab Emirates which are viewed from camelback. In a ten-day trek with Apa Sherpa, Google documented Khumbu, Nepal with its Mount Everest, Sherpa communities, monasteries and schools.

Google also added landmarks in Egypt, including the Pyramids of Giza, Cairo Citadel, Saqqara, Monastery of Saint Mina, and the Citadel of Qaitbay in the 9 September 2014 release.

Many places still have limited or no coverage, including:

- The Caribbean except limited coverage in the United States Virgin Islands, and some touristic places in Martinique: Boucle d'Absalon, Habitation Clément and the south-western coast of Sainte-Anne

- Central America

- French Guiana, Guyana, Paraguay, Suriname and Venezuela in South America

- Africa except Botswana, Lesotho, South Africa, Swaziland, Uganda and some city views in Madagascar

- Albania, Austria, Belarus, Bosnia and Herzegovina, Kosovo, Liechtenstein, Malta, Moldova, Montenegro and much of Germany in Europe

- Asia except Bangladesh, Bhutan, Cambodia, Hong Kong, Japan, Macau, Malaysia, Singapore, Sri Lanka, Taiwan, Thailand, much of Indonesia, Kyrgyzstan, Laos, Mongolia, Philippines, Russia and some locations in South Korea (such as Seoul and Busan)

- The Middle East except Israel, Palestine, Turkey and the United Arab Emirates

- The South Pacific, except American Samoa, Australia and New Zealand

References

- Wenkart, Michael (2014-04-10). You are the target !: Or do you believe your government is always watching the others?. BoD – Books on Demand. p. 171. ISBN 9783735793553. Retrieved 2014-12-28.

- Peter John Davison. "A summary of studies conducted on the effect of motion in flight simulator pilot training" (PDF). MPL Simulator Solutions. Retrieved September 18, 2016.

- Menegus, Bryan (11 March 2016). "The New VR Coaster at Six Flags Is the Future of Vomiting". Gizmodo. Retrieved 12 July 2016.

- MacDonald, Brady (17 September 2015). "Get ready for virtual reality coasters to become a real-world reality". La Times. Retrieved 12 July 2016.

- Clark, Kristen (23 March 2016). "Virtual Reality Roller Coasters Are Here (and Everywhere)". IEEE Spectrum. Retrieved 12 July 2016.

- Pappas, Stephanie (20 April 2016). "Why Does Virtual Reality Make Some People Sick?". Live Science. Retrieved 18 June 2016.

- Janssen, Jan-Keno (18 September 2015). "Ausprobiert: Mit VR-Brille auf dem Kopf Achterbahn fahren". c´t. Retrieved 12 June 2016.

- Sheikh, Knvul (1 April 2016). "Are You Ready for America's 1st Virtual-Reality Roller Coasters?". Live Science. Retrieved 12 July 2016.

- Clark, Patrick (24 May 2016). "Six Flags reinvents older roller coaster with new VR technology". FOX 2. Retrieved 12 July 2016.

- Wesley, Yiin (10 June 2016). "Virtual reality is revolutionizing the roller coaster experience". Washington Post. Retrieved 18 June 2016.

- Popper, Ben (15 June 2016). "Adding virtual reality to a roller coaster sounds dumb, but works amazingly well". The Verge. Retrieved 18 June 2016.

- MacDonald, Brady (15 December 2015). "Virtual reality rides set to invade theme parks in 2016". La Times. Retrieved 18 June 2016.

- Anstey, Tom (15 January 2016). "Universal debuts company's first VR coaster at Japanese park". Attractions Management. Retrieved 18 June 2016.

- "Superman The Ride VR Coaster Media Day Six Flags New England". Theme Park Review. 11 June 2016. Retrieved 18 June 2016.

- Nalawadi, Shailesh (2012-09-18). "An easier way to find panoramic interior imagery in Google Maps". Google-latlong.blogspot.co.il. Retrieved 2013-12-23.

- McCracken, Harry (April 11, 2011). "Alas, There Will Be No More Google Street View in Germany". Techland.time.com. Retrieved December 16, 2011.

- "India IT hub orders Google to suspend Street View service – International Business Times". Hken.ibtimes.com. June 21, 2011. Retrieved December 16, 2011.

- Fly Away Simulation (12 July 2010). "Flight Simulator Technology Through the Years". Archived from the original on 12 October 2011. Retrieved 20 April 2011.

6

An Integrated Study of Computer-Mediated Reality

The reality created by the ability to add, subtract and/or manipulate a person's perception through the use of technology like wearable computer or handheld devices like smartphones is known as computer-mediated reality. The chapter aids the reader in understanding the concepts of mixed reality, simulated reality, extended reality, augmented reality and computer-mediated reality with clarity.

Computer-Mediated Reality

Computer-mediated reality refers to the ability to add to, subtract information from, or otherwise manipulate one's perception of reality through the use of a wearable computer or hand-held device such as a smartphone.

Art installation illustrating the mediated reality concept. First we display what's really there, and then this allows a computer to be inserted into the "reality stream" to modify it.

Typically, it is the user's *visual* perception of the environment that is mediated. This is done through the use of some kind of electronic device, such as an EyeTap device or smart phone, which can act as a visual filter between the real world and what the user perceives.

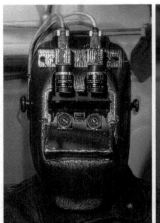

MannGlas welding helmet ("Digital Eye Glass") implements HDR (High dynamic Range) Imaging to augment the image in dark areas and diminish it in bright areas, thus implementing.

Mediated Reality application running on Apple iPhone

Computer-mediated reality has been used to enhance visual perception as an aid to the visually impaired. This example achieves a mediated reality by altering a video input stream light that would have normally reached the user's eyes, and computationally altering it to filter it into a more useful form.

It has also been used for interactive computer interfaces.

The use of computer-mediated reality to *diminish* perception, by the removal or masking of visual data, has been used for architectural applications, and is an area of ongoing research.

The long-term effects of altering perceived reality have not been thoroughly studied, and negative side effects of long-term exposure might be possible.

As a Seeing Aid

In the 1970s and 1980s, Steve Mann introduced the Generation-1 and Generation-2 "Digital Eye Glass", initially as a vision aid to help people see better, as a welding helmet, and as a general-purpose seeing aid for everyday life as outlined in IEEE Technology & Society 31(3) and the supplemental material entitled "GlassEyes".

In this sense, mediated reality is a proper superset of mixed reality, augmented reality, and virtual reality, as it also includes, for example, diminished reality.

Window Managers

One common window manager in mediated reality is the "Reality Window Manager".

Wireless Mediated Reality

Bluetooth devices are often used with mediated reality.

With wireless communications, mediated reality can also become a communications medium among different communities.

With the use of EyeTap, such interaction is called *"seeing eye-to-eye"*.

Applications

Applications of mediated reality include devices that help people see better, as well as devices for gaming and equipment repair, telemedicine, remote expert advice interfaces, and wayfinding. Mediated reality is also used in robotics and drawing applications such as the "Loose and Sketchy" drawing package.

Related Concepts

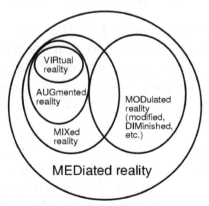

Mixed reality and augmented reality are special cases of mediated reality

Mediated reality is related to other concepts such as augmented reality (which is a special case of mediated reality), virtual reality, etc.

Mixed Reality

Mixed reality (MR), sometimes referred to as hybrid reality, is the merging of real and virtual worlds to produce new environments and visualizations where physical and digital objects co-exist and interact in real time. Mixed reality takes place not only in the physical world or the virtual world, but is a mix of reality and virtual reality, encompassing both augmented reality and augmented virtuality.

An Example Mixed Reality: Virtual characters mixed into a live video stream of the real world.

Definition

Virtuality continuum and mediality continuum

In 1994 Paul Milgram and Fumio Kishino defined a mixed reality as "...anywhere between the extrema of the *virtuality continuum*." (VC), where the virtuality continuum extends from the completely real through to the completely virtual environment with augmented reality and augmented virtuality ranging between.

This continuum is one of the two axes in Steve Mann's concept of mediated reality as implemented by various welding helmets and wearable computers and wearable photographic systems he created in the 1970s and early 1980s, the second axis being the *mediality continuum*, which includes, for example, Diminished Reality (as implemented in a welding helmet or eyeglasses that can block out advertising or replace real-world ads with useful information)

"The conventionally held view of a Virtual Reality (VR) environment is one in which the participant-observer is totally immersed in, and able to interact with, a completely synthetic world. Such a world may mimic the properties of some real-world environments, either existing or fictional; however, it can also exceed the bounds of physical reality by creating a world in which the physical laws ordinarily governing space, time, mechanics, material properties, etc. no longer hold. What may be overlooked in this view, however, is that the VR label is also frequently used in association with a variety of other environments, to which total immersion and complete synthesis do not necessarily pertain, but which fall somewhere along a virtuality continuum. In this paper we focus on a particular subclass of VR related technologies that involve the merging of real and virtual worlds, which we refer to generically as Mixed Reality (MR)."

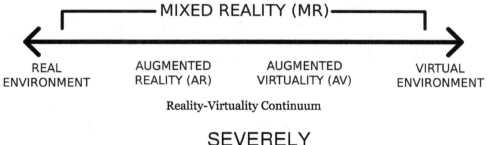

Reality-Virtuality Continuum

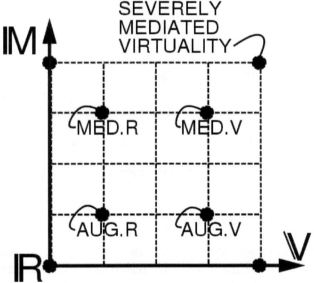

Virtuality axis (left-to-right) and mediality axis (bottom to top) of the mediated reality continuum. Here four example points are shown: augmented reality, augmented virtuality, mediated reality, and mediated virtuality on the virtuality and mediality axes. This includes, for example, diminished reality (e.g. computerized welding helmets that filter out and diminish certain parts of a scene)

Interreality Physics

In a physics context, the term "interreality system" refers to a virtual reality system coupled to its real-world counterpart. A paper in the May 2007 issue of Physical Review E describes an interreality system comprising a real physical pendulum coupled to a pendulum that only exists in virtual reality. This system apparently has two stable states of motion: a "Dual Reality" state in which the motion of the two pendula are uncorrelated and a "Mixed Reality" state in which the pendula exhibit stable phase-locked motion which is highly correlated. The use of the terms "mixed reality" and "interreality" in the context of physics is clearly defined but may be slightly different from in other fields.

Augmented Virtuality

Augmented virtuality (**AV**), is a subcategory of mixed reality which refers to the merging of real world objects into virtual worlds.

As an intermediate case in the virtuality continuum, it refers to predominantly virtual spaces, where physical elements, e.g. physical objects or people, are dynamically integrated into, and can interact with, the virtual world in real time. This integration is achieved with the use of various techniques. Often streaming video from physical spaces (e.g., via webcam) or using 3-dimensional digitalisation of physical objects.

The use of real-world sensor information (e.g., gyroscopes) to control a virtual environment is an additional form of augmented virtuality, in which external inputs provide context for the virtual view.

Applications

A topic of much research, MR has found its way into a number of applications, evident in the arts and entertainment industries. However, MR is also branching out into the business, manufacturing and education worlds with systems such as these:

- IPCM – Interactive Product Content Management

Moving from static product catalogs to interactive 3D smart digital replicas. Solution consists of application software products with scalable license model.

- SBL – Simulation Based Learning

Moving from e-learning to s-learning—state of the art in knowledge transfer for education. Simulation/VR based training, interactive experiential learning. Software and display solutions with scalable licensed curriculum development model.

- Military Training

Combat reality is simulated and represented in complex layered data through HMD.

- Real Asset Virtualization Environment (RAVE)

3D Models of Manufacturing Assets (for example process manufacturing machinery) are incorporated into a virtual environment and then linked to real-time data associated with that asset. Avatars allow for multidisciplinary collaboration and decision making based on the data presented in the virtual environment. This example of Mixed Reality was pioneered and demonstrated by Kevyn Renner of Chevron Corporation for which a United States Patent 8,589,809, B2 "Methods and Systems for Conducting a Meeting in a Virtual Environment" was granted November 19, 2013. One of the earliest patents describing mixed reality is shown by Michael DeLuca in United States Patent 6,064,354 "Stereoscopic user interface method and apparatus" granted May 16, 2000.

Display Technologies

Here are some more commonly used MR display technologies:

Cave Automatic Virtual Environment	Head-up display	Head-mounted display

Augmented Reality

Samsung SARI AR SDK markerless tracker used in the *AR EdiBear* game (Android OS)

AR Tower Defense game on the Nokia N95 smartphone (Symbian OS) uses fiducial markers

Augmented reality (AR) is a live direct or indirect view of a physical, real-world environment whose elements are *augmented* (or supplemented) by computer-generated sensory input such as sound, video, graphics or GPS data. It is related to a more general concept called mediated reality, in which a view of reality is modified (possibly even diminished rather than augmented) by a computer. As a result, the technology functions by enhancing one's current perception of reality. By contrast, virtual reality replaces the real world with a simulated one. Augmentation is conventionally in real-time and in semantic context with environmental elements, such as sports scores on TV during a match. With the help of advanced AR technology (e.g. adding computer vision and object recognition) the information about the surrounding real world of the user becomes interactive and digitally manipulable. Information about the environment and its objects is overlaid on the real world. This information can be virtual or real, e.g. seeing other real sensed or measured information such as electromagnetic radio waves overlaid in exact alignment with where they actually are in space.

Technology

Hardware

Hardware components for augmented reality are: processor, display, sensors and input devices. Modern mobile computing devices like smartphones and tablet computers contain these elements which often include a camera and MEMS sensors such as accelerometer, GPS, and solid state compass, making them suitable AR platforms.

Display

Various technologies are used in Augmented Reality rendering including optical projection systems, monitors, hand held devices, and display systems worn on the human body.

Head-mounted

A head-mounted display (HMD) is a display device paired to the forehead such as a harness or helmet. HMDs place images of both the physical world and virtual objects over the user's field of view. Modern HMDs often employ sensors for six degrees of freedom monitoring that allow the system to align virtual information to the physical world and adjust accordingly with the user's head movements. HMDs can provide users immersive, mobile and collaborative AR experiences.

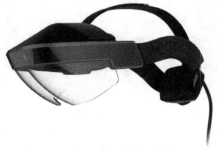

Meta 2 Headset

In January 2015, Meta launched a $1 project led by Horizons Ventures, Tim Draper, Alexis Ohanian, BOE Optoelectronics and Garry Tan. On February 17, 2016, Meta announced their second-generation product at TED, Meta 2. The Meta 2 head-mounted display headset uses a sensory array for hand interactions and positional tracking, visual field view of 90 degrees (diagonal), and resolution display of 2560 x 1440 (20 pixels per degree), which is considered the largest field view (FOV) currently available.

Eyeglasses

AR displays can be rendered on devices resembling eyeglasses. Versions include eyewear that employ cameras to intercept the real world view and re-display its augmented view through the eye pieces and devices in which the AR imagery is projected through or reflected off the surfaces of the eyewear lens pieces.

HUD

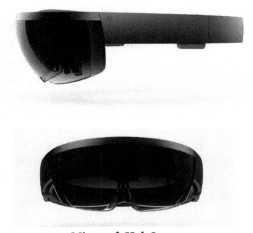

Microsoft HoloLens

Near eye augmented reality devices can be used as portable head-up displays as they can show data, information, and images while the user views the real world. Many definitions of augmented reality only define it as overlaying the information. This is basically what a head-up display does; however, practically speaking, augmented reality is expected to include tracking between the superimposed information, data, and images and some portion of the real world.

CrowdOptic, an existing app for smartphones, applies algorithms and triangulation techniques to photo metadata including GPS position, compass heading, and a time stamp to arrive at a relative significance value for photo objects. CrowdOptic technology can be used by Google Glass users to learn where to look at a given point in time.

In January 2015, Microsoft introduced HoloLens, which is an independent smartglasses unit. Brian Blau, Research Director of Consumer Technology and Markets at Gartner, said that "Out of all the head-mounted displays that I've tried in the past couple of decades, the HoloLens was the best in its class.". First impressions and opinions have been generally that HoloLens is a superior device to the Google Glass, and manages to do several things "right" in which Glass failed.

Contact Lenses

Contact lenses that display AR imaging are in development. These bionic contact lenses might contain the elements for display embedded into the lens including integrated circuitry, LEDs and an antenna for wireless communication. The first contact lens display was reported in 1999 and subsequently, 11 years later in 2010/2011 Another version of contact lenses, in development for the U.S. Military, is designed to function with AR spectacles, allowing soldiers to focus on close-to-the-eye AR images on the spectacles and distant real world objects at the same time. The futuristic short film *Sight* features contact lens-like augmented reality devices.

Virtual retinal Display

A virtual retinal display (VRD) is a personal display device under development at the University of Washington's Human Interface Technology Laboratory. With this technology, a display is scanned directly onto the retina of a viewer's eye. The viewer sees what appears to be a conventional display floating in space in front of them.

EyeTap

The EyeTap (also known as Generation-2 Glass) captures rays of light that would otherwise pass through the center of a lens of an eye of the wearer, and substitutes synthetic computer-controlled light for each ray of real light. The Generation-4 Glass (Laser EyeTap) is similar to the VRD (i.e. it uses a computer controlled laser light source) except that it also has infinite depth of focus and causes the eye itself to, in effect, function as both a camera and a display, by way of exact alignment with the eye, and resynthesis (in laser light) of rays of light entering the eye.

Handheld

Handheld displays employ a small display that fits in a user's hand. All handheld AR solutions to date opt for video see-through. Initially handheld AR employed fiducial markers, and later GPS units and MEMS sensors such as digital compasses and six degrees of freedom accelerometer–gyroscope. Today SLAM markerless trackers such as PTAM are starting to come into use. Handheld display AR promises to be the first commercial success for AR technologies. The two main advantages of handheld AR is the portable nature of handheld devices and ubiquitous nature of camera phones. The disadvantages are the physical constraints of the user having to hold the handheld device out in front of them at all times as well as distorting effect of classically wide-angled mobile phone cameras when compared to the real world as viewed through the eye.

Spatial

Spatial Augmented Reality (SAR) augments real world objects and scenes without the use of special displays such as monitors, head mounted displays or hand-held devices. SAR makes use of digital projectors to display graphical information onto physical objects. The key difference in SAR is that the display is separated from the users of the system. Because the displays are not associated with each user, SAR scales naturally up to groups of users, thus allowing for collocated collaboration between users.

Examples include shader lamps, mobile projectors, virtual tables, and smart projectors. Shader lamps mimic and augment reality by projecting imagery onto neutral objects, providing the opportunity to enhance the object's appearance with materials of a simple unit- a projector, camera, and sensor.

Other applications include table and wall projections. One innovation, the Extended Virtual Table, separates the virtual from the real by including beam-splitter mirrors attached to the ceiling at an adjustable angle. Virtual showcases, which employ beam-splitter mirrors together with multiple graphics displays, provide an interactive means of simultaneously engaging with the virtual and the real. Many more implementations and configurations make spatial augmented reality display an increasingly attractive interactive alternative.

A SAR system can display on any number of surfaces of an indoor setting at once. SAR supports both a graphical visualisation and passive haptic sensation for the end users. Users are able to touch physical objects in a process that provides passive haptic sensation.

Tracking

Modern mobile augmented-reality systems use one or more of the following tracking technologies: digital cameras and/or other optical sensors, accelerometers, GPS, gyroscopes, solid state compasses, RFID and wireless sensors. These technologies offer varying levels of accuracy and precision. Most important is the position and orientation of the user's head. Tracking the user's hand(s) or a handheld input device can provide a 6DOF interaction technique.

Input Devices

Techniques include speech recognition systems that translate a user's spoken words into computer instructions and gesture recognition systems that can interpret a user's body movements by visual detection or from sensors embedded in a peripheral device such as a wand, stylus, pointer, glove or other body wear. Some of the products which are trying to serve as a controller of AR Headsets include Wave by Seebright Inc. and Nimble by Intugine Technologies.

Computer

The computer analyzes the sensed visual and other data to synthesize and position augmentations.

Software and Algorithms

A key measure of AR systems is how realistically they integrate augmentations with the real world. The software must derive real world coordinates, independent from the camera, from camera images. That process is called image registration which uses different methods of computer vision, mostly related to video tracking. Many computer vision methods of augmented reality are inherited from visual odometry. Usually those methods consist of two parts.

First detect interest points, or fiducial markers, or optical flow in the camera images. First stage can use feature detection methods like corner detection, blob detection, edge detection or thresholding and/or other image processing methods. The second stage restores a real world coordinate system from the data obtained in the first stage. Some methods assume objects with known geometry (or fiducial markers) present in the scene. In some of those cases the scene 3D structure should be precalculated beforehand. If part of the scene is unknown simultaneous localization and mapping (SLAM) can map relative positions. If no information about scene geometry is available, structure from motion methods like bundle adjustment are used. Mathematical methods used in the second stage include projective (epipolar) geometry, geometric algebra, rotation representation with exponential map, kalman and particle filters, nonlinear optimization, robust statistics.

Augmented Reality Markup Language (ARML) is a data standard developed within the Open Geospatial Consortium (OGC), which consists of an XML grammar to describe the location and appearance of virtual objects in the scene, as well as ECMAScript bindings to allow dynamic access to properties of virtual objects.

To enable rapid development of Augmented Reality Application, some software development kits (SDK) have emerged. A few SDK such as CloudRidAR leverage cloud computing for performance improvement. Some of the well known AR SDKs are offered by Vuforia, ARToolKit, Catchoom CraftAR, Mobinett AR, Wikitude, Blippar Layar, and Meta.

Applications

Augmented reality has many applications. First used for military, industrial, and medical applications, it has also been applied to commercial and entertainment areas.

Literature

In 2011, there were works using AR poetry made by ni_ka from the Sekai Camera in Japan, Tokyo. The rose of these works come from Paul Celan, "Die Niemandsrose", and express the mourning of 3.11, 2011 Tōhoku earthquake and tsunami.

Archaeology

AR can be used to aid archaeological research, by augmenting archaeological features onto the modern landscape, enabling archaeologists to formulate conclusions about site placement and configuration.

Another application given to AR in this field is the possibility for users to rebuild ruins, buildings, landscapes or even ancient characters as they formerly existed.

Architecture

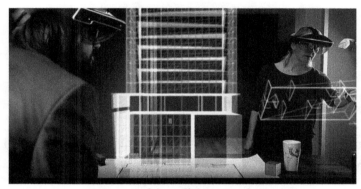
Meta 2 used for collaborative design

AR can aid in visualizing building projects. Computer-generated images of a structure can be superimposed into a real life local view of a property before the physical building is constructed there; this was demonstrated publicly by Trimble Navigation in 2004. AR can also be employed within an architect's work space, rendering into their view animated 3D visualizations of their 2D drawings. Architecture sight-seeing can be enhanced with AR applications allowing users viewing a building's exterior to virtually see through its walls, viewing its interior objects and layout.

Visual Art

AR technology has helped disabled individuals create visual art by using eye tracking to translate a user's eye movements into drawings on a screen. An item such as a commemorative coin can be designed so that when scanned by an AR-enabled device it displays additional objects and layers of information that were not visible in a real world view of it. In 2013, L'Oreal used CrowdOptic technology to create an augmented reality at the seventh annual Luminato Festival in Toronto, Canada.

AR in visual art opens the possibility of multidimensional experiences and interpretations of reality. Augmenting people, objects, and landscapes is becoming an art form in itself. In 2011, artist Amir Bardaran's *Frenchising the Mona Lisa* infiltrates Da Vinci's painting using an AR mobile application called Junaio. Aim a Junaio loaded smartphone camera at any image of the Mona Lisa and watch as Leonardo's subject places a scarf made of a French flag around her head. The AR app allows the user to train his or her smartphone on Da Vinci's *Mona Lisa* and watch the mysterious Italian lady loosen her hair and wrap a French flag around her in the form a (currently banned) Islamic *hijab*.

iGreet's augmented reality greeting card suddenly becomes alive and hidden digital content appears when being viewed through the app.

Greeting Cards

AR technology has been used in conjunction with greeting cards. They can be implemented with digital content which users are able to discover by viewing the illustrations with certain mobile applications or devices using augmented reality technology. The digital content could be 2D & 3D animations, standard video and 3D objects with which the users can interact.

In 2015, the Bulgarian startup iGreet developed its own AR technology and used it to make the first premade "live" greeting card. It looks like traditional paper card, but contains hidden digital content which only appears when users scan the greeting card with the iGreet app.

Commerce

View Description image 1

AR can enhance product previews such as allowing a customer to view what's inside a product's packaging without opening it. AR can also be used as an aid in selecting products from a catalog or through a kiosk. Scanned images of products can activate views of additional content such as customization options and additional images of the product in its use. AR is used to integrate print and video marketing. Printed marketing material can be designed with certain "trigger" images that, when scanned by an AR enabled device using image recognition, activate a video version of the promotional material. A major difference between Augmented Reality and straight forward image recognition is that you can overlay multiple media at the same time in the view screen, such as social media share buttons, in-page video even audio and 3D objects. Traditional print only publications are using Augmented Reality to connect many different types of media.

Construction

With the continual improvements to GPS accuracy, businesses are able to use augmented reality to visualize georeferenced models of construction sites, underground structures, cables and pipes using mobile devices. Augmented reality is applied to present new projects, to solve on-site construction challenges, and to enhance promotional materials. Examples include the Daqri Smart Helmet, an Android-powered hard hat used to create augmented reality for the industrial worker, including visual instructions, real time alerts, and 3D mapping.

Following the Christchurch earthquake, the University of Canterbury released, CityViewAR, which enabled city planners and engineers to visualize buildings that were destroyed in the earthquake. Not only did this provide planners with tools to reference the previous cityscape, but it also served as a reminder to the magnitude of the devastation caused, as entire buildings were demolished.

Education

Augmented reality applications can complement a standard curriculum. Text, graphics, video and audio can be superimposed into a student's real time environment. Textbooks, flashcards and other educational reading material can contain embedded "markers" that, when scanned by an AR device, produce supplementary information to the student rendered in a multimedia format. Students can participate interactively with computer generated simulations of historical events, exploring and learning details of each significant area of the event site. On higher education, there are some applications that can be used. For instance, Construct3D, a Studierstube system, allows students to learn mechanical engineering concepts, math or geometry. This is an active learning process in which students learn to learn with technology. AR can aid students in understanding chemistry by allowing them to visualize the spatial structure of a molecule and interact with a virtual model of it that appears, in a camera image, positioned at a marker held in their hand. It can also enable students of physiology to visualize different systems of the human body in three dimensions. Augmented reality technology also permits learning via remote collaboration, in which students and instructors not at the same physical location can share a common virtual learning environment populated by virtual objects and learning materials and interact with another within that setting.

App iSkull, an augmented human skull for education (iOS OS)

App iWow, a mobile device based augmented reality enhanced world globe

This resource could also be of advantage in Primary School. Children can learn through experiences, and visuals can be used to help them learn. For instance, they can learn new knowledge about astronomy, which can be difficult to understand, and children might better understand the solar system when using AR devices and being able to see it in 3D. Further, learners could change the illustrations in their science books by using this resource. For teaching anatomy, teachers could visualize bones and organs using augmented reality to display them on the body of a person.

Mobile apps using augmented reality are emerging in the classroom. The mix of real life and virtual reality displayed by the apps using the mobile phone's camera allows information to be manipulated and seen like never before. Many such apps have been designed to create a highly engaging environment and transform the learning experience. Examples of the mobile apps, that leverage augmented reality to aid learning, include SkyView for studying astronomy and AR Circuits for building simple electric circuits.

Emergency Management/Search and Rescue

Augmented reality systems are used in public safety situations – from super storms to suspects at large. Two interesting articles from *Emergency Management* magazine discuss the power of the technology for emergency management. The first is "Augmented Reality--Emerging Technology for Emergency Management" by Gerald Baron. Per Adam Crowe: "Technologies like augmented reality (ex: Google Glass) and the growing expectation of the public will continue to force professional emergency managers to radically shift when, where, and how technology is deployed before, during, and after disasters."

LandForm+ is a geographic augmented reality system used for search and rescue, and emergency management.

Another example, a search aircraft is looking for a lost hiker in rugged mountain terrain. Augmented reality systems provide aerial camera operators with a geographic awareness of forest road names and locations blended with the camera video. As a result, the camera operator is better able to search for the hiker knowing the geographic context of the camera image. Once found, the operator can more efficiently direct rescuers to the hiker's location.

Everyday

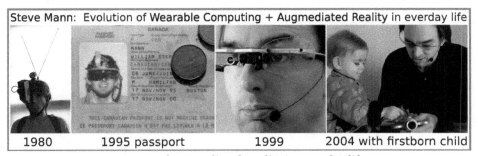

30 years of Augmediated Reality in everyday life.

Since the 1970s and early 1980s, Steve Mann has been developing technologies meant for everyday use i.e. "horizontal" across all applications rather than a specific "vertical" market. Examples include Mann's "EyeTap Digital Eye Glass", a general-purpose seeing aid that does dynamic-range management (HDR vision) and overlays, underlays, simultaneous augmentation and diminishment (e.g. diminishing the electric arc while looking at a welding torch).

Video Games

Lyteshot in action

Merchlar's mobile game *Get On Target* uses a trigger image as fiducial marker

Augmented reality allows video game players to experience digital game play in a real world environment. Companies and platforms like Niantic and LyteShot emerged as augmented reality gaming creators. Niantic is notable for releasing the record-breaking *Pokémon Go* game.

Industrial Design

AR can help industrial designers experience a product's design and operation before completion. Volkswagen uses AR for comparing calculated and actual crash test imagery. AR can be used to visualize and modify a car body structure and engine layout. AR can also be used to compare digital mock-ups with physical mock-ups for finding discrepancies between them.

Medical

Since 2005, a device that films subcutaneous veins, processes and projects the image of the veins onto the skin has been used to locate veins. This device is called a near-infrared vein finder.

Augmented Reality can provide the surgeon with information, which are otherwise hidden, such as showing the heartbeat rate, the blood pressure, the state of the patient's organ, etc. AR can be used to let a doctor look inside a patient by combining one source of images such as an X-ray with another such as video.

Examples include a virtual X-ray view based on prior tomography or on real time images from ultrasound and confocal microscopy probes, visualizing the position of a tumor in the video of an endoscope, or radiation exposure risks from X-ray imaging devices. AR can enhance viewing a fetus inside a mother's womb. It has been also used for cockroach phobia treatment. Also, patients wearing augmented reality glasses can be reminded to take medications.

Beauty

In 2014 the company L'Oreal Paris started developing a smartphone and tablet application called "Makeup Genius", which lets users try out make-up and beauty styles utilizing the front-facing camera of the endpoint and its display.

Spatial Immersion and Interaction

Augmented reality applications, running on handheld devices utilized as virtual reality headsets, can also digitalize human presence in space and provide a computer generated model of them, in a virtual space where they can interact and perform various actions. Such capabilities are demonstrated by "Project Anywhere" developed by a postgraduate student at ETH Zurich, which was dubbed as an "out-of-body experience".

Military

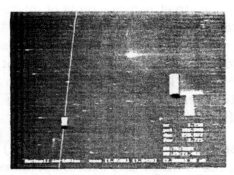

Rockwell WorldView Console showing space surveillance telescope video map overlay of satellite flight tracks from a 1993 paper.

In combat, AR can serve as a networked communication system that renders useful battlefield data onto a soldier's goggles in real time. From the soldier's viewpoint, people and various objects can be marked with special indicators to warn of potential dangers. Virtual maps and 360° view camera imaging can also be rendered to aid a soldier's navigation and battlefield perspective, and this can be transmitted to military leaders at a remote command center.

An interesting application of AR occurred when Rockwell International created video map overlays of satellite and orbital debris tracks to aid in space observations at Air Force Maui Optical System. In their 1993 paper "Debris Correlation Using the Rockwell WorldView System" the authors describe the use of map overlays applied to video from space surveillance telescopes. The map overlays indicated the trajectories of various objects in geographic coordinates. This allowed telescope operators to identify satellites, and also to identify – and catalog – potentially dangerous space debris.

Screen capture of SmartCam3D in picture in picture (PIP) mode. This helps sensor operators maintain a broader situation awareness than a telescopic camera "soda-straw". It was shown to essentially double the speed at which points can be located on the ground.

Starting in 2003 the US Army integrated the SmartCam3D augmented reality system into the Shadow Unmanned Aerial System to aid sensor operators using telescopic cameras to locate people or points of interest. The system combined both fixed geographic information including street names, points of interest, airports and railroads with live video from the camera system. The system offered "picture in picture" mode that allows the system to show a synthetic view of the area surrounding the camera's field of view. This helps solve a problem in which the field of view is so narrow that it excludes important context, as if "looking through a soda straw". The system displays real-time friend/foe/neutral location markers blended with live video, providing the operator with improved situation awareness.

Researchers at USAF Research Lab (Calhoun, Draper et al.) found an approximately two-fold increase in the speed at which UAV sensor operators found points of interest using this technology. This ability to maintain geographic awareness quantitatively enhances mission efficiency. The system is in use on the US Army RQ-7 Shadow and the MQ-1C Gray Eagle Unmanned Aerial Systems.

Navigation

LandForm video map overlay marking runways, road, and buildings during 1999 helicopter flight test.

AR can augment the effectiveness of navigation devices. Information can be displayed on an automobile's windshield indicating destination directions and meter, weather, terrain, road conditions and traffic information as well as alerts to potential hazards in their path. Aboard maritime vessels, AR can allow bridge watch-standers to continuously monitor important information such as a ship's heading and speed while moving throughout the bridge or performing other tasks.

The NASA X-38 was flown using a Hybrid Synthetic Vision system that overlaid map data on video to provide enhanced navigation for the spacecraft during flight tests from 1998 to 2002. It used the LandForm software and was useful for times of limited visibility, including an instance when the video camera window frosted over leaving astronauts to rely on the map overlays. The LandForm software was also test flown at the Army Yuma Proving Ground in 1999. In the photo at right one can see the map markers indicating runways, air traffic control tower, taxiways, and hangars overlaid on the video.

Office Workplace

AR can help facilitate collaboration among distributed team members in a work force via conferences with real and virtual participants. AR tasks can include brainstorming and discussion meetings utilizing common visualization via touch screen tables, interactive digital whiteboards, shared design spaces, and distributed control rooms.

Sports and Entertainment

AR has become common in sports telecasting. Sports and entertainment venues are provided with see-through and overlay augmentation through tracked camera feeds for enhanced viewing by the audience. Examples include the yellow "first down" line seen in television broadcasts of American football games showing the line the offensive team must cross to receive a first down. AR is also used in association with football and other sporting events to show commercial advertisements overlaid onto the view of the playing area. Sections of rugby fields and cricket pitches also display sponsored images. Swimming telecasts often add a line across the lanes to indicate the position of the current record holder as a race proceeds to allow viewers to compare the current race to the best performance. Other examples include hockey puck tracking and annotations of racing car performance and snooker ball trajectories.

AR can enhance concert and theater performances. For example, artists can allow listeners to augment their listening experience by adding their performance to that of other bands/groups of users.

The gaming industry has benefited a lot from the development of this technology. A number of games have been developed for prepared indoor environments. Early AR games also include AR air hockey, collaborative combat against virtual enemies, and an AR-enhanced pool games. A significant number of games incorporate AR in them and the introduction of the smartphone has made a bigger impact.

Task Support

Complex tasks such as assembly, maintenance, and surgery can be simplified by inserting additional information into the field of view. For example, labels can be displayed on parts of a system to clarify operating instructions for a mechanic who is performing maintenance on the system. Assembly lines gain many benefits from the usage of AR. In addition to Boeing, BMW and Volkswagen are known for incorporating this technology in their assembly line to improve their manufacturing and assembly processes. Big machines are difficult to maintain because of the multiple layers or structures they have. With the use of AR the workers can complete their job in a much easier way because AR permits them to look through the machine as if it was with x-ray, pointing them to the problem right away.

Television

Weather visualizations were the first application of augmented reality to television. It has now become common in weathercasting to display full motion video of images captured in real-time from multiple cameras and other imaging devices. Coupled with 3D graphics symbols and mapped to a common virtual geo-space model, these animated visualizations constitute the first true application of AR to TV.

Augmented reality has also become common in sports telecasting. Sports and entertainment venues are provided with see-through and overlay augmentation through tracked camera feeds for enhanced viewing by the audience. Examples include the yellow "first down" line seen in television broadcasts of American football games showing the line the offensive team must cross to receive a first down. AR is also used in association with football and other sporting events to show commercial advertisements overlaid onto the view of the playing area. Sections of rugby fields and cricket pitches also display sponsored images. Swimming telecasts often add a line across the lanes to indicate the position of the current record holder as a race proceeds to allow viewers to compare the current race to the best performance. Other examples include hockey puck tracking and annotations of racing car performance and snooker ball trajectories.

Augmented reality is starting to allow Next Generation TV viewers to interact with the programs they are watching. They can place objects into an existing program and interact with these objects, such as moving them around. Avatars of real persons in real time who are also watching the same program.

Tourism and Sightseeing

Augmented reality applications can enhance a user's experience when traveling by providing real time informational displays regarding a location and its features, including comments made by previous visitors of the site. AR applications allow tourists to experience simulations of historical events, places and objects by rendering them into their current view of a landscape. AR applications can also present location information by audio, announcing features of interest at a particular site as they become visible to the user.

Translation

AR systems can interpret foreign text on signs and menus and, in a user's augmented view, re-display the text in the user's language. Spoken words of a foreign language can be translated and displayed in a user's view as printed subtitles.

Marketing

Usage of AR is increasing in the field of Marketing.Games like POKEMON GO have helped businesses to increase the number of foot falls to their shop. For clothing, accessory, and makeup companies, AR presents a new way to show customers what it will be like to use or wear their products.Virtual dressing rooms are recent trends in e commerce.

Privacy Concerns

The concept of modern augmented reality depends on the ability of the device to record and analyze the environment in real time. Because of this, there are potential legal concerns over privacy. While the First Amendment to the United States Constitution allows for such recording in the name of public interest, the constant recording of an AR device makes it difficult to do so without also recording outside of the public domain. Legal complications would be found in areas where a right to certain amount of privacy is expected or where copyrighted media are displayed. In terms of individual privacy, there exists the ease of access to information that one should not readily possess about a given person. This is accomplished through facial recognition technology. Assuming that AR automatically passes information about persons that the user sees, there could be anything seen from social media, criminal record, and marital status.

Extended Reality

Extended reality (XR) is a term referring to all real-and-virtual combined environments and human-machine interactions generated by computer technology and wearables. It includes representative forms such as augmented reality (AR), augmented virtuality (AV) and virtual reality (VR), and the areas interpolated among them. The levels of virtuality range from partially sensory inputs to immersive virtuality, also called VR.

XR is a superset which includes the entire spectrum from "the complete real" to "the complete virtual" in the concept of reality–virtuality continuum introduced by Paul Milgram. Still, its connotation lies in the extension of human experiences especially relating to the senses of existence (represented by VR) and the acquisition of cognition (represented by AR). With the continuous development in human–computer interactions, this connotation is still evolving.

Simulated Reality

Simulated reality is the hypothesis that reality could be simulated—for example by computer simulation—to a degree indistinguishable from "true" reality. It could contain conscious minds which may or may not be fully aware that they are living inside a simulation. This is quite different from the current, technologically achievable concept of virtual reality. Virtual reality is easily distinguished from the experience of actuality; participants are never in doubt about the nature of what they experience. Simulated reality, by contrast, would be hard or impossible to separate from "true" reality. There has been much debate over this topic, ranging from philosophical discourse to practical applications in computing.

Types of Simulation

Brain-Computer Interface

In brain-computer interface simulations, each participant enters from outside, directly connecting their brain to the simulation computer. The computer transmits sensory data to the participant, reads and responds to their desires and actions in return; in this manner they interact with the simulated world and receive feedback from it. The participant may be induced by any number of possible means to forget, temporarily or otherwise, that they are inside a virtual realm (e.g. "passing through the veil", a term borrowed from Christian tradition, which describes the passage of a soul from an earthly body to an afterlife). While inside the simulation, the participant's consciousness is represented by an avatar, which can look very different from the participant's actual appearance.

Virtual People

In a virtual-people simulation, every inhabitant is a native of the simulated world. They do not have a "real" body in the external reality of the physical world. Instead, each is a fully simulated entity, possessing an appropriate level of consciousness that is implemented using the simulation's own logic (i.e. using its own physics). As such, they could be downloaded from one simulation to another, or even archived and resurrected at a later time. It is also possible that a simulated entity could be moved out of the simulation entirely by means of mind transfer into a synthetic body.

Arguments

Simulation Argument

The simulation hypothesis was first published by Hans Moravec. Later, the philosopher Nick Bostrom developed an expanded argument examining the probability of our reality being a simulacrum. His argument states that at least one of the following statements is very likely to be true:

1. Human civilization is unlikely to reach a level of technological maturity capable of producing simulated realities, or such simulations are physically impossible to construct.

2. A comparable civilization reaching aforementioned technological status will likely not produce a significant number of simulated realities (one that might push the probable existence of digital entities beyond the probable number of "real" entities in a Universe) for any of a number of reasons, such as, diversion of computational processing power for other tasks, ethical considerations of holding entities captive in simulated realities, etc.

3. Any entities with our general set of experiences are almost certainly living in a simulation.

In greater detail, Bostrom is attempting to prove a tripartite disjunction, that at least one of these propositions must be true. His argument rests on the premise that given sufficiently advanced technology, it is possible to represent the populated surface of the Earth without recourse to digital physics; that the qualia experienced by a simulated consciousness is comparable or equivalent to that of a naturally occurring human consciousness; and that one or more levels of simulation within simulations would be feasible given only a modest expenditure of computational resources in the real world.

If one assumes first that humans will not be destroyed nor destroy themselves before developing such a technology, and, next, that human descendants will have no overriding legal restrictions or moral compunctions against simulating biospheres or their own historical biosphere, then it would be unreasonable to count ourselves among the small minority of genuine organisms who, sooner or later, will be vastly outnumbered by artificial simulations.

Epistemologically, it is not impossible to tell whether we are living in a simulation. For example, Bostrom suggests that a window could *pop up* saying: "You are living in a simulation. Click here for more information." However, imperfections in a simulated environment might be difficult for the native inhabitants to identify, and for purposes of authenticity, even the simulated memory of a blatant revelation might be purged programmatically. Nonetheless, should any evidence come to light, either for or against the skeptical hypothesis, it would radically alter the aforementioned probability.

Computationalism

Computationalism is a philosophy of mind theory stating that cognition is a form of computation. It is relevant to the Simulation hypothesis in that it illustrates how a simulation could contain conscious subjects, as required by a "virtual people" simulation. For example, it is well known that physical systems can be simulated to some degree of accuracy. If computationalism is correct, and if there is no problem in generating artificial consciousness or cognition, it would establish the theoretical possibility of a simulated reality. However, the relationship between cognition and phenomenal qualia of consciousness is disputed. It is possible that consciousness requires a vital substrate that a computer cannot provide, and that simulated people, while behaving appropriately, would be philosophical zombies. This would undermine Nick Bostrom's simulation argument; we cannot be a simulated consciousness, if consciousness, as we know it, cannot be simulated. However, the skeptical hypothesis remains intact, we could still be envatted brains, existing as conscious beings within a simulated environment, even if consciousness cannot be simulated.

Some theorists have argued that if the "consciousness-is-computation" version of computationalism and mathematical realism (or radical mathematical Platonism) are true then consciousnesses is computation, which in principle is platform independent, and thus admits of simulation. This argument states that a "Platonic realm" or ultimate ensemble would contain every algorithm, including those which implement consciousness. Hans Moravec has explored the simulation hypothesis and has argued for a kind of mathematical Platonism according to which every object (including e.g. a stone) can be regarded as implementing every possible computation.

Dreaming

A dream could be considered a type of simulation capable of fooling someone who is asleep. As a result, the "dream hypothesis" cannot be ruled out, although it has been argued that common sense and considerations of simplicity rule against it. One of the first philosophers to question the distinction between reality and dreams was Zhuangzi, a Chinese philosopher from the 4th century BC. He phrased the problem as the well-known "Butterfly Dream," which went as follows:

Once Zhuangzi dreamt he was a butterfly, a butterfly flitting and fluttering around, happy with himself and doing as he pleased. He didn't know he was Zhuangzi. Suddenly he woke up and there he was, solid and unmistakable Zhuangzi. But he didn't know if he was Zhuangzi who had dreamt he was a butterfly, or a butterfly dreaming he was Zhuangzi. Between Zhuangzi and a butterfly there must be *some* distinction! This is called the Transformation of Things. (2, tr. Burton Watson 1968:49)

The philosophical underpinnings of this argument are also brought up by Descartes, who was one of the first Western philosophers to do so. In *Meditations on First Philos-*

ophy, he states "... there are no certain indications by which we may clearly distinguish wakefulness from sleep", and goes on to conclude that "It is possible that I am dreaming right now and that all of my perceptions are false".

Chalmers (2003) discusses the dream hypothesis, and notes that this comes in two distinct forms:

- that he is *currently* dreaming, in which case many of his beliefs about the world are incorrect;

- that he has *always* been dreaming, in which case the objects he perceives actually exist, albeit in his imagination.

Both the dream argument and the simulation hypothesis can be regarded as skeptical hypotheses; however in raising these doubts, just as Descartes noted that his own thinking led him to be convinced of his own existence, the existence of the argument itself is testament to the possibility of its own truth. Another state of mind in which some argue an individual's perceptions have no physical basis in the real world is called psychosis though psychosis may have a physical basis in the real world and explanations vary.

Computability of Physics

A decisive refutation of any claim that our reality is computer-simulated would be the discovery of some uncomputable physics, because if reality is doing something that no computer can do, it cannot be a computer simulation. (*Computability* generally means computability by a Turing machine. Hypercomputation (super-Turing computation) introduces other possibilities which will be dealt with separately.) In fact, known physics is held to be (Turing) computable, but the statement "physics is computable" needs to be qualified in various ways, as a recent result shows.

Before symbolic computation, a number, thinking particularly of a real number, one with an infinite number of digits, was said to be computable if a Turing machine will continue to spit out digits endlessly, never reaching a "final digit". This runs counter, however, to the idea of simulating physics in real time (or any plausible kind of time). Known physical laws (including those of quantum mechanics) are very much infused with real numbers and continua, and the universe seems to be able to decide their values on a moment-by-moment basis. As Richard Feynman put it:

"It always bothers me that, according to the laws as we understand them today, it takes a computing machine an infinite number of logical operations to figure out what goes on in no matter how tiny a region of space, and no matter how tiny a region of time. How can all that be going on in that tiny space? Why should it take an infinite amount of logic to figure out what one tiny piece of space/time is going to do? So I have often made the hypotheses that ultimately physics will not require a mathematical statement, that in the end the machinery will be revealed, and the laws will turn out to be simple, like the chequer board with all its apparent complexities".

The objection could be made that the simulation does not have to run in "real time". It misses an important point, though: the shortfall is not linear; rather it is a matter of performing an infinite number of computational steps in a finite time. Note that these objections all relate to the idea of reality being *exactly* simulated. Ordinary computer simulations as used by physicists are always approximations.

These objections do not apply if the hypothetical simulation is being run on a hyper-computer, a hypothetical machine more powerful than a Turing machine. Unfortunately, there is no way of working out if computers running a simulation are capable of doing things that computers in the simulation cannot do. The laws of physics inside a simulation and those outside it do not have to be the same, and simulations of different physical laws have been constructed. The problem now is that there is no evidence that can conceivably be produced to show that the universe is *not* any kind of computer, making the simulation hypothesis unfalsifiable and therefore scientifically unaccept-able, at least by Popperian standards.

All conventional computers, however, are less than hypercomputational, and the sim-ulated reality hypothesis is usually expressed in terms of conventional computers, i.e. Turing machines. Roger Penrose, an English mathematical physicist, presents the ar-gument that human consciousness is non-algorithmic, and thus is not capable of being modeled by a conventional Turing machine-type of digital computer. Penrose hypoth-esizes that quantum mechanics plays an essential role in the understanding of human consciousness. He sees the collapse of the quantum wavefunction as playing an import-ant role in brain function.

CantGoTu Environments

In his book *The Fabric of Reality*, David Deutsch discusses how the limits to comput-ability imposed by Gödel's Incompleteness Theorem affect the Virtual Reality render-ing process. In order to do this, Deutsch invents the notion of a CantGoTu environment (named after Cantor, Gödel, and Turing), using Cantor's diagonal argument to con-struct an 'impossible' Virtual Reality which a physical VR generator would not be able to generate. The way that this works is to imagine that all VR environments renderable by such a generator can be enumerated, and that we label them VR1, VR2, etc.

Slicing time up into discrete chunks we can create an environment which is unlike VR1 in the first timeslice, unlike VR2 in the second timeslice and so on. This environment is not in the list, and so it cannot be generated by the VR generator. Deutsch then goes on to discuss a universal VR generator, which as a physical device would not be able to render all possible environments, but would be able to render those environments which can be rendered by all other physical VR generators. He argues that 'an environment which can be rendered' corresponds to a set of mathematical questions whose answers can be calculated, and discusses various forms of the Turing Principle, which in its initial form refers to the fact that it is possible to build a universal computer which can be programmed to execute any computation that any other machine can do. Attempts to capture the process of virtual reality rendering provides us with a version which states: "It is possible to build a virtual-reality generator, whose repertoire includes every physically possible environment". In other words, a single, buildable physical object can mimic all the behaviours and responses of any other physically possible process or object. This, it is claimed, is what makes reality comprehensible.

Later on in the book, Deutsch goes on to argue for a very strong version of the Turing principle, namely: "It is possible to build a virtual reality generator whose repertoire includes every *physically possible* environment." However, in order to include *every physically possible environment*, the computer would have to be able to include a recursive simulation of the environment containing *itself*. Even so, a computer running a simulation need not have to run every possible physical moment to be plausible to its inhabitants.

Nested Simulations

The existence of simulated reality is unprovable in any concrete sense: any "evidence" that is directly observed could be another simulation itself. In other words, there is an infinite regress problem with the argument. Even if we are a simulated reality, there is no way to be sure the beings running the simulation are not themselves a simulation, and the operators of *that* simulation are not a simulation.

"Recursive simulation involves a simulation, or an entity in the simulation, creating another instance of the same simulation, running it and using its results" (Pooch and Sullivan 2000).

Consequences

If we are living in a simulation, then it's possible that our simulation could get shut down. Some futurists have speculated about how we can avoid this outcome. Ray Kurzweil argues in *The Singularity is Near* that we should be interesting to our simulators, and that bringing about the Singularity is probably the most interesting event that could happen. The philosopher Phil Torres has argued that the simulation argument itself leads to the conclusion that, if we run simulations in the future, then there almost certainly exists a stack of nested simulations, with ours located towards the bottom. Since annihilation is inherited downwards, any terminal event in a simulation "above" ours would also be a terminal event for us. If there are many simulations above us, then the risk of an existential catastrophe could be significant.

In Fiction

Simulated reality in fiction has been explored by many authors, game designers, and film directors.

References

- Grasset, R.; Gascuel, J. -D.; Schmalstieg (2003). "Interactive Mediated Reality". The Second IEEE and ACM International Symposium on Mixed and Augmented Reality, 2003. Proceedings. pp. 302–303. doi:10.1109/ISMAR.2003.1240731. ISBN 0-7695-2006-5.

- R. Behringer, G. Klinker,. D. Mizell. Augmented Reality – Placing Artificial Objects in Real Scenes. Proceedings of IWAR '98. A.K.Peters, Natick, 1999. ISBN 1-56881-098-9.

- Pooch, U.W.; Sullivan, F.J. (2000). "Recursive simulation to aid models of decisionmaking". Simulation Conference (Winter ed.). 1. doi:10.1109/WSC.2000.899898. ISBN 0-7803-6579-8.

- Chapman, Lizette (2015-01-28). "Augmented-Reality Headset Maker Meta Secures $23 Million". Wall Street Journal. Retrieved 2016-02-29.

- Matney, Lucas (2016-03-02). "Hands-on with the $949 mind-bending Meta 2 augmented reality headset". TechCrunch. Retrieved 2016-03-02.

- Brewster, Signe (2015-01-28). "Meta raises $23M Series A to refine its augmented reality glasses". Gigaom. Retrieved 2016-02-29.

- Davis, Nicola (January 7, 2015). "Project Anywhere: digital route to an out-of-body experience". The Guardian. Retrieved September 21, 2016.

- Bond, Sarah (July 17, 2016). "After the Success Of Pokémon Go, How Will Augmented Reality Impact Archaeological Sites?". Retrieved July 17, 2016.

- "TED 2016: Meta augmented reality headset demoed at TED". British Broadcast Corporation. BBC. Retrieved 28 May 2016.

- "What is Augmented Reality (AR): Augmented Reality Defined, iPhone Augmented Reality Apps and Games and More". Digital Trends. Retrieved 2015-10-08.

- Berinato, Scott (January 29, 2015). "What HoloLens Has That Google Glass Didn't". Harward Business Preview. Retrieved 15 February 2015.

- Kosner, Anthony Wing (29 July 2012). "Sight: An 8-Minute Augmented Reality Journey That Makes Google Glass Look Tame". Forbes. Retrieved 3 August 2015.

- O'Dell, J. (27 July 2012). "Beautiful short film shows a frightening future filled with Google Glass-like devices". Retrieved 3 August 2015.

- Lee, Kangdon (March 2012). "Augmented Reality in Education and Training" (PDF). Techtrends: Linking Research & Practice To Improve Learning. 56 (2). Retrieved 2014-05-15.

- Stuart Eve. "Augmenting Phenomenology: Using Augmented Reality to Aid Archaeological Phenomenology in the Landscape". Retrieved 2012-09-25.

- Noelle, S. (2002). "Stereo augmentation of simulation results on a projection wall". Mixed and Augmented Reality, 2002. ISMAR 2002. Proceedings.: 271–322. Retrieved 2012-10-07.

- Verlinden, Jouke; Horvath, Imre. "Augmented Prototyping as Design Means in Industrial Design Engineering". Delft University of Technology. Retrieved 2012-10-07.

7

Various File formats used in Virtual Reality

Virtual reality uses a wide array of software to simulate the user's perception. This chapter details the various file formats used in VR like VRML, COLLADA, X3D, universal3D, 3DMLW etc. These specialized file formats help in dynamic and interactive digital content creation-graphics, textures etc.

VRML

VRML (Virtual Reality Modeling Language, pronounced *vermal* or by its initials, originally—before 1995—known as the Virtual Reality Markup Language) is a standard file format for representing 3-dimensional (3D) interactive vector graphics, designed particularly with the World Wide Web in mind. It has been superseded by X3D.

WRL File Format

VRML is a text file format where, e.g., vertices and edges for a 3D polygon can be specified along with the surface color, UV mapped textures, shininess, transparency, and so on. URLs can be associated with graphical components so that a web browser might fetch a webpage or a new VRML file from the Internet when the user clicks on the specific graphical component. Animations, sounds, lighting, and other aspects of the virtual world can interact with the user or may be triggered by external events such as timers. A special Script Node allows the addition of program code (e.g., written in Java or ECMAScript) to a VRML file.

VRML files are commonly called "worlds" and have the *.wrl extension (for example island.wrl). VRML files are in plain text and generally compress well using gzip, useful for transferring over the internet more quickly (some gzip compressed files use the *.wrz extension). Many 3D modeling programs can save objects and scenes in VRML format.

Standardization

The Web3D Consortium has been formed to further the collective development of the format. VRML (and its successor, X3D), have been accepted as international standards by the International Organization for Standardization (ISO).

The first version of VRML was specified in November 1994. This version was specified from, and very closely resembled, the API and file format of the Open Inventor software component, originally developed by SGI. The current and functionally complete version is VRML97 (ISO/IEC 14772-1:1997). VRML has now been superseded by X3D (ISO/IEC 19775-1)

Emergence, Popularity, and Rival Technical Upgrade

The term VRML was coined by Dave Raggett in a paper called "Extending WWW to support Platform Independent Virtual Reality" submitted to the First World Wide Web Conference in 1994, and first discussed at the WWW94 VRML BOF established by Tim Berners-Lee, where Mark Pesce presented the Labyrinth demo he developed with Tony Parisi and Peter Kennard. In October 1995, at Internet World, Template Graphics Software (TGS) demonstrated a 3D/VRML plug-in for the beta release of Netscape 2.0 by Netscape Communications.

In 1997, a new version of the format was finalized, as VRML97 (also known as VRML2 or VRML 2.0), and became an ISO standard. VRML97 was used on the Internet on some personal homepages and sites such as "CyberTown", which offered 3D chat using Blaxxun Software. The format was championed by SGI's Cosmo Software; when SGI restructured in 1998 the division was sold to the VREAM Division of Platinum Technology, which was then taken over by Computer Associates, which did not develop or distribute the software. To fill the void a variety of proprietary Web 3D formats emerged over the next few years, including Microsoft Chrome and Adobe Atmosphere, neither of which is supported today. VRML's capabilities remained largely the same while realtime 3D graphics kept improving. The VRML Consortium changed its name to the Web3D Consortium, and began work on the successor to VRML—X3D.

SGI ran a web site at vrml.sgi.com on which was hosted a string of regular short performances of a character called "Floops" who was a VRML character in a VRML world. Floops was a creation of a company called "Protozoa".

H-Anim is a standard for animated Humanoids, which is based around VRML, and later X3D. The initial version 1.0 of the H-Anim standard was scheduled for submission at the end of March 1998.

VRML provoked much interest but has never seen much serious widespread use. One reason for this may have been the lack of available bandwidth. At the time of VRML's popularity, a majority of users, both business and personal, were using slow dial-up internet access.

VRML experimentation was primarily in education and research where an open specification is most valued. It has now been re-engineered as X3D. The MPEG-4 Interactive Profile (ISO/IEC 14496) was based on VRML (now on X3D), and X3D is largely backward-compatible with it. VRML is also widely used as a file format for interchange of

3D models, particularly from CAD systems.

A free cross-platform runtime implementation of VRML is available in OpenVRML. Its libraries can be used to add both VRML and X3D support to applications, and a GTK+ plugin is available to render VRML/X3D worlds in web browsers.

In the 2000s, many companies like Bitmanagement improved the quality level of virtual effects in VRML to the quality level of DirectX 9.0c, but at the expense of using proprietary solutions. All main features like game modeling are already complete. They include multi-pass render with low level setting for Z-buffer, BlendOp, AlphaOp, Stencil, Multi-texture, Shader with HLSL and GLSL support, realtime Render To Texture, Multi Render Target (MRT) and PostProcessing. Many demos shows that VRML already supports lightmap, normalmap, SSAO, CSM and Realtime Environment Reflection along with other virtual effects.

Alternatives

- 3DMLW: 3D Markup Language for Web
- COLLADA: managed by the Khronos Group
- O3D: developed by Google
- U3D: Ecma International standard ECMA-363
- Unity: a game engine which can be used online via a browser plugin
- X3D: successor of VRML

COLLADA

COLLADA (*COLLAborative Design Activity*) is an interchange file format for interactive 3D applications. It is managed by the nonprofit technology consortium, the Khronos Group, and has been adopted by ISO as a publicly available specification, ISO/PAS 17506.

COLLADA defines an open standard XML schema for exchanging digital assets among various graphics software applications that might otherwise store their assets in incompatible file formats. COLLADA documents that describe digital assets are XML files, usually identified with a .dae (digital asset exchange) filename extension.

History

Originally created at Sony Computer Entertainment by Rémi Arnaud and Mark C. Barnes, it has since become the property of the Khronos Group, a member-funded industry consortium, which now shares the copyright with Sony. The COLLADA schema and specification are freely available from the Khronos Group. The COLLADA DOM uses the SCEA Shared Source License.

Several graphics companies collaborated with Sony from COLLADA's beginnings to create a tool that would be useful to the widest possible audience, and COLLADA continues to evolve through the efforts of Khronos contributors. Early collaborators included Alias Systems Corporation, Criterion Software, Autodesk, Inc., and Avid Technology. Dozens of commercial game studios and game engines have adopted the standard.

In March 2011, Khronos released the COLLADA Conformance Test Suite (CTS). The suite allows applications that import and export COLLADA to test against a large suite of examples, ensuring that they conform properly to the specification. In July 2012, the CTS software was released on GitHub, allowing for community contributions.

ISO/PAS 17506:2012 *Industrial automation systems and integration -- COLLADA digital asset schema specification for 3D visualization of industrial data* was published in July 2012.

Software Tools

COLLADA was originally intended as an intermediate format for transporting data from one digital content creation (DCC) tool to another application. Applications exist to support the usage of several DCCs, including:

- 3ds Max (ColladaMax)
- Adobe Photoshop
- Allplan
- ArtiosCAD
- Blender
- Bryce
- Carrara
- Cheddar Cheese Press (model processor)
- Chief Architect Software
- Cinema 4D (MAXON)
- CityEngine
- CityScape
- Clara.io

- DAZ Studio

- Delphi

- E-on Vue 9 xStream

- Esko Studio

- FreeCAD

- FormZ

- GPure

- Houdini (Side Effects Software)

- iBooks Author

- LightWave 3D (v 9.5)

- MakeHuman

- Maya (ColladaMaya)

- MeshLab

- Mobile Model Viewer (Android)

- Modo

- OpenRAVE

- Poser Pro (v 7.0)

- Presagis Creator

- Robot Operating System

- SAP Visual Enterprise Author

- Shade 3D (E Frontier, Mirye)

- SketchUp (v 8.0) – KMZ file is a zip file containing a KML file, a COLLADA file, and texture images

- Softimage|XSI

- Strata 3D

- Ürban PAD

- Vectorworks

- Visual3D Game Development Tool for Collada scene and model viewing, editing, and exporting

- Wings 3D
- Xcode (v 4.4)

Game Engines

Although originally intended as an interchange format, many game engines now support COLLADA natively, including:

- Ardor3D
- Blender Game Engine
- C4 Engine
- CryEngine 2
- FireMonkey
- GamePlay
- Godot
- GLGE
- Irrlicht Engine
- OpenSimulator
- Panda3d
- SceneKit
- ShiVa
- Spring
- Torque 3D
- Turbulenz
- Unigine
- Unity
- Unreal Engine
- Vanda Engine
- Visual3D Game Engine

- Neoaxis 3d Game Engine

- HPL Engine

Applications

Some games and 3D applications have started to support COLLADA:

- ArcGIS

- Autodesk InfraWorks

- Google Earth (v 4) – users can simply drag and drop a COLLADA file on top of the virtual Earth

- JanusVR

- Kerbal Space Program - .dae files for 3d model mods.

- Maple (software) - 3D plots can be exported as COLLADA

- Open Wonderland

- OpenSimulator

- Mac OS X 10.6's Preview

- NASA World Wind

- SAP Visual Enterprise Author – supports import and export .dae files.

- Second Life

- SketchUp - import .dae files.

- Systems Tool Kit (STK) - utilizes .dae files for 3d models

- TNTmips

Libraries

There are several libraries available to read and write COLLADA files under programmatic control:

- COLLADA DOM (C++) - The COLLADA DOM is generated at compile-time from the COLLADA schema. It provides a low-level interface that eliminates the need for hand-written parsing routines, but is limited to reading and writing only one version of COLLADA, making it difficult to upgrade as new versions are released.

- FCollada (C++) - A utility library available from Feeling Software. In contrast to the COLLADA DOM, Feeling Software's FCollada provides a higher-level interface. FCollada is used in ColladaMaya, ColladaMax, and several commercial game engines. The development of the open source part was discontinued by Feeling Software in 2008. The company continues to support its paying customers and licenses with improved versions of its software.

- OpenCOLLADA (C++) - The OpenCOLLADA project provides plugins for 3ds Max and Maya and the sources of utility libraries which were developed for the plugins.

- pycollada (Python) - A Python module for creating, editing and loading COLLADA. The library allows the application to load a COLLADA file and interact with it as a Python object. In addition, it supports creating a COLLADA Python object from scratch, as well as in-place editing.

- Scene Kit (Objective-C) - An Objective-C framework introduced in OS X 10.8 Mountain Lion that allows reading, high-level manipulation and display of COLLADA scenes.

- GLGE (JavaScript) - a JavaScript library presenting COLLADA files in a web browser using WebGL.

- Three.js (JavaScript) - a 3D Javascript library capable of loading COLLADA files in a web browser.

- StormEngineC (JavaScript) - Javascript 3D graphics library with option of loading COLLADA files.

Physics

As of version 1.4, physics support was added to the COLLADA standard. The goal is to allow content creators to define various physical attributes in visual scenes. For example, one can define surface material properties such as friction. Furthermore, content creators can define the physical attributes for the objects in the scene. This is done by defining the rigid bodies that should be linked to the visual representations. More features include support for ragdolls, collision volumes, physical constraints between physical objects, and global physical properties such as gravitation.

Physics middleware products that support this standard include Bullet Physics Library, Open Dynamics Engine, PAL and NVIDIA's PhysX. These products support by reading the abstract found in the COLLADA file and transferring it into a form that the middleware can support and represent in a physical simulation. This also enables different middleware and tools to exchange physics data in a standardized manner.

The Physics Abstraction Layer provides support for COLLADA Physics to multiple physics engines that do not natively provide COLLADA support including JigLib, OpenTissue, Tokamak physics engine and True Axis. PAL also provides support for COLLADA to physics engines that also feature a native interface.

3DMLW

3DMLW (*3D Markup Language for Web*) is an open-source project, and a XML-based Markup Language for representing interactive 3D and 2D content on the World Wide Web.

The project has been inactive since 2009; as of 2016, the website, including the documentation, is no longer available.

3DMLW Platform

The 3DMLW platform is an open-source software suite aimed at showing dynamic 3D content. It included its own scripting language for software design, and a format support for 3D models.

3DMLW Language

3DMLW is an XML standard 1.0 based markup language that allows for data exchange between applications linked with 3DMLW plug-in interface. A schema definition is provided for verifying the notation with 3rd party software such as jEdit or other XML editors capable of checking XSD constraints.

3DMLW Renderer

The rendering engine uses industry standard OpenGL. It can be plugged into 3DMLW Plug-in Interface and consists of a scene library and a graphics library, which provides an optimized rendering pipeline for the scene library structures. The scene library can be utilized independently for the manipulation or conversion of meshes without rendering them.

3DMLW Plug-in Interface

The plug-in interface mediates input events and output from host windows (e.g. web browsers) or an independent output window. It is extendible to allow integration into 3rd party software. Native support has been implemented for common web browsers.

3DMLW Server Toolset

The toolset provides batch conversion for several filetypes (.obj, .3ds, .xyz, .pts) and texture atlas generation capable of processing multiple models concurrently. It can be employed server-side to provide automatic conversion of 3D models and textures.

3DMLW File Format

A 3DMLW file is a simple text file containing instructions confined to 3DMLW language syntax:

```
<?xml version='1.0' standalone='no'?>

<document>

        <content2d>

                <area width='200' height='100' color='#C0C0C0FF' texture='flow-
er.png' />

        </content2d>

        <content3d id='content' camera='{#cam}'>

                <camera id='cam' class='cam_rotation' y='10' z='40' viewy='10'/>

                <box name='ground' width='100' height='2' depth='100' col-
or='green' class='ground' />

                <box name='dynamic' y='20' width='10' height='10' depth='10' col-
or='blue' />

        </content3d>

</document>
```

In 3DMLW 2D and 3D content are handled independently from each other, but they are free to overlap. For animating 3D scenes and handling different events a Lua scripting facility is provided. The following script snippet demonstrates colour fading:

```
<script type='text/x-lua'><![CDATA[

        receiver = Reference.get("@receiver");

        c = receiver:attributeColor("color");

        c:setAlpha(c:getAlpha()+1);

        if c:getAlpha()>255 then

                c:setAlpha(0);

        end

        receiver:putAttribute("color", tostring(c));

        ]]>

</script>
```

The use of 3D models in .3ds, .obj, .an8, and .blend file formats is supported, but 3DMLW Plug-in interface allows for easy extension to include other formats.

3DMLW files use .3dmlw (e.g. filename.3dmlw) as extension and can be linked together similar to HTML.

Displaying 3DMLW

3DMLW content could be viewed using applications provided by 3D Technologies R&D, including plug-ins for Internet Explorer and NPAPI compatible browsers (Mozilla Firefox, Opera etc.). However, these applications are not available anymore.

Usage of 3DMLW

3DMLW was used for Tallinn's old town 3D application. 3D Technologies R&D also is using some parts of 3DMLW engine in their 3D Wayfinder application.

X3D should not be confused with 3DXML, which is a proprietary 3D file format.

X3D is a royalty-free ISO standard XML-based file format for representing 3D computer graphics. It is successor to the Virtual Reality Modeling Language (VRML). X3D features extensions to VRML (e.g. CAD, Geospatial, Humanoid animation, NURBS etc.), the ability to encode the scene using an XML syntax as well as the Open Inventor-like syntax of VRML97, or binary formatting, and enhanced application programming interfaces (APIs).

The X3D extension supports multi-stage and multi-texture rendering; it also supports shading with lightmap and normalmap. Starting in 2010, X3D has supported deferred rendering architecture. Now X3D can import SSAO, CSM and Realtime Environment Reflection/Lighting. The user can also use optimizations including BSP/QuadTree/ OctTree or culling in the X3D scene.

X3D can work with other open source standards including XML, DOM and XPath.

Standardization

X3D defines several profiles (sets of components) for various levels of capability including X3D Core, X3D Interchange, X3D Interactive, X3D CADInterchange, X3D Immersive, and X3D Full. Browser makers can define their own component extensions prior to submitting them for standardisation by the Web3D Consortium. Formal review and approval is then performed by the International Organization for Standardization (ISO).

Liaison and cooperation agreements are also in place between the Web3D Consortium and the World Wide Web Consortium (W3C), Open Geospatial Consortium (OGC), Digital Imaging and Communications in Medicine (DICOM) and the Khronos Group.

A subset of X3D is XMT-A, a variant of XMT, defined in MPEG-4 Part 11. It was designed to provide a link between X3D and 3D content in MPEG-4 (BIFS).

The abstract specification for X3D (ISO/IEC 19775) was first approved by the ISO in 2004. The XML and ClassicVRML encodings for X3D (ISO/IEC 19776) were first approved in 2005.

Applications

There are several applications, most of which are open-source software, which natively parse and interpret X3D files, including the 3D graphics and animation editor Blender and the Sun Microsystems virtual world client Project Wonderland. An X3D applet is a software program that runs within a web browser and displays content in 3D, using OpenGL 3D graphics technology to display X3D content in several different browsers (IE, Safari, Firefox) across several different operating systems (Windows, Mac OS X, Linux). However, X3D has not received as wide acceptance as that of other, more notable software applications.

In the 2000s, many companies such as Bitmanagement improved the quality level of virtual effects in X3D to quality level of DirectX 9.0c, but at the expense of using proprietary solutions. All main features including game modeling are already complete. They include multi-pass render with low level setting for Z-buffer, BlendOp, AlphaOp, Stencil, Multi-texture, Shader with HLSL and GLSL support, real-time Render To Texture, Multi Render Target (MRT) and post-processing. Many demos shows that X3D already supports lightmap, normalmap, SSAO, CSM and real-time environment reflection along with other virtual effects.

Striving to become the 3D standard for the Web, X3D is designed to be as integrated into HTML5 pages as other XML standards such as MathML and SVG. X3DOM is a proposed syntax model and its implementation as a script library that demonstrates how this integration can be achieved without a browser plugin, using only WebGL and JavaScript.

Example

```
<?xml version="1.0" encoding="UTF-8"?>

<!DOCTYPE X3D PUBLIC "ISO//Web3D//DTD X3D 3.2//EN"

 "http://www.web3d.org/specifications/x3d-3.2.dtd">


<X3D profile="Interchange" version="3.2"

  xmlns:xsd="http://www.w3.org/2001/XMLSchema-instance"

    xsd:noNamespaceSchemaLocation="http://www.web3d.org/specifications/x3d-3.2.xsd">

<Scene>
```

```
<Shape>
  <IndexedFaceSet coordIndex="0 1 2">
    <Coordinate point="0 0 0 1 0 0 0.5 1 0"/>
  </IndexedFaceSet>
</Shape>
</Scene>
</X3D>
```

Universal 3D

Universal 3D (U3D) is a compressed file format standard for 3D computer graphics data.

The format was defined by a special consortium called *3D Industry Forum* that brought together a diverse group of companies and organizations, including Intel, Boeing, HP, Adobe Systems, Bentley Systems, Right Hemisphere and others whose main focus had been the promotional development of 3D graphics for use in various industries, specifically at this time manufacturing as well as construction and industrial plant design. The format was later standardized by Ecma International in August 2005 as ECMA-363.

The goal is a universal standard for three-dimensional data of all kinds, to facilitate data exchange. The consortium promoted also the development of an open source library for facilitating the adoption of the format.

The format is natively supported by the PDF format and 3D objects in U3D format can be inserted into PDF documents and interactively visualized by Acrobat Reader (since version 7).

Editions

There are four editions to date.

The first edition is supported by many/all of the various applications mentioned below. It is capable of storing vertex based geometry, color, textures, lighting, bones, and transform based animation.

The second and third editions correct some errata in the first edition, and the third edition also adds the concept of vendor specified blocks. One such block widely deployed is the RHAdobeMesh block, which provides a more compressed alternative to the mesh blocks defined in the first edition. Deep Exploration, 3D PDF Converter for Acrobat Pro and PDF3D-SDK can author this data, and Adobe Acrobat and Reader 8.1 can read this data.

The fourth edition provides definitions for higher order primitives (curved surfaces).

Application Support

Applications which support PDFs with embedded U3D objects include:

- Adobe Acrobat Extended allows PDF creation and conversion of various file formats to U3D within the PDF. Acrobat Pro allows PDF creation and embedding of pre-created U3D files.

- Adobe Photoshop CS3, CS4 and CS5 Extended are able to export a 3D Layer as a U3D file.

- ArchiCAD allows export of U3D files.

- Bluebeam Revu Allows PDF creation and embedding of U3D within the PDF. Comes packaged with plugins that can export 3D PDFs from Revit and Solidworks.

- DAZ Studio

- iText open source Java library allows creation of PDF containing U3D

- Jreality, an open source mathematical visualization package with 3D-PDF and U3D export

- MeshLab

- MeVisLab supports export of U3D models for biomedical images.

- MicroStation allows export of PDF containing U3D.

- Poser 7

- Autodesk Inventor allows saving of files to 3D PDF containing U3D. Soon available since version 2017.

- SolidWorks allows saving of files to 3D PDF containing U3D.

- ArtiosCAD allows saving of files to 3D PDF containing U3D.

- SimLab Composer allows importing and exporting U3D and embedding U3D in 3D PDF.

- SpaceClaim allows the opening and saving of 3D PDF format comprising U3D.

- SAP VE Author allows saving of files to 3D PDF containing U3D.

References

- "Simplified Generation of Biomedical 3D Surface Model Data for Embedding into 3D Portable Document Format (PDF) Files for Publication and Education". Retrieved 2015-09-25.

- "Towards an easier creation of three-dimensional data for embedding into scholarly 3D PDF (Portable Document Format) files". Retrieved 2015-09-25.

- "ISO/PAS 17506:2012 Industrial automation systems and integration -- COLLADA digital asset schema specification for 3D visualization of industrial data". Retrieved March 30, 2013.

- Dave Raggett (1994). "Extending WWW to support Platform Independent Virtual Reality". Retrieved April 2, 2012.

Permissions

Index